The World is Your Burger

David Michaels

The World is Your Burger

A Cultural History

Contents

Preface

My love for burgers began years ago when I was a teenager in Baltimore. I would throw punk-rock barbecues for all my friends. I was always the Que-Master. Later, as my career in photography grew, so did my passion for burgers. After college I took many cross-country trips. One thing you realize on the road is there aren't a lot of restaurant options, mainly local diners. Usually these diners have laminated menus with clip-art photos of food on them. I have always been fascinated by these menus. Where do people get these photos? I can't even imagine where they come from. Almost jokingly, I thought that I wanted to be the guy that photographed those images for the menus. One day in Los Angeles with that idea still on my brain I thought, "Why not? I can do that. I can be that guy." I took the idea and turned it into an art piece. I decided to do a series of burgers using an 8 x 10 camera with Polaroid film. Later I connected directly with Polaroid to use their 20 x 24 camera to create giant burger photos.

My idea was that we don't actually look at burgers that much when we eat them. We don't stop and consider what they look like, in person, before we stuff them into our face. In our mind the image of the burger comes from fast-food ad campaigns, not from reality. Using Polaroid film flipped the idea of mass-produced Pop Art on its head and brought it back to the individual item, the individual burger.

The hamburger has such resonance, I think, because it is so American. It is more American than apple pie. A photo of a burger is practically like the image of the American flag. It represents us as a people so well. You can't look at a burger and not think of America and all the things it represents, the ideas of overabundance and decadence, but also the fact that burgers are inexpensive and available to all. The iconic nature of the burger has a kind of universality, though, an appeal that goes beyond this American nature. You only have to look at how popular this incredibly American food item is across the world to see that.

Because of my photo series, I know a lot more about burgers than most people do. But anyone can get into them because they're such a wonderful food and so readily available. Personally, my favorite burgers are the ones I cook at home for my barbecues. Luckily, we have an amazing butcher, McCall's, down the street from where I live that has a fantastic house-burger blend. Cooking for the Fourth of July or any other occasion and having friends over is the best reason to have a great burger. This book collects the personal and the public and shows the burger in all its glory and variety. There's history and recipes and great burger joints and art, but at the center is the idea that people love eating great, juicy burgers. Because we do, everywhere. Whatever the burger means to people, however it's presented and talked about, at heart it's just a very satisfying, tasty thing to eat. The universal and the personal: the world really is your burger.

Jeff Vespa

Introduction

Introduction

I ate my first burger when I was seven. I remember it so clearly. My mother took me to the local Wimpy Bar in London. After that I would drive her crazy to take me there as often as possible; I just couldn't get enough of stuffing my face with delicious cheeseburgers. When I was twelve years old, on vacation in Amsterdam, I experienced my first McDonald's. I can still taste that first bite of a Quarter Pounder with Cheese and it's fair to say that was the moment my lifelong passion for the humble hamburger was born. Since then, it's been a mission of mine to root out the world's finest burgers and it's been my privilege to travel the globe and enjoy my favorite food all across the world.

This book has been about ten years in the making and is a genuine labor of love. The idea first came to me when eating a burger, naturally, and I started thinking about the variety, the history, the huge number of people to whom the burger means so much: childhood, friends, family, something around which to come together, something to enjoy.

Tackling such a huge subject, and one so close to my heart, was daunting to start with, but I also had a clear idea of some of the people who needed to be part of the book. It's been a privilege to hear from some of the greatest chefs at work across the globe at the moment, but also to delve into the world of independent burger joints. I researched and visited places and ate many burgers to whittle down an enormous list to the tastiest, most interesting, and most burger-y restaurants around. I've covered the history of household names like McDonald's, White Castle, and Burger King; delved into the genesis of market leaders like Five Guys and Shake Shack; and explored how burger joints like In-N-Out Burger achieve cult status.

Of course, the burger isn't just for eating. It has a rich cultural and iconographic history, bound up in the very narratives that make its home, America, what it is today, but the burger is also a place where ideas of consumption and capitalism are explored, and where advertising has found a distinctive voice. This book contains richly detailed interviews with some of the top food writers and burger experts, and conversations with visual artists who use the burger in their work. Ultimately, the burger is one of the most versatile and tasty food items in the world, and in this book you'll see it's also vastly more than that. I dedicate this book to all burger lovers and to the genius who first decided to place a meat patty between two round slices of bread.

David Michaels

Origins

1ST

Isicia Omentata
Rome

The first stirrings of what came to resemble a hamburger, this ground- (minced-) meat dish contained pine nuts, pepper, and flavorings of wine and garum.

Steak Tartare
The Steppes

The Mongols were fierce horsemen who conquered most of Eurasia with thick slabs of beef tucked under their saddles, eaten after being tenderized by a day's riding.

13TH

CENTURY AD

1747

"Hamburg" Sausage
London

Hannah Glasse's *The Art of Cookery* is published, describing this smoked sausage of ground (minced) beef, suet, pepper, cloves, nutmeg, garlic, vinegar, salt, red wine, and rum, to be served on toast.

1802

The English language's foremost lexicon describes Hamburg steak as "a hard slab of salted, minced [ground] beef, often slightly smoked, mixed with onions and bread crumbs."

The Meat Grinder
Virginia

G. A. Coffman created and patented his Machine for Cutting Sausage-Meat, which featured rotating blades under a spiral feeder, akin to modern meat grinders (mincers).

1845

1885

The Menches Brothers
Erie County Fair, New York

There are dubious and conflicting claims that at this fair in New York State the brothers ran out of pork sausages and so put beef into a sandwich, thereby creating a burger.

1885

Charlie Nagreen
Seymour Fair, Wisconsin

Nagreen, affectionately known as "Hamburger Charlie," apparently squashed a beef meatball between slices of bread so his customers could walk around eating—a concoction he claimed was the first hamburger.

Oscar Weber Bilby
Bowden, Oklahoma

The first documented appearance of flame-grilled beef patties in a sourdough bun, created by Bilby and his wife Fanny to celebrate the Fourth of July.

1891

1900

Louis Lassen
New Haven, Connecticut

The United States Library of Congress credits Lassen with creating the first hamburger, but doubt remains, as his beef patty was served between two slices of toast rather than the bun that the true burger demands.

1904

Fletcher Davis
St. Louis World's Fair, Missouri

Davis claimed to have been serving beef in sandwiches since the 1880s and to have sold out of his "hamburgers" at this world-famous exposition.

The Jungle
Chicago, Illinois

Upton Sinclair's novel about the meat-packing industry led many Americans to distrust the quality of ground (minced) beef, even though that was not Sinclair's aim at all.

1906

1916

Walter Anderson
Wichita, Kansas

Anderson, one of the two geniuses behind White Castle, originally started trading from a food cart, serving burgers with specifically created buns and using his own handmade spatula.

1921

White Castle
Wichita, Kansas

Cook Walter Anderson and entrepreneur Billy Ingram opened their first restaurant and changed the course of hamburger history, with innovations in design, cooking, and serving.

The Cheese Hamburger
Pasadena, California

Lionel Sternberger, running his father's diner, The Rite Spot, claimed to be the first man to put cheese over a patty in a bun, which he called a Cheese Hamburger.

1925

1931

Wimpy
Fleischer Studios

The New York-based animation house created the famous hamburger-eating comic character J. Wellington Wimpy for the *Popeye* series; the restaurant was later named after him.

1934

"A New Tang"
Louisville, Kentucky

That was how Kaelin's Restaurant described the taste when they melted cheese over patties, which they claimed to be the first proper cheeseburger.

1935

Cheese-burger™?
Denver, Colorado

Louis Ballast submitted a trademark for "The Cheeseburger" for his now defunct Humpty Dumpty Drive-In, though historians query whether he was ever granted it.

1937

The Big Boy
Glendale, California

Bob Wian founded Bob's Pantry in 1936 and within a year had gone for broke, slicing a bun into three and using two patties to create the first double-decker burger.

1948

McDonald's
San Bernardino, California

Though the McDonald brothers had run a barbecue shack since 1940, in 1948 they changed to serving hamburgers and started what became the largest fast-food chain in the world.

Burger King
Miami, Florida

David Edgerton and James McLamore purchased the floundering Insta-Burger King and renamed it, creating the biggest challenger to McDonald's fast-food crown.

1954

Wimpy
London

J. Lyons and Co. bought franchise rights to run Wimpy burger bars in England and opened their first as a concession in a Lyons Corner House restaurant on Coventry Street in Central London.

1954

1955

Ray Kroc
Des Plaines, Illinois

Ray Kroc, erstwhile milkshake-machine salesman, joined the McDonald brothers before eventually buying them out and transforming the brand into a global phenomenon.

The Big Mac
Pittsburgh, Pennsylvania

Though it wasn't introduced nationwide until a year later, 1967 saw the invention by Jim Delligatti of what has become one of McDonald's signature items, the Big Mac.

1967

1969

Wendy's
Columbus, Ohio

For a long time the third-biggest hamburger retailer in the world, Wendy's was a later starter when created by former Kentucky Fried Chicken head chef Dave Thomas.

Humble Beginnings

The history of the burger is shrouded in conjecture, in claims that cannot be substantiated, in myth. For a food item so universally recognized and almost as universally loved, the exact definition of a burger is not as clear as our immediate recognition of its form. Of course, when you invent something that will potentially change the world, you don't always realize that this is what you are doing, and so much of our historicization of the burger is, naturally, retrospective. What is perhaps more interesting is the fervor with which the various claims are offered. Those who would provide primary evidence for their place in the history or folklore of the burger do so with a passion that is at odds with much of the rest of food history, and crucial when considering why such importance is placed on the beginnings of what is still, in effect, a slab of meat in between some bits of bread.

The reason for this is, of course, that the burger is not just a burger. It is a symbol, culturally resonant. When something has this resonance, it is natural that people want to make claims about it, to see it as an object to which they connect. It's a basic human urge to plant such cultural flags, and mythmaking is one of the most obvious ways that symbols like the hamburger are appropriated.

The origin and history of the burger, then, are subject to fiercely competing claims, some even fairly recent and all of them taking place in the shadow of the question of what, in fact, constitutes the burger. It is, almost certainly, not enough to say that the first burger was a meat patty, made of ground (minced) beef, flavored or seasoned and browned before eating. In this way, a recent discovery that attempts to credit the Romans with the invention of the burger is, while not erroneous, certainly incomplete. A Roman recipe book, *Apicius*, written by an unknown author or collection of authors, describes how to fashion the Isicia Omentata, a dish of ground meat, pepper, and pine nuts, flavored with wine and a rich fish sauce called garum. The book, named after a famous Roman gourmet of the first century AD, Marcus Gavius Apicius, was known in later printed editions as *De re coquinaria* (On the subject of cooking), and is divided into ten sections, one of which is called *Sarcoptes*, the meat grinder (mincer). It's not surprising then that some sort of burger-like creation should be found nestled in its pages.

Annie Gray, a well-regarded food historian, observes that the hustle and bustle of Roman life created a demand for street food that would feel very familiar to us moderns. She describes the Isicia Omentata as "decidedly more upmarket" and "richer and more complex" than what we might understand as the meat patty component of the hamburger, though it's also worth noting that the addition of a fishy element has a rich tradition in earlier modern recipes. But this is no hamburger, bereft as it is of a bun. The naked burger is not a burger, it is a ground (minced) beef steak, also known in the United States as a Salisbury steak.

The origins of ground meat are also assigned to a later, but equally competent, set of conquerors, the horsemen of The Steppes of Eastern Europe and Central Asia, from the pre-Roman Scythians and Huns to the thirteenth-century Mongols and Tartars, from whom steak tartare gets its name. In *The Primal Cheeseburger*, food writer Elisabeth Rozin reports that "these warriors, it is said, stashed slabs of meat under their saddles as they dashed about the world on their ponies, pillaging, looting, and conquering. After a long day's ride the meat was pounded to a pulp and seasoned to boot with a hefty dose of saddle oil, not to mention a soupçon of sweat from the horse's rump!" This is amusingly congruent with the actions of some latter-day warriors, the cyclists who compete in the annual Tour de France, who in the earlier days of the race used to stuff a steak down their heavy woolen cycling shorts to prevent saddle sores, but with the bonus of a tenderized hunk of meat to consume once the day's stage had been completed. There is, though, no suggestion that the *rouleurs* of the Tour de France made beef patties from the fragrant remnants of their day's work.

Of course, the cooking of meat itself takes us further back in time and, indeed, Rozin evocatively imagines a hunter-gatherer female coming across a charring animal corpse on a grass plain in Africa and noticing that it smells wonderful, suggesting that what we would come to know as cooking had its origins in a serendipitous discovery. This sort of thread-pulling back through time, from the burger we find on our plate to *Homo erectus* pottering about and discovering that browned meat smells delicious, is the sort of historicization noted above:

Above: Advertisement
for the Halstead
Company Beef and Pork
Packers, New York,
featuring cowboys
rounding up cattle
and other livestock.

it is an urge to go further back in the narrative of the hamburger, to uncover its roots and create a myth about its origins, as if almost to validate the importance placed upon it now.

With any history, of course, questions about origins are both interesting and contentious. This is relevant to the history of the hamburger because the fact that food historians are prepared to venture so far into the question of its origins shows how tightly contested the history of the hamburger is. That can only be the case because the answer is so important within the social history of the United States.

The reasons for this are many and various, but perhaps they can most succinctly be explained by the fact that within the burger are meshed several crucial narratives of the very founding of the United States as the sprawling global powerhouse we recognize today. The burger's creation coincided with and was born out of the growth of industrialization, the taming of the plains, and the incorporation of immigrants. Later developments in the burger industry and the narrative of individual achievement and the growth of capitalism—that is to say, the American Dream—are also part of this heady mixture:

To the West, to the West! to the land of the free
Where mighty Missouri rolls down to the sea,
Where a man is a man if he's willing to toil,
And the humblest may gather the fruits of the soil.
Where children are blessings, and he who hath most
Has aid for his fortune and riches to boast;
Where the young may exult, and the aged may rest
Away, far away, to the land of the West!

—Nineteenth-century English song

The period in which the burger starts to form into something we might recognize today was one of immense upheaval in America. Out of the ruinous but formative Civil War, according to historian Hugh Brogan, "there entered the twentieth century a continental nation, hugely rich and productive, populous, harshly urbanized, heavily industrialized, infinitely various in its ethnic origins, its religions, languages and cultures, transformed

into the first fully modern society by its rapidly evolving technology." This nascent superpower's industrial tendrils, the railroads, spread across the country, usurping the great cattle drives that forged such a strong, pioneering narrative of the American West. In so doing, they opened up the beef market to all corners of the country and by 1865 Chicago was the meat-packing nexus of the world. The fertile lands of the plains, now brutally purged of their indigenous population, were not only open to cattle farmers, but also connected at speed to the cities that could take their produce and render it into easy-to-move, easy-to-consume, and easy-to-buy meat. Of course, this increased organization, a growth of system and industry, robbed the beef farmers of their romance but, as British nature writer Tim Dee notes in his book *Four Fields*, it was a natural marriage of idealism and practicality:

THE TENSION BETWEEN THE DESIRE TO PUSH ON, THE SENSE THAT BETTER THINGS LIE OVER THE NEXT HILL, AND THE URGE TO MAKE CAMP—TO OPEN THE GROUND AND LIVE ON IT—RUN THROUGH THE INTERLEAVED HISTORY OF AMERICANS AND AMERICAN GRASS.

LANDLESS BUT ENCLOSED PEOPLE LEFT ONE CONTINENT FOR ANOTHER AND THERE SOUGHT FENCES. OUT OF EUROPE CAME BODIES AND MINDS THAT HAD REGISTERED WHAT HEDGING MEANT, THAT UNDERSTOOD THE WISH TO BE BORDERED, AND THAT ADMIRED THE PIONEER BUT LOVED ALSO TO SIT DOWN.

Indeed, there are parallels to be drawn with this in the construction of the burger itself. The roving, pioneering, adventure-laden beef is contained, but augmented, by the agrarian, fenced-in, wheat-based bun. It is as if the burger's architecture encapsulates the transition from one form of Americana to another, growing into a single symbol of the resultant synthesis, an all-consuming, all-encompassing food item that is also a cultural archetype of taste, consumerism, and the delivery of comfort.

The reason for the expansion into the plains was to feed an already existing love of beef, a love brought from Europe in various forms, and sustained by the growth of farming done, by and large, by immigrants to feed a growing industrial workforce of, by and large, immigrants.

These immigrants not only assimilated into the American way of life but also maintained their own cultural and culinary traditions.

The introduction of the Hamburg steak itself, a collection of beef scrapings patted together and browned, may not have come from the Hamburg shipping line but did certainly emerge from among the many German immigrants who flocked to the New World in the late nineteenth century and, like them, it spread widely and quickly. As these immigrants either moved out to farms across the central belt of the United States, or stayed in the growing urban sprawls to support and sustain the burgeoning industrial sector, they took their food habits with them: Elisabeth Rozin notes, for example, the love of pickled items common in the United States now, which has its origins in German and Eastern European migrants.

But while many of the foodstuffs, such as the Hamburg steak and the Frankfurter, were imported, a very American spirit of entrepreneurial innovation drove developments in how they were served: as factories and newspaper offices increasingly stayed open twenty-four hours a day, new wagons sprang up outside their gates to serve food throughout the day; as technology developed, some of these were fitted with grills so that they could offer hot food, including Frankfurters and Hamburg steaks. The "fast food" aspect of the hamburger has its origins in these roadside vendors, created to sustain the ever-churning wheels of American industrialism (a workforce, as much as an army, marches on its stomach). But these early fast-food joints were not serving hamburgers as we now know them, even if bread was added as an accompaniment. For a hamburger to be a hamburger, it needs a bun!

Various places have staked their claim to be the home of the first proper hamburger, some even successfully lobbying to have it enshrined in law. Athens, a city in Texas, claims that Fletcher Davis created the burger at his lunch counter in the 1880s; Seymour, Wisconsin, makes similar claims for the work of Charlie Nagreen. Louis Lassen, the first owner of Louis' Lunch in New Haven, Connecticut, has his advocates, as do the Menches brothers and their stall at New York state's Erie County Fair. The mobile dining wagon of Reno, Nevada's Tom

The Butcher.

Origins

Cooking

Fraker was celebrated in 1893 for its Hamburger steak sandwiches, though evidence suggests these used toasted bread, rather than a bun; the same is said of Louis Lassen's product. The late American food historian Josh Ozersky (see page 329) put it starkly: "Louis serves a ground [minced] beef sandwich on sliced bread, in this case toast. And that is not a hamburger."

Ozersky also shed further light on the claim of Fletcher Davis, whose Athens, Texas-born burgers are supposed to have made such a splash at the 1904 St. Louis World's Fair, according to Frank Tolbert, a former reporter for the *Dallas Morning News*, in his book *Tolbert's Texas*. Tolbert cites a *New York Tribune* article from 1904 to support his claims about Davis's ur-Burger status, but Ozersky was confident enough to say quite plainly that this article "does not exist, [though it] has been quoted everywhere; its real source seems to Tolbert himself."

Ozersky actually maintained that the best-documented claim belonged to the Bilby family of Tulsa, Oklahoma, who founded a drive-in burger restaurant in 1933. He wrote that "Weber's claims that its family patriarch, Oscar Bilby, had been serving hamburgers on buns at huge picnics on the family farm for over forty years before the restaurant's founding," quoting a Weber's publicity piece that made the following rather grand claim: "On the fourth of July, 1891, Oscar probably made his most significant contribution to society when he forged a piece of iron into a 3" x 4" grill.... His wife, Fanny, made sour dough buns while Oscar pattied up some black angus all-beef patties and proceeded to grill the patties on his new hand-made grill."

The reason this was so important to Ozersky is that it explicitly mentions a bun rather than bread, that crucial casing that makes the hamburger as we now know it different from the humble Hamburg steak or Salisbury sandwich; the bun is, as Rozin says, "the essential structure that holds everything together." She goes further in her argument, stating that the bun is necessary "as the crucial support system of the cheeseburger" because, unlike much bread, it is unobtrusive on the olfactory glands, "a suitably bland base for the savory contents ... nothing about the bun gets in the way of the

For a hamburger to be a hamburger, it needs a bun!

WHY PAY RENT?
Better Own a FARM & Start NOW!

1895
Thousands of Acres of fertile lands, capable of raising the finest quality of farm products in luxurious abundance.
Are FOR SALE, Upon Reasonable Terms
In Wisconsin, Minnesota, South Dakota, Iowa, Nebraska, and Wyoming. Reference to reliable statistics will demonstrate the fact that the pursuits of agriculture, stock-raising, and dairying in these States are attended with profitable results.

CHICAGO & NORTH-WESTERN RAILWAY

THE NORTH WESTERN LINE

Affords EASY Access to Unfailing Markets

Correspondence solicited from intending settlers.

Send for free copy of *The North-Western Home Seeker*.

H. R. McCULLOUGH, General Traffic Manager.
W. B. KNISKERN, Gen'l Pass'r and Ticket Agt.
CHICAGO.

burger itself, no crusty exterior, no yeasty bready aroma, no chewy texture."

It's clear, then, that the bun-ness of the burger is part of its essential form; without a bun, a burger is just a piece of meat prepared in a certain way and whether it's on toast, on a trencher, or straight off the plate, it cannot be seen as a burger.

Having seen how important the burger was to the foundation myth of the United States, it is hardly surprising to find such varied and insistent claims for the creation of the first one. Perhaps, though, as with many myths or mysterious parts of early history, it might be better to step away, to allow the swirl of conjecture and competing assertions to exist without making any definitive statements. In fact, it is better to say that this very mystery, this very uncertainty is, in fact, totally appropriate for the sprawling, embryonic America, where wild self-determination was endemic, where competing narratives coexisted and threads were pulled together, out of which grew the nation we recognize today. The burger is no different. Indeed, if we want a sensible, solid place to jump when it comes to discussing the origins of the hamburger as we now know it, that place is the northwest corner of First and Main, in Wichita, Kansas.

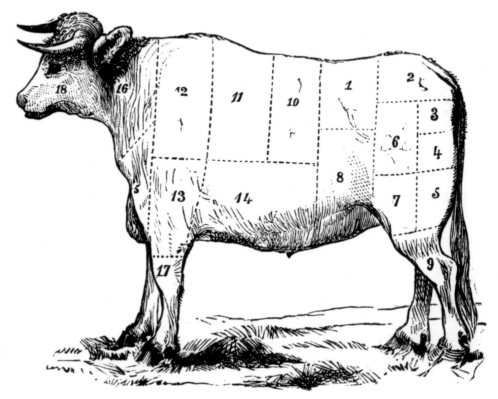

OX, SHOWING THE MODE OF CUTTING UP THE VARIOUS JOINTS.

861. *The Names of the Several Joints* are as follows :—

HIND QUARTER.

1. Sirloin.
2. Rump.
3. Aitchbone.
4. Buttock.
5. Mouse-round
6. Veiny piece.
7. Thick flank.
8. Thin flank.
9. Leg.

FORE QUARTER.

10. Fore rib (5 ribs).
11. Middle rib (4 ribs).
12. Chuck rib (3 ribs).
13. Leg of mutton piece.
14. Brisket.
15. Clod.
16. Neck.
17. Shin.
18. Cheek.

White Castle

Origins

First location:
Wichita, Kansas, USA
1921

On September 13, 1921, a chef named Walter Anderson and a former real-estate broker turned entrepreneur named Billy Ingram opened the very first White Castle hamburger restaurant, selling what they called the five-cent slider. It was a squared-off patty of beef, pressed thin with a specially designed spatula of Anderson's own creation, served between two halves of a burger bun, with onions and a slice of pickle (gherkin). It was, in other words, a genuine hamburger and White Castle was the first restaurant of its kind to open, the first fast-food joint. The place's exterior design was based on that of the Chicago Water Tower, one of the few buildings to survive the 1871 fire. Gleaming white, with turrets and crenellations, it was a resounding riposte to those who thought hamburgers were associated only with grubby, transitory fast-food carts and, even, a lack of moral fiber.

It's no exaggeration to say that what Ford did for the motorcar, Ingram and Anderson did for the burger: White Castle revolutionized the whole concept. Of course, mention of Ford invokes images of the production line, of systemization, of the beginnings of an industrial design that effectively moved men and women into a semiautomated process, where training meant that those men and women were interchangeable and could fulfill various functions in the line. White Castle's effects on the processes behind the counter—and at it—were equally crucial. But what Ingram and Anderson did moves beyond that, beyond the way that products were created, and into the realm of consumer choice and consumption. Ford famously said that his customers could have any color of the Model T as long as it was black; Anderson and Ingram's only initial concession to customer choice was that they could add condiments like ketchup or mustard of their own volition. Everything else in the production of the burger and the rest of the limited menu was preordained, its production tightly controlled.

The origins of this process lay in Anderson's own experience as a short-order cook. From 1916 until 1921, a grill geek who was constantly innovating, he had run first one and then a series of hamburger stands. The square-shaped burger was a result of working out how best to maximize space on the grill, its thinness a way of speeding up the cooking process. Anderson, proclaimed by the Wichita *Eagle* as the "King of the Hamburger," also sought to minimize the negative perceptions around the quality of meat in burgers. According to American food authority Andrew F. Smith, a lot of the meat used in products sold from food carts was of questionable provenance; he notes wryly that the expression "hot dog" was coined by waggish Yale students who were implying (strongly) that our canine friends made up much of the content of the Frankfurters sold around the university. Smith says that Anderson "arranged for beef to be delivered twice a day, and sometimes more often, and he ground [minced] his own beef so that customers could watch him do so through glass windows."

This fastidious approach both to supply and hygiene was clearly visible in the first White Castle venue: the very name was designed, quite deliberately, to evoke cleanliness (a consistent obsession for fast-food restaurants from that time onward), and standards were set and kept very high. White Castle was also the first chain to finance and develop its own meat-processing factories, a move that meant Anderson and Ingram retained tight control over the means of production and thus could guarantee the quality of the meat they served. They also owned the factories that supplied their paper plates, napkins, and other sundries.

Anderson's experience at the sharp, hot end of burger production had taught him a huge amount but, like many businessmen at the time, he struggled to get together sufficient capital to expand. Ingram was able to throw his considerable cash and business acumen behind him. Indeed, for all Anderson's culinary innovations, it was Ingram's development of what came to be known as the "White Castle System" that really accelerated the success of both the brand itself and the fast-food industry in general. Indeed, it is fair to say that before White Castle there was no fast-food industry beyond the carts that clustered in centers of employment in the major cities of the United States. Ingram's system brought industrial

What Ford did for the motorcar, Ingram and Anderson did for the burger.

Opposite: Exterior view of White Castle number 1, Wichita, Kansas.

Origins

A hearty Yuletide Welcome from White Castle

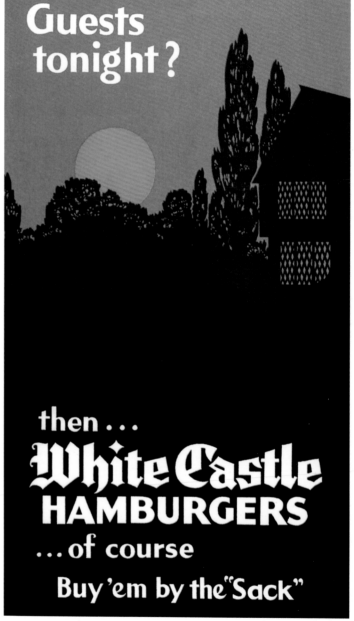

Guests tonight?

then . . . White Castle HAMBURGERS . . . of course

Buy 'em by the "Sack"

Opposite (left): White Castle Christmas advertisement.

Opposite (right): White Castle advertising poster.

Left: White Castle billboard advertisement, Louisville, Kentucky.

Next spread (top left): Exterior view of White Castle number 10, Wichita, Kansas.

Next spread (bottom left): White Castle appearance chart titled "Look Yourself Over" gives instructions to male employees on how they should be dressed at work.

Next spread (right): R. C. Decker & Co. meat delivery truck for White Castle, New York City.

thinking to the production of the burger in ways that had never been applied to food of any kind: he came up with what Andrew F. Smith describes as "efficiency and economy (nickel hamburgers, a limited menu and mass volume); standardization and simplification of the food-preparation process; prominent locations near mass-transit stops; a uniform and distinctive architecture; aggressive expansion of outlets; and a pleasant setting conducive to the customer's enjoyment." They were also proud of their open kitchens, intended to show cleanliness to their customers.

The progress made by Anderson and Ingram—and, after Anderson sold out in 1925, by Ingram alone—was nothing short of spectacular. Within nine years, White Castle had 116 restaurants that each had, according to Josh Ozersky, "an exquisite machine, dynamically engineered to allow one man to sell coffee and hamburgers, supremely efficient and gleaming with chrome and white enamel." Part of the system was a newsletter, first called *Hot Hamburger* and then rebranded as the *White Castle House Organ*, maybe one of the few things they got wrong. It encouraged company employees to innovate themselves and send in suggestions, such as this brilliant way of speeding up the cooking process, quoted by Ozersky in his book *The Hamburger* and reproduced here with the original spelling, punctuation, and capitalization:

I HAVE DISCOVERED BY PUTTING THIS HOLE IN THE MEAT, IT WILL COOK FASTER IT ALSO ALLOWES THE STEAM TO COME UP THROUGH THE HOLE AND STILL RETAIN ALL OF IT'S FLAVOUR, I HAVE TIMED THIS PROSSESS OF COOKING THE HAMBURGERS AND I BELIEVE IT IS A THIRD FASTER, IF THIS HOLE WAS PROSSESSED IN IT WHILE BEING MANUFACTORED IT WOULD BE BETTER, OTHERWISE IT WOULD BE TO SLOW TO DO IT OUR SELVES, BY THE HOLE IN THE MEAT IT DOES ALLOW IT TO COOK FASTER THAT IS THE IDEA I AM TRYING TO EXPLAIN.

This sort of creative thinking, in thrall to the larger idea of making more and quicker, meant that White Castle could not help but succeed—becoming, as Ozersky put it, a "mighty engine of prosperity." According to him, the

"The day of the dirty, greasy hamburger is past."

➡ Billy Ingram

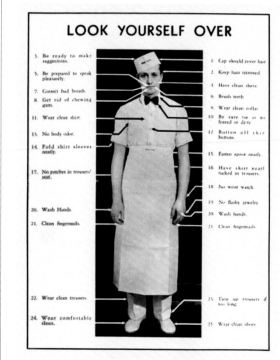

Origins

creation and development of the inexpensive hamburger meal "was a worthy goal, a universal meal that would be completely American, unmarred by distinctions of region, class, or ethnicity. Out of many, one—just like the meat of a well-ground hamburger."

Ingram strongly resisted franchising, feeling that it would lessen his control of the system, but there were benefits to remaining part of the White Castle empire: it was the first fast-food chain to set up a profit-sharing bonus system and a fund for employee medical expenses.

It was also the first to use advertising and propaganda: in 1930, Ingram even arranged for a University of Minnesota medical student to live exclusively on White Castle food for thirteen weeks to prove how healthy it was.

In short, White Castle's innovations set the tone for what would become the fiercely competitive fast-food market, whether in the kitchen, in the boardroom, or on the newsstand. It even instituted its own Hall of Fame, including members such as the rock star Alice Cooper. Despite Cooper's reputation for extreme behavior, throughout his career, his love of the Castle's famous sliders has remained steadfast. Already a member of the Rock 'n' Roll equivalent at the time of his induction in 2014, Cooper said that many of his fellow musicians would be jealous of his newer accolade and, indeed, getting into the annals of White Castle's history is arguably a tougher ask. Cooper's affection for the simple White Castle burger kept him grounded even as his rock career took off on its trajectory.

In 2014, *Time* magazine declared the White Castle slider the most influential burger of all time. It's hard to argue.

Opposite: White Castle customers at counter.

Above: Exterior view of White Castle number 18, St. Louis, Missouri.

Texas Tavern

Origins

First (and only) location: Roanoke, Virginia, USA 1930

The Texas Tavern is so steeped in American history of a certain era that even if the burgers weren't delicious it would be worth a visit. Nick Bullington, whose family still owns and runs the diner, opened it in 1930. He had been an "advance" man (even possessing his own personal railroad car) for the Ringling Brothers Circus, traveling to all the towns the circus would be visiting and sorting out business and logistical matters before everyone else arrived. In the course of his travels, he experienced a wide variety of cuisines and began to file away his own recipes. In the 1920s, many counter-style hamburger stands were opening up and Bullington decided that this was a growing trend: he left the circus to create a diner.

He began by opening the tiny seven-stool Texas Tavern in New Castle, Indiana, in 1928. Sadly, the Great Depression hit shortly afterward and Bullington decided to move to the fast-growing, progressive city of Roanoke, Virginia. Here he opened the Texas Tavern in February 1930, and the rest is history. The restaurant is now under the watchful eye of its fourth generation of Bullingtons—the owner is Nick's great-grandson Matt—and celebrated its eighty-fifth anniversary in 2015.

The Tavern is open twenty-four hours a day and seven days a week. In the classic diner style, it retains its original counter, grill, and ten stools that were there in 1930. As Matt Bullington told me, "If ain't broken, don't fix it!" The restaurant places a huge amount of importance on its welcome and natural charm, as Bullington explained: "We're known as Roanoke's Millionaire's Club, because no matter if you're white collar, blue collar, or no collar, you get treated like a millionaire when you walk through the door of the Texas Tavern."

The signature burger is the Cheesy Western (known simply as a "Cheesy" to regulars), a cheeseburger topped with a fried egg and including the Tavern's secret-recipe mustard-based relish, pickles (gherkins), and onions.

Adventurous diners can opt for a Double Meat Cheesy Western, which is the same as a Cheesy but with an extra hamburger patty, and the Tavern is also known for its World Famous Texas Tavern Chile, of which it has served over twenty million bowls. It also serves thousands of Coney Island Hotdogs each week, topped with relish, mustard, onions, and its secret hot dog chile recipe, proving that it's not just burgers that make the Tavern an institution.

Bullington describes the burger as one of the great "equalizer" foods" and is very proud of the restaurant's diverse clientele: "At any given moment, you can walk in my restaurant and see a big burly biker sitting next to a little old lady who is rubbing elbows with a preacher, next to a judge on his lunch break, sitting next to a guy who just got out of jail. It is truly a melting pot."

Opposite: Exterior, Texas Tavern, Roanoke, Virginia.

Right: Signage, Texas Tavern, Roanoke, Virginia.

Wimpy

Origins

First location: Bloomington, Indiana, USA 1934

In existence in the U.S. since 1934, when Edward Gold created it in Bloomington, Indiana, Wimpy was the first American-style fast-food restaurant to open in London. It started business in the United Kingdom in 1954 when the first restaurant opened as part of a Lyons Corner House on Coventry Street in Central London. Today, the Wimpy chain no longer exists in the United States because, according to a 1978 *Chicago Tribune* article, no one had purchased the trademarked name from the Gold estate.

Wimpy now has eighty-two restaurants in the United Kingdom, focusing on "providing all of our customers with a freshly cooked meal at outstanding value," according to Brand Manager Alexia Mavro. Describing the company's usual customer as "loyal" makes a lot of sense, especially when you consider that it once served a celebratory meal for a multi-million-pound lottery winner.

The chain has undergone some upheaval, having moved from table service to counter service in the 1970s as it began to lose ground to McDonald's. It has also changed from largely company-owned to franchise restaurants and is now owned by Famous Brands, which also runs the South African Wimpy chain. In the UK, Wimpy is traditionally found in coastal locations such as the Isle of Wight, Southsea in Hampshire, and Clacton-on-Sea, Essex, evocative of traditional British seaside vacations. It still serves up some of the original menu items including the Wimpy Egg Burger, Wimpy Kingsize, and Bender Frankfurter Burger, as well as its classic Cheeseburger and the Wimpy Grill.

Until 2007, Mr. Wimpy, a character whose costume was based on the Beefeaters who guard the Tower of London, fronted the Wimpy chain. He even appeared in a computer game, *The Hamburger Game*, released in 1984, his enormous nose and grin peeking out from beneath a wide-brimmed red hat. The *Popeye* cartoon character, J. Wellington Wimpy, has not actually featured in the

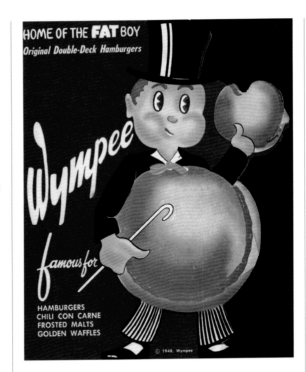

company's advertising, despite being the inspiration for its name (see page 340).

Wimpy sees the burger as "a meal in a bun, which can be adapted and innovated to capture a complete range of flavors." It's little surprise that the company believes the burger will go "from strength to strength, being enjoyed by future generations ... it remains the 'hero' product within our range and is the future of the brand." Described as "a British institution" by *Vice* magazine in 2014, there's no doubt that Wimpy will be around for a long time to come.

(see page 340).

Opposite: Wimpy, corner of Clark and Madison Streets, Chicago, Illinois, 1958.

Left: Menu for Wympee reads "Wympee, Home Of The Fat Boy, Original Double-Deck Hamburgers," U.S., 1948.

HOME OF THE **FAT** BOY
Original Double-Deck Hamburgers

Wympee

famous for

HAMBURGERS
CHILI CON CARNE
FROSTED MALTS
GOLDEN WAFFLES

© 1948, Wympee

Carl's Jr.

Origins

First location: Anaheim, California, USA 1945

Carl's Jr. was founded in 1941 by Carl and Margaret Karcher as a hot dog stand in Los Angeles, funded by $311 borrowed with their car as collateral and $15 that Margaret had in her purse. In 1945, when Carl was only twenty-eight years old, the couple opened their first permanent location, a restaurant called Carl's Drive-in Barbeque, in Anaheim, California. By 1954, the chain had expanded and been renamed Carl's Jr., the premise being a series of smaller, more fast-food-style burger joints with smaller menus. By 1981 there were over three hundred Carl's Jr. restaurants, predominantly in the west and southwest of the United States; there are now over a thousand. In 1997, Carl's Jr. merged with Hardee's, which was owned by the same parent company, CKE Restaurants, creating a chain of almost four thousand locations. Carl's Jr. also operates restaurants in a number of other countries, including Mexico, Russia, and Singapore.

The chain's signature items include the Tex Mex Bacon Thickburger, an 8-ounce (225-gram) charbroiled (chargrilled) patty with fire-roasted bell peppers and onions, bacon, Pepper Jack cheese, and spicy Santa Fe sauce; and the Six Dollar Burger, which comes with American cheese, tomato, red onions, pickles (gherkins), mustard, mayonnaise, and ketchup. It is so named because Carl's Jr. says you would have to pay that much in a sit-down restaurant for a burger of the same quality—when it was introduced in 2001 it cost a bargain $3.99.

Carl's Jr. is known as much for its provocative advertising as for its food. A campaign from the early 1990s showed children eating burgers from the chain and getting covered in sauce and burger juice, with the slogan "If it doesn't get all over the place, it doesn't belong in your face." In 2005, it launched a series of rather more risqué ads featuring celebrities and models eating burgers in what might be described as a suggestive manner. This campaign was kicked off with Paris Hilton, decked out in

Origins

Far left: Hardee's
restaurant, c. 1963.

Left: Free Sausage
Biscuit Day,
Cheyenne, Wyoming.

a black swimsuit, washing and writhing against a Bentley, before eating a Spicy BBQ Six Dollar Burger and declaring, "That's hot." In another ad, model Kate Upton cavorts with a Southwest Patty Melt in the back of a classic car. Other models to have featured include Heidi Klum and Emily Ratajkowski.

Kim Kardashian has also advertised for the chain, as has former National Football League star Terrell Owens; in addition Carl's Jr. used YouTube stars such as Smosh and iJustine to promote its food, the first time a fast-food chain had delved into that form of digital marketing.

While the campaigns have attracted criticism, the chain seems resolutely behind its flamboyant style, airing an ad featuring model Charlotte McKinney in one of the renowned Super Bowl advertising slots in 2015, and demonstrating that it has a sense of humor in its promotion of the Most American Thickburger. A voiceover asks, "What's more American than a cheese-burger?" before answering, with admirable brio as the camera pans away for a series of reveals, "This cheese-burger, loaded with a hot dog and potato chips [crisps], in the hands of all-American model Samantha Hoopes, in a hot tub, in a pick-up truck, driven by an American bull-rider, on an aircraft carrier, under the gaze of Lady Liberty." It's silly and funny and irreverent.

Above: Carl Karcher, founder of Carl's Jr., outside restaurant signage, 1960.

Opposite: Carl's Jr. waitress, 1983.

"That's hot."

⬇

Paris Hilton, star of Carl's Jr. advertise-ments

Fatburger

"**The club be poppin' so I'm stoppin' at the Fatburger.**"

↓

rapper Tupac Shakur, "Late Night"

First location: Los Angeles, California, USA 1948

Fatburger was born as Mr. Fatburger in Los Angeles in 1948. Lovie Yancey, the restaurant's creator, loved burgers and she loved her boyfriend, so when she created the burger joint she named it after him—his nickname was Fat. Happily for Lovie, and for us, her relationship with burgers lasted longer than the one with the boyfriend; when they split in 1952, Mr. Fatburger dropped the gendered title and became, simply, Fatburger.

Over the next half-century the brand went from strength to strength, gaining a cult following for its blend of juicy burgers and music, throwing out a wonderfully danceable mix of rock 'n' roll, hip-hop, and soul that had customers burning off calories as quickly as they consumed them. Fatburger was ripe for expansion, so in 2006, when basketball legend Magic Johnson and singer Janet Jackson part-owned the chain, current chairman and CEO Andy Wiederhorn bought them out. He took a company that had 40 restaurants and transformed it; today there are 200 locations in 19 countries, with a further 350 in development. There are Fatburgers in casinos, Fatburgers with bars, and in 2008 the company even opened a Fatburger in the Arizona Diamondbacks' Chase Field stadium, their first in a sports arena.

Fatburger, which goes by the tagline "The Last Great Hamburger Stand," cooks its burgers to order and takes pride in the fact that it is "all about the burger." It's not inflexible about the form it comes in, though, and has adapted its menus to suit international venues—for example, serving lamb and buffalo in India. It also sells vast numbers of turkey and vegetarian burgers, and halal options are available.

While the company's signature item is the Fatburger, served with oodles of fries (chips), it has plenty of other popular options. The Triple X is a burger of gargantuan proportions, three 8-ounce (225-gram) patties and all the rest; Fatburger sees finishing the behemoth as a contest

and, if you manage it, a t-shirt and a picture on the wall await you. The brand also serves the cheekily named Hypocrite, a vegetarian burger with two rashers of bacon tucked inside.

Fatburger has a close relationship with hip-hop music and its musicians, and features in a number of tracks by Notorious B.I.G, Ice Cube, and Tupac Shakur. Kanye West's restaurant company also owned several Fatburgers in Chicago for a while. Rapper Pharrell Williams partnered with Fatburger to expand the chain into China in 2007. If it's good enough for Ice Cube at two o'clock in the morning, it's good enough for the rest of us.

Opposite (top):
Exterior, Fatburger,
West Hollywood,
California.

Opposite (bottom):
Interior, Fatburger,
Laughlin, Nevada.
2012.

Right: Lovie Yancey,
founder of Fatburger,
1947.

51

McDonald's

Origins

First location: San Bernardino, California, USA 1948

Two brothers who were much taken with the business model as evinced by White Castle and its pale imitators were Maurice and Richard McDonald: together with the irrepressible and extraordinarily gifted Ray Kroc, they took the humble drive-thru and perfected a combination of industrial design, menu, service, and advertising that has led some to give McDonald's quasi-divine status among brands. The brothers McDonald opened their first proper restaurant as a drive-in burger bar that, while good, was a long way from what the franchise would evolve into. While the drive-in element represented the growing centrality of the car to American life, "the place was still burdened by the customs of pre-automotive dining: knives, forks, plates, a big menu, slow-smoked meats, and all the rest of it," to quote Josh Ozersky.

This first McDonald's also had carhops, lissome young women who carried orders out to waiting customers but often, according to Andrew F. Smith, "seemed more interested in socializing than selling burgers" and according to Ozersky, "attracting good-for-nothing teenage boys who would loiter around and not order anything." History has not judged the carhops kindly, perhaps because their removal was the first step toward the McDonald brothers achieving the speed of service for which the brand became legendary.

The brothers worked out that by dispensing with silverware (cutlery) and plates, and by getting customers to come to the counter to be served, and then dispose of their own waste in discreet and carefully sanitized bins, they could save time. When this was combined with the fiercely rapid (and open) kitchen set-up, the fast could really be put into fast food. Such volumes of burgers and shakes were being sold that Ray Kroc, seller of Multimixer shake machines, was intrigued by the supposedly small-time San Bernardino outfit that had ordered so many of them. He visited the restaurant in 1954, a couple

Left: Exterior, McDonald's drive-thru, c. 1970.

Above: McDonald's owner Ray Kroc, eating a hamburger outside restaurant.

Origins

of years later than Matthew Burns and Keith Kramer, who would go on to found Insta-Burger King in Florida, which eventually became Burger King.

Kroc was amazed by the McDonald brothers' success and within a short time had negotiated a deal for McDonald's franchises, changing the typical playing field by selling the brand to individual stores. He brought in Harry Sonneborn, who had run franchising for "soft-serve" ice-cream chain Tastee-Freez, and the two of them created an operation even slicker than the kitchen of the original McDonald's restaurant. Every detail was regulated and checked, from menu and service to restaurant design and branding. McDonald's proliferated, an army of burger vendors marching under Kroc's banner of "Quality, Service, Cleanliness, and Value," so that by 1959 there were more than one hundred franchises across the country, run by carefully selected and trained managers. In 1961, the famous Hamburger University, which awards graduates a Bachelor of Hamburgerology, opened in Illinois, part of Kroc's drive to create a professionalized managerial group within the brand who were fully educated in the ethos and management theory he had developed and evangelized. It is still in operation, and Burger King runs a similar program to train its managers.

Kroc drove the McDonald's brand into the nascent suburban America, a land of opportunity opened up by an extensive national program of interstate highways and local road building and the increase in car ownership, and significantly, an area untapped by chains like White Castle. By 1963 McDonald's was selling over one million hamburgers a day; by 1965 there were over seven hundred restaurants across the United States and two years later the group began to go global, opening franchises in Canada and Puerto Rico. The first recognizably American food item was well and truly established.

And that sense of the burger being American, a product of time and place and spirit, has never left it. As food writer Elisabeth Rozin says in *The Primal Cheeseburger*, the hamburger is "wholeheartedly and uncontestedly American, a fact made no less true by its popularity in Paris, Rio, and Beijing." She describes it, in fact,

as "a characteristic culinary expression of the American experience."

Indeed, as the hamburger spread around the globe, and took on localized forms and flavors, it did so riding on the back of American commercialism. Whether serving a burger from a beachfront shack to surfers in Australia or shucking out mass-produced vegetarian patties in a McDonald's in New Delhi, the burger and its multifarious incarnations have retained the taste of Americana and its cultural imprint. The burger has, and always will have, its roots in that murky story about not only the food itself but also the nation that gave birth to it.

Ever since the McDonald brothers founded that first restaurant in San Bernardino, the name has been synonymous with the hamburger and the global spread of fast food. Today the empire serves tens of millions customers across the world, with over 35,000 locations in 119 countries.

The diverse menu ranges from classic burgers like the signature Big Mac and the Quarter Pounder to the vegetarian McAloo Tikki in India, McRice in Indonesia, and the hot chicken Mighty Wings, hugely popular in China and Spain.

A recent advertising campaign called "The Cow" rebutted general myths about the low quality of the produce fast-food restaurants use. Using an animated cow and bright coloring, "The Cow" asserted that McDonald's only used good-quality beef. Interestingly, the ad also mentioned that the claims it was making had to be true because the Advertising Standards Authority required it.

Fast-food advertising often stays close to the core message that its wares engender a feeling of togetherness and happiness. McDonald's is no exception to this: a recent ad for its limited-edition BBQ Chicken Legend burger, entitled "My Dad," features a young boy describing the high-quality ingredients he would use to create such an item, then giving his Dad a McDonald's burger of that type and saying, "My Dad's a legend and that's the least he deserves."

Opposite: Employee, McDonald's, 1979.

Many of the various ads run by McDonald's under the "i'm lovin' it" slogan, devised in 2003 by Heye & Partner, McDonald's German agency, which then took the campaign global, have also featured this sort of family-oriented, feel-good approach. "Good Times," run in 2015 on British television, shows a young boy named Harry being told off in stores for various enthusiasms such as jumping on beds and touching glass display cabinets, before finally being allowed to enjoy himself in McDonald's with his parents. Harry's playfulness is only unconfined in the restaurant and there are smiles all round as the family enjoys its light-hearted moments while enjoying burgers. Both "Good Times" and "My Dad" play on the familiar themes of family togetherness, bonding over a burger, appealing to the emotions that the food evokes in many of us.

The company isn't averse to bringing romance into its advertising, either. A 2015 campaign called "Lonely Hearts" shows a blind date between John and Emma, which proceeds clumsily. Various things go wrong, including Emma entering John's name as Steve at a bowling alley, then the two ruefully go their separate ways. But, by happy chance, they meet again in a McDonald's and overhear each other ordering exactly the same meal, right down to the choice of sauce. A meaningful look is exchanged and the audience understands that a shared interest in something can bring people together, even when they least expect it.

Romance and family are mingled in a 2014 McDonald's ad from the Philippines, in which two brothers, the younger of whom has Down Syndrome, go for breakfast at the restaurant, and trade advice on how flirt with one of the women who works there. The brothers bond over pancakes and the older one urges his younger sibling to smile flirtatiously, advising him on just how broad his grin should be. It's a classic fast-food mélange of family and love and food, hitting all the notes of communality, warmth, and friendship that resonate with our associations with burgers.

McDonald's has also successfully used an array of celebrities in its advertising: Justin Timberlake sang the jingle for the "i'm lovin' it" campaign and appeared in

several ads, while the chain sponsored his 2003 European tour; basketball legend Kobe Bryant advertised the Big N' Tasty in 2001; and Destiny's Child worked with the brand in 2003–4, including an ad that raised awareness of McDonald's charitable work through the Ronald McDonald House charities. The imLovinIt24 event, in 2015, used Ne-Yo's performance of "Every Day With Love," a song for which the lyrics had been crowd-sourced from McDonald's customers. McDonald's took its relationship with recording artists a step further by sponsoring the McDonald's Lounge at the SXSW Festival in Austin, Texas: here visitors could see how the brand is pushing into the digital world, while listening to various artists performing live.

The chain can also lay claim to perhaps the most heartfelt of celebrity endorsements for a fast-food restaurant: actor James Franco's open love letter to McDonald's in *The Washington Post* in 2015. Between the chain's founding in the 1940s and 2000, one-eighth of the potential American working population had been employed by McDonald's at some point. This is a staggering figure and it seems Hollywood heartthrobs are no exception. As Franco wrote, "All I know is that when I needed McDonald's, McDonald's was there for me. When no one else was." He used the time as a drive-thru attendant to hone his theatrical skills: "I refrained from reading on the job, but soon started putting on fake accents with the customers to practice for my scenes in acting." He remembers this time very fondly and with a touch of humor: "I hate to whistleblow, but *everyone* ate straight from the fry hopper. You'd walk by and snag a fry and pop it in your mouth. So easy."

Franco's nostalgic piece is shot with affection and is a fine reminder that McDonald's, or other fast-food joints, forms part of a fabric of their lives. As Franco said, "When I was hungry for work, they fed the need. I still love the simplicity of the McDonald's hamburger and its salty fries." This sort of advocacy is PR gold dust, of course, but you get the impression from reading it that Franco wrote from a genuine warmth toward the brand, not as an endorsement.

In terms of sponsorship, McDonald's is closely affiliated to soccer, having long-standing arrangements with FIFA,

Opposite (top left): U.S. President John F. Kennedy outside McDonald's, 1962.

Opposite (bottom left): Mariah Carey at McDonald's, Times Square, New York City, 2014.

Opposite (right): British Prime Minister Margaret Thatcher with McDonald's Big Mac, 1983.

the world governing body, for events such as the World Cup, and with UEFA, the European governing body, for the European Championships. The company has also created and sustained sports coaching in Malawi and helped small clubs in the United Kingdom.

The global proliferation of McDonald's has resulted in several interesting academic offshoots. The Big Mac, launched in 1968, became such a symbol of the McDonald's brand that in 1986, *The Economist* launched "The Big Mac Index," a measure of currency valuation based on its purchasing power. Effectively assuming that a Big Mac should cost the same in raw terms wherever it was and that it would be universally recognizable to its readers, *The Economist* compared prices of the burger globally and used the data to show which currencies were under- or overvalued. The Big Mac Index has now been updated to take labor costs into account and is a widely recognized economic metric.

In 1999, Thomas L. Friedman's book *The Lexus and the Olive Tree* posited what is known as the Golden Arches Theory of Conflict Prevention, essentially that no two countries in which McDonald's operated a franchise had ever fought a war against each other. This was argued to be a reflection of such countries' advanced capitalist state, which made conflict unnecessary as a result of economic development. While Friedman has subsequently said the theory was slightly tongue-in-cheek, and various conflicts seem to disprove the idea, the fact that McDonald's was seen as such a strong indicator of global capitalist development shows how widely the brand has spread and how strongly it is identified with economic progress.

In-N-Out Burger

Origins

First location: Baldwin Park, California, USA 1948

In-N-Out Burger has an almost legendary status among burger aficionados. Its secret menu (available only to those in the know), tasty food, and socially responsible approach guaranteeing huge numbers of fans extends well beyond its West Coast home.

Founded by married couple Harry and Esther Snyder, the first In-N-Out opened in Baldwin Park, California, in 1948; many credit it as the home of the drive-thru, despite McDonald's making similar claims. It is still run as a family business, has never gone public, and has never solicited bids to run its restaurants as franchises.

When Harry and Esther created their first burger shack, which was about 10 square feet (1 square meter) in area, they used to collect all their ingredients from local producers. The current management at In-N-Out prides itself on the fact that none of its food travels more than 500 miles (800 kilometers) and that it is never frozen. Rather than outsourcing any of the supply chain, the restaurants are supplied by the company's own commissaries, so the food is effectively shipped fresh to over 230 separate In-N-Outs along the West Coast. This is why In-N-Out has never expanded further east than Texas, so as to remain near the distribution centers.

Alongside the standard offerings of hamburger, cheeseburger, and the Double Double (two patties and two slices of cheese), In-N-Out is famous for its not-so-secret menu (see page 67), which includes having your burger "Animal Style," with additional pickles (gherkins), mustard, grilled onions, and extra "spread" (similar to Thousand Island dressing) grilled onto the patty. Because the company makes every order from scratch, it also allows for variations in the number of patties. Though after some customers ordered a 100 x 100, the In-N-Out code for a hundred patties and a hundred slices of cheese

Opposite: Replica of an early In-N-Out drive-thru.

Above: In-N-Out drive-thru, Baldwin Park, California, 1948.

in a burger, the company vowed never to make anything larger than a 4 × 4 again.

In-N-Out is also renowned for its legions of celebrity fans, who appreciate it both for its inherently Californian cool and the kudos of the secret menu, and because the food is sublime. Michelin-starred chefs such as Gordon Ramsay and Thomas Keller, and Anthony Bourdain and the late Julia Child have all spoken volubly of their love of In-N-Out Burger. Ramsay said in an interview in 2008, "In-N-Out burgers were extraordinary. I was so bad, I sat in the restaurant, had my double cheeseburger, then minutes later I drove back round and got the same thing again to take away."

The ethos of In-N-Out doubtless helps as well. The menu has hardly changed since the company first opened, adding low-fat meals in the 1970s, but otherwise staying very close to the basic template of well-crafted burgers, fries (chips), and shakes. As Stacy Perman, author of *In-N-Out Burger: An Unauthorized Behind-The-Counter Look at the Fast-Food Chain That Breaks All the Rules*, notes, "It's taken In-N-Out 60 years to add 7-Up and Dr. Pepper." Add to that a famously competitive wage by the standards of the fast-food sector, which leads to a very low staff turnover, and the emphasis on local produce, especially beef, and you can understand why In-N-Out has a reputation as the most ethical of fast-food joints. The fact that it is a privately owned company means that the owners and managers aren't under pressure to overcommit to expansion or to change the company's core values. It also means that In-N-Out will be able to stay that way for as long as it wants. And that includes keeping "Animal Style" on the not-so-secret menu. Just don't tell everyone.

Generally regarded as the hottest ticket in town, even harder to get invited to than the Academy Awards ceremony itself, *Vanity Fair*'s post-Oscars bash is fueled by celebrity chat, martinis, and In-N-Out burgers. Over a thousand burgers were served at the party in 2016 hosted by *Vanity Fair*'s editor Graydon Carter, demonstrating once again that no matter how refined the atmosphere, a burger always hits the spot.

Right: In-N-Out restaurant signage, Camarillo, California.

Origins

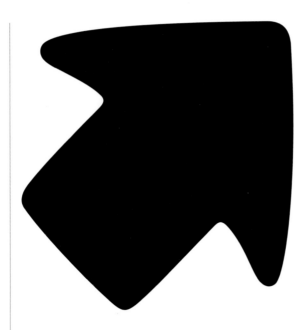

In-N-Out's "Not-So-Secret Menu"

Double Meat

Two 100-percent pure beef patties, hand-leafed lettuce, tomato, spread, with or without onions, stacked high on a freshly baked bun.

4 × 4

Four 100-percent pure beef patties, hand-leafed lettuce, tomato, spread, four slices of American cheese, with or without onions, stacked high on a freshly baked bun.

Protein Style

Your favorite burger wrapped in hand-leafed lettuce instead of a bun.

3 × 3

Three 100-percent pure beef patties, hand-leafed lettuce, tomato, spread, three slices of American cheese, with or without onions, stacked high on a freshly baked bun.

Grilled Cheese

Two slices of melted American cheese, hand-leafed lettuce, tomato, spread, with or without onions, on a freshly baked bun.

Animal Style

Burger of your choice with hand-leafed lettuce, tomato, a mustard-cooked beef patty; add pickles (gherkins), extra spread with grilled onions.

Far left: In-N-Out drive-thru menu.

Left: Helen Mirren eating an In-N-Out Cheeseburger at the *Vanity Fair* Oscar Party, 2007.

Jack in the Box

Origins

First location: San Diego, California, USA 1951

Jack in the Box was born in San Diego in 1951, the brainchild of businessman Robert O. Peterson. It served eighteen-cent hamburgers and used a drive-thru window with an early version of the intercom, to connect customers in the comfort of their own cars to the restaurant workers. Today, there are more than 2,250 Jack in the Box locations, spread across 21 American states and Guam. Many of these are open twenty-four hours a day "to satisfy our guests' cravings any time day or night," says Senior Vice President Keith Guilbault.

The brand aims to "provide a unique menu with craveable, mouthwatering products that range from the familiar to the unexpected." Its signature item is the Buttery Jack, a beef patty and bun, smothered in melted garlic butter and Provolone cheese, with the option of adding hickory-smoked bacon and Swiss cheese. The chain also serves breakfast all day, every day, offering a Supreme Croissant sandwich with egg, bacon, and American cheese, and a Late Night menu that features tacos. With that kind of variety, it's no wonder that Guilbault says, "The hamburger is unique as it represents infinite possibilities, but can also be great on its own."

The company hit nationwide headlines when a famously tongue-in-cheek commercial aired in the classic prime-of-all-times slot in the 2012 Super Bowl. "Marry Bacon" shows an absurdly earnest young man telling his mother he is about to be married—to bacon. There follows a series of humorous wedding clichés, in which the man is accompanied by a strip of bacon rather than a wife, before the ad culminates in a priest telling him, "You may now eat the bride!"

Guilbault has always loved burgers, so it's not a surprise he ended up working for a hamburger restaurant. The relationship began early: "One of my favorite burgers of all time has to be the one my Dad used to make at our family barbecues when I was a kid. It was his master grilling that

"There are no weird orders at Jack in the Box, only creative ones."

→ Keith Guilbault

Left: Exterior, Jack in the Box drive-thru, c. 1953.

71

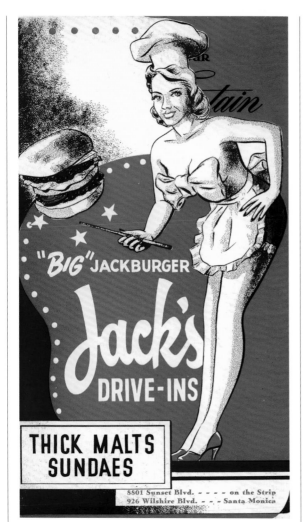

"BIG" JACKBURGER

Jack's DRIVE-INS

THICK MALTS SUNDAES

8801 Sunset Blvd. ~ ~ ~ ~ on the Strip
926 Wilshire Blvd. ~ ~. ~ Santa Monica

kick-started my unending love for burgers!" The person he'd most like to share a burger with now, he says, is Will Ferrell, "but only dressed as Ron Burgundy [his famous *Anchorman* character]—he knows good food and loves San Diego, just like us."

For Guilbault, the burger is only going to improve in terms of quality and creativity. Its essential versatility encourages that creativity, as he sees it: "There are many different ways to prepare a burger, and the options to put on the burger are even longer. In our industry, we have seen some crazy innovation, and that's what makes the burger so exciting—it's an empty, delicious canvas and can be accompanied by so many different flavors."

Nonetheless, it's this essential, basic love of burgers that means they can be explored, experimented with, even messed with, and still retain their place in our affections. As Guilbault says, "Burgers are hot, juicy, and delicious and can be eaten just about anywhere—in the car at a drive-in or at the ballpark; they're an American classic."

The All-American Diner & Drive-In

Is there another structure as uniquely American as the diner? Almost always of prefabricated stainless steel, sometimes in a decommissioned railroad car, these bastions of late-night, low-key dining sprang up across the East Coast of the United States in the late nineteenth century and have been a fixture across the country since. A man named Walter Scott is widely credited with establishing the first diner, in Providence, Rhode Island, in 1872. It was a horse-drawn wagon with windows on either side that allowed customers to walk up and order, then eat on the street. The success of Scott's wagon, which fed the hungry employees of the *Providence Journal* as they started to work all night to make the newspaper, soon led to imitators in Worcester, Massachusetts, where Thomas Buckley set up a series of White House Café wagons from 1887 onward. In 1891, Charles Palmer patented the horse-drawn "night lunch wagon" and ran a number of them successfully in the area until 1901.

In 1939, Roland Stickney created the first diner in the shape of a railroad car, using the Sterling Streamliner as a model. Two such diners remain in their original form, in Salem, Massachusetts, and in Pawtucket, Rhode Island. As the popularity of fast-food restaurants grew post-World War II, many of these diners and others were superseded, but there are still plenty in current use, especially in the northeastern United States.

Most diners are built to similar specifications, including a long service counter, often opposite the door, with large banks of windows. When Uma Thurman's character in the film *Kill Bill* staggers across the road from the graveyard where she has been buried, to order a coffee, the layout of a typical diner affords the terrified server a view of her ghostly approach. She then plunks herself down at an otherwise empty bar, as if there were nothing at all strange about her disheveled appearance. As we shall see in more detail later (see page 368), director Quentin Tarantino often uses diners in his films, both because of their iconic, resonant place in the American psyche and as the natural setting for his often transient or peripheral characters. Diners are at once egalitarian and available, but also afford a certain anonymity; people pass in and out without ever really being noticed.

Right: Drive-in food tray, 1950s.

Next spread: Drive-in carhop waitress on roller skates, serving burgers and milkshakes to couple in Ford Thunderbird, 1955.

This anonymity, coupled with a quintessentially American optimism, is reflected in two famous paintings, Edward Hopper's *Nighthawks* (1942) and Norman Rockwell's *The Runaway* (1958). In the first, an employee in gleaming white overalls serves three patrons of a late-night diner, awash with light against the shaded background of the city. The occupants are almost faceless, drawn together like moths to the diner's lights, but sealed away from the rest of the city by its vast windows. In Rockwell's painting, a young boy with a knapsack is chatting to a jovial police officer. He has clearly run away from somewhere, attracted to the diner as a transient's stop-off, but welcomed and befriended by a symbol of protection and safety.

The diners of the 1950s were a focal point for social gatherings, especially for American teenagers. Often sporting a jukebox, they were ideal spots for a get-together, especially as, unlike bars, they had no age restrictions, and were open just as late, if not twenty-four hours a day. Their low cost and relaxed atmosphere made them a vibrant social melting pot.

Their popularity increased still further with the spread of the automobile. Although the first drive-in diner, Kirby's Pig Stand, had been opened in 1921 in Dallas, Texas, the idea took off in the 1950s as people sought out meeting spots that catered for the new ubiquity of the car. In the TV series *Happy Days*, set in the 1950s, Arnold's Drive-In is just such a meeting place for the characters. While their popularity has declined, drive-in diners such as Mel's, a chain based in California, still flourish, their garishly beautiful neon signs as iconic as their rotunda style of building design and their food.

The diner is a vibrant hub of American communities. It is as central to the American narrative as its main offering, the hamburger.

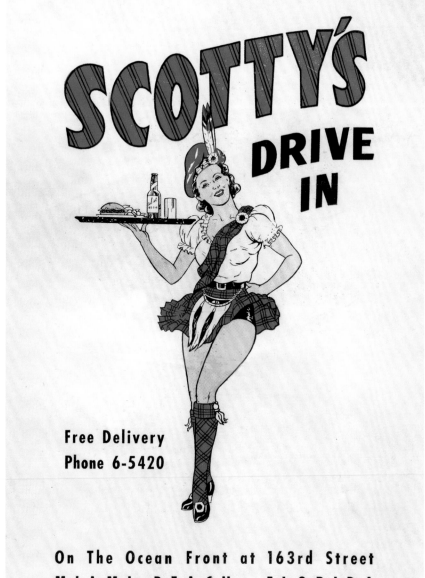

Above: Menu for
Scotty's Drive In,
Miami, Florida, 1955.

Above: Menu for
Oscar's, U.S., 1951.

Above: Menu for
Simon's Drive In,
U.S., 1936.

Origins

Left: Exterior,
Rosie's Diner,
Rockford, Michigan,
1945.

Opposite: Dining car,
New York City, 1920.

Left: Two carhops stand
under the "Drive-in
Restaurant" sign at
the Ox-in-Flames in
Farnborough, UK, 1960.

Sonic Drive-In

Origins

First location: Shawnee, Oklahoma, USA 1953

Sonic, so-called because it delivers food at (almost) the speed of sound, began life in 1953 as Top Hat Drive-In in Shawnee, Oklahoma. Top Hat was the creation of Troy Smith, Sr., who, in 1959, developed curbside speakers that allowed customers to order without leaving their cars. That same year he changed the company name to Sonic to reflect the existing catchy slogan.

The chain has bucked the general trend in American fast food by continuing to employ carhops, who at Sonic deliver food to customers on roller skates and, if the customers remain in the parking lot to eat, also skate back over to ensure everything was good. While many other drive-ins abandoned carhops and moved their employees inside, Sonic prides itself on this unique aspect of its customer service.

The company now serves about 3 million customers across over 3,500 locations, with a menu that centers on the burger but includes a range of other options. The carhop uniforms have changed; candy-striped waistcoats and sailor-style hats were replaced by a sportier polo shirt and visor look that reflects Sonic's modernization.

Even with that evolution, Sonic's one roller-skating foot in the past continues to be enduringly popular, evocative for many of a bygone age in the United States.

Real Burger Goodness

FOOT LONG CONEY . . 30¢
Foot Long CHEESE CONEY 35¢
REGULAR CONEY . . . 20¢
Regular CHEESE CONEY 25¢
Corn-Dog-on-a-Stick . . 25¢

FRITO CHILI PIE 25c
With CHILI and GRATED CHEESE

SONIC FAMOUS
"O"NION RINGS 35c
CRISP — GOLDEN BROWN
DELICIOUS

TATER TOTS . 25¢
SHREDDED & MOLDED

FRENCH FRIES 25¢
New Krinkle Cut-Delicious-Golden Brown

SONIC HAMBURGERS
PLEASE ORDER BY NUMBER   **35¢**

No. 1 Mayonnaise, Sweet Relish, Lettuce Tomato and Onion

No. 2 Old Fashion—Mustard, Dill Pickles Lettuce, Tomato and Onion

No. 3 With Special Smoke Sauce and Sliced Tomato

CHEESE BURGERS 45¢

SONIC SPECIALS
GRILLED CHEESE . . . . 30¢
BAR-B-Q BEEF Large with Relish **45¢**

THE WHOPPER 40¢
"That didn't get away"
Slab Boneless Fish on Toasted Bun
Shredded Lettuce — Tartar Sauce

Distinctive Desserts
Dish of Vanilla 10c
Sundaes Strawberry, Chocolate, Pineapple **25c**
Home Made Fried Pies . . . 25c
SERVED PIPING HOT — Apple, Cherry, Apricot
Fried Pie a la mode 35c

Fountain favorites
ROOT BEER . . .	10c	15c	20c
COCA-COLA . .	10c	15c	20c
DR. PEPPER . . .	10c	15c	20c
PEPSI-COLA . .	.10c	15c	20c
LIMEADE PLAIN WATER	10c	15c	20c
ICED TEA	10c	15c	20c
ICE COLD MILK			15c
COFFEE HOT – FRESH			10c
Rich, Creamy Hot Chocolate			15c
GRAPE SLUSH	10c	15c	20c
ORANGE SLUSH	10c	15c	20c

Shakes-Malts 30¢
★ Thick and Rich ★
Vanilla, Strawberry, Chocolate
Pineapple

Frosties 30¢
Root Beer - Coke - Dr. Pepper

FLOATS
Root Beer - Coke
Dr. Pepper
25¢

Above: First Sonic
Drive-In menu, 1953.

Above: Sonic Drive-In
signage, 2016.

Burger King

Origins

First location:
Miami, Florida, USA
1954

It's appropriate that if you are going to vie for the position of foremost in the world of anything, you pick something regal as your symbol. Burger King and McDonald's have been slugging it out since the dawn of hamburger time, and Burger King's innovations and brand development have been as important to the growth of the burger as anyone—literally.

Keith Kramer and Matthew Burns founded the chain's progenitor, Insta-Burger King, in Jacksonville, Florida, in 1953. The name was derived from a broiling (grilling) conveyor belt on which the burgers were cooked, giving an open-air flavor to the food, which tapped into an American, and especially Southern, love of outdoors cooking.

Insta-Burger King shack quickly franchised but ran into financial difficulties and so David Edgerton and James McLamore, two franchise owners from Miami, bought the company in 1954 and renamed it Burger King in 1956.

Edgerton and McLamore were to Burger King what Ray Kroc was to McDonald's and Billy Ingram to White Castle. They quickly set about refining the cooking method, improving the Insta-Broiler into the Flame Broiler, which was both more reliable and produced more flavor. It was so effective that the company did not replace it until forty years later, and even then the upgrade was based on the same cooking principle.

Edgerton and McLamore's biggest innovation was the development of the Whopper. McLamore had observed that while the United States was flourishing with a rampant form of consumerism, burgers had stayed small, largely a result of the initial popularity of White Castle's sliders and the concept of the burger as more of a snack than a full meal. McLamore decided to offer a monster of a burger: "I suggested that we call our product a *Whopper*, knowing that would convey imagery of something *big*," he helpfully explains in his autobiography *The Burger King*.

Left: Burger King
magazine advertisement,
U.S., 1966.

Opposite: Burger King
magazine advertisement,
U.S., 1982.

Where 60-second service begins with a smile...

...and ends with one

Burger King – the nation's fastest growing chain of self-service restaurants – is so delightfully different, no wonder it has caught America's fancy. Not a drive-in...not a cafeteria...not a diner – Burger King is a unique concept in restaurants, designed for America-on-the-move.

At Burger King, there are no waiters, no waiting, no tipping. Give your order and in just about 60-seconds, your hot food is ready to enjoy. The atmosphere is home-like, casual, relaxed. And you can eat inside where the weather is perfect for comfort.

The whole family will enjoy the good tasting, nourishing food – like the famous open-flame broiled *Whopper* an exclusive Burger King creation that's a nutritionally balanced meal-in-itself –

big enough to satisfy a healthy appetite. And the kids will love those super-size shakes, too.

Wherever you go...look for the sign of the happy King-on-a-Bun. It's the sign of good food...60-second service and pleasingly low prices. That's Burger King – Home of the *Whopper*.

America's fastest-growing chain of self-service restaurants

ALABAMA
Birmingham · Mobile

COLORADO
Colorado Springs · Denver

CONN. · Waterbury

DEL. · Wilmington

FLORIDA
Fort Lauderdale · Hialeah
Greater Miami · Hollywood
Jacksonville · Key West
Ocala · Pensacola
Pompano · W. Palm Beach

GEORGIA
Atlanta · Augusta
Savannah

ILLINOIS
Champaign
Chicagoland (44 stores)

INDIANA · Gary

KANSAS · Kansas City

KENTUCKY · Louisville

LOUISIANA
Baton Rouge · New Orleans
Shreveport

MASSACHUSETTS
Greater Boston

MICHIGAN
Ann Arbor · Flint
Lansing · Detroit

MINNESOTA
Minneapolis/St. Paul

MISSOURI · St. Louis

NEW JERSEY · Edison

NEW YORK · Queens
Hempstead, L. I.

NORTH CAROLINA
Asheville · Charlotte
Greensboro · High Point
Winston Salem

OHIO · Cincinnati

PENNSYLVANIA
Broomall · Conshohocken
Harrisburg · King of Prussia

SOUTH CAROLINA
Anderson
Charleston · Columbia
Greenville · Spartanburg

TENNESSEE
Knoxville · Nashville
Memphis (Jolly King)

TEXAS
Dallas · Denton · Houston

VIRGINIA
Fairfax · Norfolk

WISCONSIN · Milwaukee

PUERTO RICO
Greater San Juan

International Headquarters:
Miami, Florida

BURGER KING®
HOME OF THE **WHOPPER**

Story of the
Battle of the Burgers

Once upon a time, Burger King® was perplexed. Millions of people knew that the "Home of the Whopper®" served the best food in the land. But there were millions and millions of others that didn't.

Then, one day, an idea: conduct taste tests coast-to-coast and spread the news far and wide.

The rest is history. Everyone knows that the Whopper® Sandwich beat the competition, and that Flame Broiling beat frying. Suddenly, the "Home of the Whopper®" became the "Home of the Winner."

And that made the competition very unhappy. Because more and more people began switching to Burger King® In fact, MILLIONS have switched!* Clearly,

The Switch is on!

BURGER KING Aren't You Hungry?™

introducing **THE PROUD WHOPPER**

Other advertising has sought to engage the glamour of celebrity, sometimes with odd consequences. The Burger King marketing team engaged a young Ben Affleck in an ad that involved an old car phone. On the other end is a young woman who wants a Burger King Chef Salad. Affleck gladly delivers it but, as the woman comes onto the porch to collect it in a scene reminiscent of a teen slasher film, he is forced to take a call from his father and return home. The slogan? "Sometimes, you've gotta break the rules."

A viral campaign in 2005–6 saw model and actress Brooke Burke "date" the Burger King "King," with paparazzi-style pictures and features on their engagement and subsequent break-up placed in gossip magazines and online. The supposed allure of the King was also used in a spoof viral campaign for a Burger King fragrance that smelled, enticingly, of flame-grilled meat. One version of this campaign even saw Piers Morgan posing in front of a fire, wearing a Burger King medallion. While perhaps not everyone's idea of tasteful, the campaign generated significant traction, and the use of the somewhat controversial and outspoken Morgan showed the brand's willingness to take risks in the pursuit of engagement.

Burger King's promotional work with *Star Wars* in 1977 set a precedent that had the whole film industry fumbling to catch up. Posters, glasses, and sticker sets were offered that depicted scenes and characters from the film, and this continued across the first trilogy, including for the release of the films on DVD. Burger King also cross-promoted the 2008 release of *Indiana Jones and the Kingdom of the Crystal Skull*, another Lucasfilm production, and has had a deal with *The Simpsons* via Fox since 1990.

Given that families are such a significant market for hamburger restaurants, the rights to cross-promote with Disney have been hotly contested between the two biggest chains. McDonald's worked with Disney until the early 1990s, when Burger King took over the rights, including those to the hugely successful *The Lion King* (1994) and *Toy Story* (1995). The natural alliance of fast food's basic appeal to children and the family experience of movie-going with entertainment is richly mined by both

"A trip to Burger King was the biggest thing in the world to me. Heaven."

⬇

Dave Grohl, rock musician

An increased volume meant an increased price, too, something of a risk given that the burger was as much associated with a low price point as it was with convenience, but the thick, tasty patty and salad crunch of the Whopper were enormously popular. Since its introduction in 1957 it has become the chain's iconic offering.

Advertising and cross-promotion have been significant planks of Burger King's success. It was the first fast-food chain to name a competitor with its advertising, leading to the so-called Burger Wars of the early 1980s: in 1981 it ran a number of ads featuring a four-year-old Sarah Michelle Gellar, later of vampire-slaying fame. It was the first of these that garnered the most attention, naming McDonald's as a competitor and stating that their burgers were smaller than Burger King's. This led to a lawsuit by McDonald's, including against Gellar, who was named in the court action and was banned from visiting McDonald's restaurants for a while. The matter was eventually settled before trial.

Opposite: The
Proud Whopper.

Right: Burger King's
full-page newspaper
advertisement
addressed to
McDonald's, the
New York Times,
August 26, 2015.

Next spread: Exterior,
Burger King, London,
1989.

Pages 96-7: Billboard
advertisement
for McWhopper.

AN OPEN LETTER
FROM BURGER KING
TO MCDONALD'S

Good morning McDonald's,

We come in peace. In fact, we come in honor of peace.
We know we've had our petty differences, but how about we
call a ceasefire on these so-called 'burger wars'?

Here's what we're thinking.

Peace One Day is a non-profit organization campaigning to make
Peace Day, September 21, an annual day of global unity.
They have a powerful rallying call – 'Who will you make peace with?' –
which has inspired us to lead by example and extend an olive branch of our own.
We'd like to propose a one-off collaboration between Burger King and McDonald's
to create something special – something that gets the world talking about Peace Day.

The McWhopper.

All the tastiest bits of your *Big Mac* and our *Whopper*, united in one delicious,
peace-loving burger. Developed together, cooked together and available in
one location for one day only – Peace Day, September 21, 2015,
with all proceeds benefiting Peace One Day. All we need from you is
a few McDonald's crew members to help combine your ingredients with ours.

We appreciate that's a lot to swallow, so we've created
mcwhopper.com to give you a better understanding of our proposal.

Let's end the beef, with beef.

Talk soon,

Origins

industries, in commercial tie-ups of lasting durability and success. Burger King's cross-promotional work with Pokémon is another more recent example.

Burger King makes significant contributions to the charitable sector, running the McLamore Foundation and the Have It Your Way Foundation, as well as supporting charities run by bitter baseball rivals the Boston Red Sox and the New York Yankees. It sponsors a number of college sports in the United States, funding the State Champions Bowl in American football and the NCAA, the governing body of college athletics. The brand also has a strong association with soccer, the world's most popular sport, sponsoring La Liga, the Spanish top flight.

In 2014, Burger King introduced the Proud Whopper, a burger wrapped with the colors of the rainbow. People flocked to Burger King to find out what was so different about this burger. But when they opened the wrapper, they found the same Whopper they had always loved. The message on the wrapper explained everything: "we are all the same inside."

In 2015, Burger King took out a full-page advertisement in the national press calling for a truce in its Burger Wars with McDonald's. It suggested they join forces to create the "McWhopper" for Peace One Day on September 21, 2015. Steve Easterbrook, McDonald's CEO, declined the offer saying, "a simple phone call will do next time."

These days, about eleven million customers visit Burger King every day and the chain operates about fourteen thousand restaurants across seventy-three countries. The Whopper is still its most popular item, proving the lasting legacy of "bigger is better."

Origins

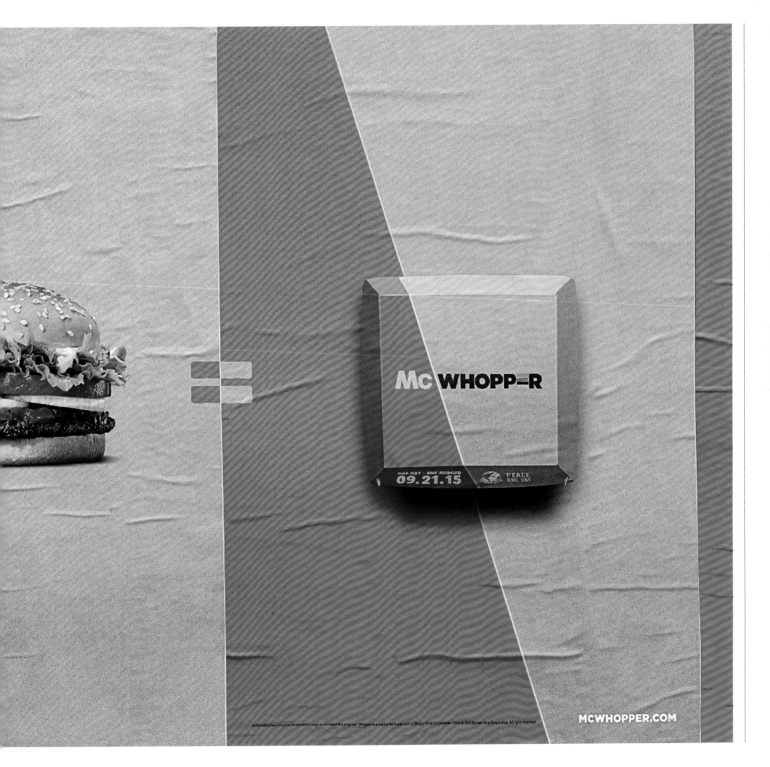

Mc WHOPP=R

ONE DAY · ONE BURGER
09.21.15   PEACE ONE DAY

MCWHOPPER.COM

97

Imagine your name is Joel Burger. You meet the love of your life, Ashley King. You propose and publish a picture of the happy occasion in front of an obvious choice of restaurant, tongue firmly in cheek. And then everyone, the restaurant included, finds out and loves it.

Joel and Ashley were married in July 2015 in Illinois. Childhood sweethearts, they had taken the picture of themselves standing behind a Burger King sign as a joke and sent it to their local newspaper with their engagement announcement, but the brand seized on the gift and offered to pay for the nuptials. The couple had photographs taken with them wearing the famous BK paper crowns, and members of the wedding party wore t-shirts bearing the restaurant's logo under their more formal attire. A spokesman for Burger King told the *New York Daily News,* "When we heard about the happy Burger-King couple, we felt an overwhelming urge to celebrate their upcoming marriage."

Mr. & Mrs. Burger-King decided on a traditional setting, the chapel in Jacksonville, Illinois. Rumors that King himself, the chain's mascot, officiated cannot be confirmed or denied.

Wendy's

Origins

First location: Columbus, Ohio, USA 1969

The Wendy's Company, or Wendy's, as everyone knows it, is the world's third-largest quick-service hamburger company and was founded in 1969. There are about 6,500 franchise or company-operated restaurants worldwide, mostly in the United States, but also across 28 other countries and U.S. territories.

As Bry Roth, Wendy's Marketing and Digital Communications Lead, explains, "Wendy's founder Dave Thomas loved two things above all else, food and people. That's why he started Wendy's. He believed in a place where you get great food, made fresh, served by nice people." It's a simple but powerful statement, and Thomas's legacy informs everything that Wendy's continues to do. He had been adopted at a very young age and his adoptive mother passed away when he was still young. He traveled widely with his adoptive father, relishing the time they spent eating out together. He began working in restaurants at age twelve and started to pick up the skills and business acumen that would help him found one of the world's most successful global hamburger brands. He named the chain after his daughter, another clear nod to the importance he placed on family.

The Wendy's signature burger is Dave's Hot 'N Juicy. In the U.S. and Canada, Dave's Hot 'N Juicy sandwich features a quarter-pound (110 grams) of 100 percent fresh North American beef, a toasted bun, red onions, tomato, lettuce, crinkle-cut pickles (gherkins), ketchup, and mayo.

The restaurant prides itself on its supply chain, as Roth told me: "The kitchens are stocked throughout the week with fresh beef and produce. In fact, in Wendy's restaurants, employees cut vegetables fresh every day for our salads, starting with full heads of iceberg and romaine (cos) lettuces and other veggies like cucumbers, bell peppers, and tomatoes."

"Where's the beef?"

↓

Clara Peller

Opposite: First Wendy's, Columbus, Ohio, 1969.

Below: Clara Peller, of Wendy's "Where's the beef?" advertising campaign, 1984.

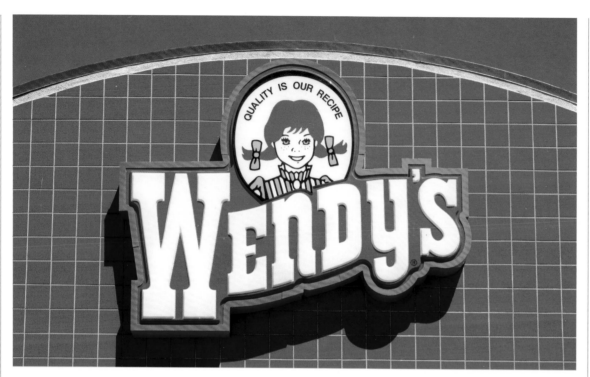

Left: Wendy's logo
on exterior restaurant
signage.

Opposite: Wendy's
drive-thru menu and
speaker, c. 1972.

This emphasis on freshness was what prompted Dave Thomas to get into burgers, as Roth explained: "Dave developed an innovative method to prepare fresh, made-to-order hamburgers. Wendy's became known for square ground (minced) beef hamburgers that hang over the bun, made with the customer's choice of toppings. Quality and fresh food are still the focus."

Roth also believes that consumers are becoming more switched on to the possibilities in what they eat, which in turn drives the brand to innovate: "Our research shows they are interested in culinary trends, different flavors and textures, and adventuresome tastes. This allows us to push the envelope with creative, upscale flavors across our menu. You'll continue to see Wendy's move the needle with consumers as to what's expected from a quick-service/fast-food chain." Nonetheless, Wendy's wants to stay close to what matters to it: "What doesn't change on a Wendy's hamburger is that iconic square shape and the quality, fresh ingredients we use to prepare it." With an emphasis on good food and nice people, informed by a

sense of family and a desire to marry the best of the new with the best of the old, it's no wonder that Wendy's continues to be loved by hamburger fans worldwide.

Gallery

Origins

Above: Double
Six Dollar Burger,
Carl's Jr.

Above: Six Dollar
Burger, Carl's Jr.

Above: Double Western
Burger, Carl's Jr.

Above: Sourdough
Bacon Cheeseburger,
Carl's Jr.

Above: Super Star
Burger, Carl's Jr.

Above: Double King
Burger, Fatburger.

Above: Quarter
Pounder, McDonald's.

Above: Double Quarter
Pounder, McDonald's.

Above: Big Mac,
McDonald's.

Above: Double Double,
In-N-Out Burger.

Above: Cheeseburger,
In-N-Out Burger.

Above: 4 x 4,
In-N-Out Burger.

Above: Jumbo Jack,
Jack in the Box.

Above: Bacon Ultimate
Cheeseburger,
Jack in the Box.

Above: Angus Classic,
Burger King.

Above: Double Whopper,
Burger King.

Above: Double
Cheeseburger, Burger
King.

Above: Double Stack,
Wendy's.

2

The Modern Burger

Modern Burgers

The first half of the twentieth century saw the founding of the big beasts of burgers, companies that have become household names and synonymous with the world's favorite fast food. You would be forgiven for thinking that the burger market was saturated by the end of the 1960s, with behemoths like McDonald's, Burger King, and Wendy's occupying the burger space with an ever-expanding range of burgers and sides. You would be wrong.

Since 1971, with the founding of Hard Rock Cafe the first restaurant in this chapter, the growth of the burger market has accelerated further. As consumer tastes have changed and developed, as the burger has become less an easy commonplace snack for families and teenagers and more of an opportunity for gastronomic experimentation, a plethora of new restaurants have been created to serve burger lovers. Even existing, sometimes high-end, restaurants have also added burgers to their menus, a move that previously would have be unimaginable.

This section captures the sheer variety of places that serve burgers, from family-owned restaurants and those serving ethically sourced burgers, to street food vendors and burger joints with a real party atmosphere to complement the food. There are themed restaurants that jumped on the burger bandwagon and gourmet venues with burgers to match. There are restaurants from America, the home of the burger, but this section also highlights the expansion of the burger across the world, with places in Europe, Australia and New Zealand, and the Far East.

There's little doubt that this panoply of burger restaurants highlights one of the most attractive aspects of the food, its versatility. The enormous range of different approaches, flavors, and inspirations that have gone to create the great variety of modern burgers available is testament both to the burger's enduring popularity and the limitless imagination that chefs have brought to bear on it.

The burger boom of the last ten years, with new household names such as Five Guys and Shake Shack emerging, has proven once again that the burger has an enduring popularity. These new chains and independent burger stores have brought new ideas, techniques, and philosophies; it's a great time to be a burger lover.

Best of all, the burger continues to shift and morph into ever-more exciting manifestations, and new places are opening all the time. This snapshot of where the burger is now, as told through the chefs and restaurants creating them, shows that over a hundred years after the first burger joints were founded, there is still no stopping the world's most popular food.

Hard Rock Cafe

The Modern Burger

First location:
London, UK
1971

Isaac Tigrett and Peter Morton were two shaggy-haired Americans who just wanted to find a good American burger while living in London. Their solution? They opened up their own American-style diner, the Hard Rock Cafe, in an old Rolls-Royce dealership on Park Lane in Mayfair, London. It was the first restaurant to bring the American-style hamburger to England and has since taken over the world with its unique combination of food and music.

In 1979, Eric Clapton, who was a big fan of the restaurant, wanted the management to hang his guitar over his regular seat in order to lay claim to his spot, and they obliged. This prompted Pete Townshend of The Who to give one of his guitars with the note "Mine's as good as his! Love Pete." And so the Hard Rock's collection of music memorabilia began, as a one-upmanship battle between two of rock's greatest guitarists.

The Hard Rock Cafe serves a range of specialty burgers including The Original Legendary Burger, S.O.B. Burger, Hickory BBQ Bacon Cheeseburger, and the Grilled Granny Smith Apple and Provolone Burger.

The excitement generated by the first cafe, an opening that quickly drew long lines of eager fans to take part in the Hard Rock Cafe's lively atmosphere, was duplicated with each additional opening of restaurants in other cities around the world and earned the brand its reputation as a popular and hot gathering spot for numerous celebrities. The Duke of Westminster often stopped by the London cafe and director Steven Spielberg ate lunch there every day during the filming of *Raiders of the Lost Ark*.

The Hard Rock Cafe has evolved into a cult global brand with over two hundred locations in sixty-eight countries.

"Love all. Serve all."

Peter Morton

STARTERS

Plenty of fresh options here, even our onion rings are hand cut and battered in house everyday.

JUMBO COMBO
A delectable array of our most popular starters that's big enough to share. Includes Santa Fe Spring Rolls, Hickory-Smoked Chicken Wings, Onion Rings, Potato Skins and Tupelo Chicken Tenders. Served with four different sauces for mixing and matching. †

SANTA FE SPRING ROLLS
Stuffed with spinach, black beans, cilantro, corn, jalapeños, diced red peppers and Jack cheese. Served with fresh homemade Hard Rock Salsa and guacamole Chipotle Ranch dressing.

TUPELO CHICKEN TENDERS
Boneless, seasoned and breaded chicken tenders, served with honey-mustard and Hickory Bar-B-Que sauces on the side or tossed in our Classic Rock, Heavy Metal, or Tangy Bar-B-Que sauces. Served with celery sticks and blue cheese dressing.†

HICKORY SMOKED CHICKEN WINGS
Colossal wings, hickory-smoked in our hardwood smoker. Have them Buffalo style or fire-grilled with your choice of Classic Rock, Heavy Metal, or Tangy Bar-B-Que sauces. Served with celery sticks and blue cheese dressing.

HARD ROCK NACHOS
Fresh corn tortilla chips piled high with Jack and Cheddar cheeses and seasoned pinto beans. Served with sour cream, chopped green onions, pico de gallo, jalapeños and a side of fresh Hard Rock Grilled Salsa. Big enough to share.
Add Grilled Chicken, Bar-B-Que Pulled Pork or Grilled Fajita Beef for an additional charge.

GRILLED CHICKEN QUESADILLA
Grilled chicken and pineapple, tossed in our own Tangy Bar-B-Que sauce with melted Jack cheese, and stuffed in a chili-dusted tortilla. Served with fresh guacamole, fresh homemade Hard Rock Salsa and sour cream.*
Substitute Grilled Fajita Beef for an additional charge.

POTATO SKINS
Large potato shells, fried golden brown, filled with Jack and Cheddar cheeses, crisp seasoned bacon and green onions. Served with a side of sour cream for dipping. which comes with celery sticks and blue cheese dressing.†

WHEN BRITISH BLUES GIANT ERIC CLAPTON SUGGESTED THAT HIS FAVORITE RESTAURANT, THE HARD ROCK CAFE, RESERVE HIS PREFERRED TABLE WITH A PLAQUE, WE SUGGESTED HIS GUITAR INSTEAD. THE REST IS HISTORY.
This humble red axe still lives at the Hard Rock London.

†Contains nuts or seeds.
Consuming raw or undercooked hamburgers, meats, poultry, seafood, shellfish or eggs may increase your risk of foodborne illness, especially if you have certain medical conditions.

Due to product availability and regulatory requirements, some menu items may not be available in every cafe. We apologize in advance if your menu selection is not available.

Previous spread: Hard
Rock Cafe, Universal
City Walk, Los
Angeles, California.

Opposite (left):
Menu, Hard Rock Cafe,
New York City.

Left: Hard Rock Cafe,
New York City.

Maxwell's

First location:
London, UK
1972

In 1972, when it was all but impossible to find a decent burger or grill in England, Brian Stein opened Maxwell's in Hampstead. "My concept was simple: a restaurant with a relaxed but vibrant atmosphere where friendly staff would serve top-class hamburgers."

In the 1980s, after a decade of the West End coming to Maxwell's, it was time to bring a bit of Hampstead to the West End: the restaurant moved to James Street in Covent Garden. It was an instant hit with a buzzy mix of residents, workers, and visitors, many of whom loyally still frequent it today. Maxwell's continues to wow customers with innovations from across the pond, including the triple-burger Stack Attack.

Below:
The Mighty Stack.

Opposite: Maxwell's Restaurant, Covent Garden, London, 1984.

"I was one of the first restaurateurs to bring the American-style burger to London."

↓

Brian Stein

MOS Burger

First location:
Tokyo, Japan
1972

MOS Burger's founder, Satoshi Sakurada, gave the company its name as an expression of his limitless love for humans and the environment, and a desire to establish a group of people committed to that ideal. MOS stands for Mountain Ocean Sun: the company's philosophy is to stand tall and firm like a mountain, to have a heart that is as broad and deep as an ocean, and to have passion like the sun that never burns out.

During its first decade, MOS rapidly grew into a nationwide franchise thanks to a combination of delicious, made-to-order burgers, including the Teriyaki Burger and several kinds of rice burgers, and cordial, friendly service. In 1991, MOS opened its first overseas spot, in Taiwan, and followed this with an aggressive expansion into the Asia Pacific region. MOS is now the second-largest fast-food franchise in Japan, after McDonald's Japan, and owns over 1,800 outlets in Japan, Singapore, Hong Kong, Thailand, Indonesia, Australia, and South Korea.

"We provide delicious and healthy food with cordial and friendly service."

⬇ Satoshi Sakurada

Opposite: MOS Burger newspaper and magazine advertisement.

今日、モス気分。

MOS BURGER®

モスで もう一度 食べたいメニュー
第1位
感動の復活

期間限定 ホットチキンバーガー ¥300

First location:
Los Angeles, California, USA
1975

Carney's started life as a traditional-style diner on Sunset Boulevard in Los Angeles. A single train car, half of which was kitchen, the other half seating, it was opened in 1975 by John Wolfe and is now run by his sons, John and Bill. Wolfe Senior had been working in radio sales and management and his sons told me, "had always wanted to open a hamburger and hot dog stand."

Today, more than forty years later, there are two locations. The Sunset Boulevard location is now one and a half train cars and a basement area; the second, in Studio City, has two full train cars, one for seating, one for cooking, and a caboose that functions as an office. Carney's burgers are also served at The Forum, a music venue in Inglewood.

The Carney's philosophy is simple, according to Wolfe Senior: "Since the beginning, Carney's slogan has been 'Probably the best hamburgers and hot dogs in the world.' To make this our reality, we use only the finest ingredients possible when making any item that is on our menu. It's never a question of price, only a question of quality." The company's signature item is its Chili Burger, which the Wolfes reckon is "the best in town." It offers a variety of sides, the most intriguing of which are the Train Wreck fries (chips), served with grilled onions, melted cheese, and Carney's own Thousand Island dressing.

The Wolfe brothers think the burger is so versatile because it works at any time, day or night: "The burger is like a meal on a bun. It can be served for breakfast, lunch, or dinner." They are very positive about the direction of the industry as well, saying, "We feel the burger business will just keep growing. Everybody loves a great burger." Their approach and fantastic location have made them a must-visit for people in LA: "We see a lot of people from all over the world. We love to get people to try our particular offerings, especially the chili, as they have never had anything like this before." Carney's reckons the secret to a great burger is "juicy, high-quality meat, a toasted, yet

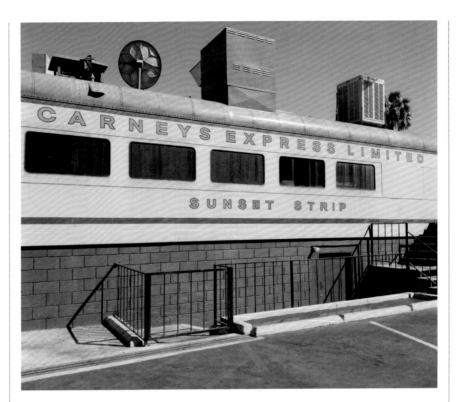

soft, bun, and super-fresh ingredients." But the Wolfes also recognize that variety is the spice of burger life, and they said, "We're not sure we could name a favorite burger; most have their own special offering."

Nonetheless, if it's an authentic, old-fashioned American dining-car experience you want, Carney's is, as they say, probably the best in town.

Opposite: Testimonial from *MAD* magazine, c. 1980.

Above: Carney's train car, Sunset Boulevard, Los Angeles, California.

"Long live the burger!"

→

John Wolfe

Right: Interior,
Carney's train car,
Sunset Boulevard, Los
Angeles, California.

WE ARE TRYING TO
GIVE YOU THE FINEST
FOOD AND SERVICE
POSSIBLE.
IF THERE IS A
PROBLEM, PLEASE
TELL THE MANAGER
OR CALL
JOHN OR BILL AT
(818) 761-9910

MGD
HAMMERS
BEWARE
OF THE
TRAINS

EXIT

Joe Allen (London)

First (and only) location: London, UK
1977

This classic American restaurant in the heart of London's theaterland is famous for its secret, off-the-menu burgers. Opened in 1977 by Joe Allen, with his partner Richard Polo, who had made money investing in musicals, the restaurant quickly established itself as the place to go for actors appearing in the nearby West End.

The burgers were always a secret, though, as General Manager Cathy Winn, who has been with the restaurant since the beginning, told me: "Joe didn't want it to be known as a burger joint. He was really nervous about putting them on the menu, people coming down and seeing that it was a New York restaurant with burgers, because he wanted to be much more than just a burger joint.... When we first started we didn't have menus, we had blackboards, and the burgers were not written down, but they were always available to those in the know."

Being "in the know" was important to Allen, who had started life as a bartender at P. J. Clarke's in New York. As Winn explains, "It was a restaurant but it had the feel of a club. Frank Sinatra and the Rat Pack used to go there for drinks. Joe loved that you had to go down an alley to get to the doorway and there were hundred-dollar bills, and this was in the 1950s, changing hands to get in."

P. J. Clarke's was to be a model for Joe Allen's first restaurant, Joe Allen (New York) in 1965. Allen wanted to create something along the same lines—a comfortable, slightly secretive haunt. Given how closely associated with the acting profession the restaurant has become, I was surprised when Winn told me, "Joe opened it because he was a sports fan. He wanted this speakeasy vibe, but he wanted it next to Madison Square Garden, which closed down three months after he had opened it!" The actors came soon after, and Joe built a connection with them during an actors' strike in the late '60s: "He gave the actors accounts, on credit, and so as they became more famous after that they remembered Joe Allen warmly. We kept having accounts here in London until the early '90s."

Left: Cheeseburger.

Next spread: Sid Vicious with girlfriend Nancy Spungen dining at Joe Allen, Covent Garden, London, 1978.

Joe had been in London with actor Roy Schneider on what Winn describes as "a lads' weekend" when he decided that the newly redeveloped Covent Garden was the ideal location for a restaurant. Joe Allen (London) opened at the height of the punk era, which led to Sid Vicious and Nancy Spungen's famous photo shoot there. Apparently they were very badly behaved, although as Winn says, "You wouldn't expect anything else."

The restaurant quickly became a success, with its off-the-menu burgers appealing especially to visiting American celebrities. It was natural that other actors would follow, especially given the popularity of Joe Allen stateside, as Winn explains: "The myth goes that they opened [in London] and there was a big American production of *A Chorus Line* and all the actors knew Joe Allen in New York, so they came here to be reminded of home, and after a couple of weeks they were all high-kicking up and down the bar in a chorus line. At that moment, we were born as a theater restaurant."

The burgers helped develop an atmosphere in which American stars could feel at home, and relax without the pressure of having to dress up or be seen: "Actors would come in after a show's performance, their launch nights, but they would also come in dressed down, coming in to relax. You'd also get people swapping ideas, chatting, having their little secret conversations." On opening nights, though, it could get a little hectic. Winn confesses: "You'd get lots of critics and journalists, and it would be an absolute nightmare on an opening night, because you'd get a flood of people climbing over each other to get in and the actors don't want to sit next to the critics and vice versa. It was a complete headache!"

Joe Allen (London) started off serving a very traditional burger: "It just used to have a big slice of onion on the patty, but people didn't seem to go for that. It was very purist." Now the restaurant offers burgers with lettuce, tomato, spicy ketchup, and mayonnaise, all packed into a brioche bun. It also serves a regular beef burger, a cheeseburger, a blue cheeseburger, a bacon burger, and bacon with the two types of cheeseburger. There are also monthly guest burgers, including the Juicy Lucy, where cheese is cooked into the patty, and a Joe Allen Massive, which has both a beef and a salt beef patty.

The burgers are very popular, according to Winn: "Any chefs that come in, Fergus Henderson from St. John [in London] for example, or Delia Smith, a British television host and cookbook writer, they usually have burgers." Americans, too "want a good, old-fashioned burger. It's evocative of home. Rod Stewart's manager Arnold Stiefel used to come in and always have a burger with our tomato relish."

Current owners Tim Healy, who used to come into the restaurant as a child, and Lawrence Hartley bought the restaurant in 2013. They have modernized, while at the same time staying true to Joe's original vision. Winn tells us, "It's a club, and people in the know get that. Maybe we used to be a bit sniffy, but we've adapted with the times: we now take bookings and credit cards and we tell people that we have burgers." But it is still very much a restaurant with a speakeasy vibe, low-key and relaxing for its array of well-known regulars. As Winn says, "People didn't really come for the food, they would come in to be seen, to network, they knew we didn't tittle-tattle. If there were paparazzi out the front we would sneak people out the back." Nonetheless, the food, and the burgers in particular, were a crucial part of Joe Allen becoming part of the heart and soul of London's theaterland. Just don't tell anyone the secret!

Fuddruckers

First Location:
San Antonio, Texas, USA
1979

Fuddruckers was founded as Freddie Fuddruckers in 1979 by Philip J. Romano in San Antonio, Texas, in a location converted to a restaurant from an old bank. He started the company with one mission: to create "the world's greatest hamburgers."

The Fuddruckers concept is to serve large hamburgers, fresh, never frozen, made with 100 percent USDA all-American premium-cut beef. Customers can choose from 1/3-, 1/2-, or 2/3-pound patties. The meat is ground (minced) on site and always grilled to order. Burgers are served on a sesame-topped bun baked from scratch in each restaurant. Once you have your masterpiece of a burger, you help yourself to a large range of toppings, including sliced sun-ripened tomatoes, lettuce, sliced onions, dill pickles, and Fudd's very own cheese sauce from the "Build Your Own" produce bar.

Fuddruckers has nearly two hundred locations in North America and has announced plans to expand into Mexico.

Above:
Fuddruckers logo.

Opposite:
Cheeseburger.

"The world's greatest ham- burgers."

↓

Philip J. Romano

Tommi's Burger Joint

First location: Reykjavik, Iceland 1981

Tommi's Burger Joint originated in Iceland, where entrepreneur Tomas "Tommi" Tómasson decided to create an informal American-style diner with burgers made to a recipe that he had perfected over many years of flipping them. In his first three years, he sold over a million burgers and grew the group to six sites before selling his interest in 1984. Over the years that followed, he ran several projects, including launching Iceland's first Hard Rock Cafe (see page 118) in Reykjavik in 1987, and in 1992 buying and renovating the Hotel Borg, which ran for ten years.

Today, Tommi's Burger Joint has fourteen sites in the group—seven in Iceland, three in London, two in Denmark, and one each in Germany, Sweden, and Norway—with more in the planning stages. The interior style is rustic and homely, cool without it feeling forced.

Tommi's classic steak burger is a succulent patty made from cuts of steak, and served with a side of Béarnaise for dipping or smearing on the burger. The cheeseburger is also a classic and the burgers are lathered with a signature cocktail sauce that has the bite of mustard and a citrus acidity that complements the meat perfectly.

Following six months of globetrotting, Tómasson returned to Iceland in 2003 and realized he would have to do something to earn a living. While he was initially reluctant to return to burgers, it is hard to stay away from something you love so much and have spent so much time around. It was almost inevitable that he should start up another restaurant and, in April 2004, the first Tommi's Burger Joint opened in Reykjavik, followed swiftly by four more across the country. Catering for everyone from business people during the lunch rush to families at the weekends, Tómasson found a style and a flavor that were popular across the board.

He takes a hands-on approach to business, working the grill and looking forward to the first bite of burger when he shows up for work in the morning. He also maintains that a good burger is healthy: "If you stop to think about it, what's in a burger? It's good beef, bread, lettuce, and tomatoes with ketchup, mustard, and a little mayonnaise." Despite spending over thirty years working at the grill, he isn't bored with the burger, saying, "It makes life worth living.... A burger is something you never get tired of: I eat one every day." And when your burgers are that good, why wouldn't you?

"The burger is like a good B movie, you're always willing to see one more."

↓

Tommi Tómasson

Opposite: Interior, Tommi's Burger Joint, Reykjavik, Iceland.

Right: Cheeseburger.

Five Guys

The Modern Burger

First location: Arlington, Virginia, USA 1986

Five Guys began when Jerry and Janie Murrell and their four sons created the brand following Jerry's advice to his boys, "Start a business or go to college." Jerry was working as a stock trader, right up until three days before the first restaurant opened and that helped provide financing as well as business acumen. He told *Inc.* magazine about being in Pittsburgh, Pennsylvania, staying in a Marriott hotel and reading the words of the chain's founder, J. W. Marriott: "He said, anyone can make money in the food business as long as they have a good product, reasonable price, and a clean place. That made sense to me."

It was a sense of what Five Guys sought to bring to the market, staying close to what it knew, using good-quality beef, chilled but never frozen, and keeping the menu small, if not simple. Indeed, with the huge variety of toppings available, there are over a quarter of a million potential variants of burger at Five Guys. The key tenet of sticking to what you know from an anecdote Jerry Murrell tells about coffee: "When we first started, people asked for coffee. We thought, Why not? This was our first lesson in humility. We served coffee, but the problem was that the young kids working for us didn't know anything about coffee. It was terrible! So we stopped serving coffee."

Five Guys certainly knows its burgers and fries (chips). It uses 80 percent lean, 20 percent fat, fresh, roll-stamped prime beef. Its buns are toasted on a grill, which adds a caramelized sweetness. Its fries are cooked in peanut (groundnut) oil and everything is made from scratch and served with a pared-down, diner aesthetic. As Murrell says, "That's why we can't do drive-thrus—it takes too long. We had a sign: 'If you're in a hurry, there are a lot of really good hamburger places within a short distance from here.' People thought I was nuts. But the customers appreciated it."

This confidence in their product, together with pretty immediate success, led the Murrells to open five more places in the Washington, D.C. metropolitan area between 1986 and 2001, before moving into franchising the following year, initially in nearby Maryland and Virginia. In 2003, they began expanding nationwide, selling rights to over three hundred locations in eighteen months. In 2013, Five Guys landed in London, opening its first restaurant in Covent Garden, famous for its long lines of people outside. There are now over 1,400 Five Guys restaurants in 9 countries. "My mother always told me that if I didn't study, I'd be flipping burgers somewhere," Murrell told *Forbes* magazine in 2012. "Little did she know...."

Far left: Five Guys restaurant counter, Middle East.

Left: Cheeseburger, fries, and milkshake.

139

FIVE GUYS®
BURGERS and FRIES

10178 Richmond Highway
Lorton, VA 22079
Tel: (703) 339-9500

OPEN 7 DAYS A WEEK! 11AM - 10PM -- ORDER ONLINE @ FIVEGUYS.COM

BURGERS
100% FRESH BEEF -- NO FILLERS OR PRESERVATIVES

HAMBURGER
CHEESEBURGER
BACON BURGER
BACON CHEESEBURGER

LITTLE HAMBURGER
LITTLE CHEESEBURGER
LITTLE BACON BURGER
LITTLE BACON CHEESEBURGER

DOGS

KOSHER STYLE HOT DOG
CHEESE DOG
BACON DOG
BACON CHEESE DOG

SANDWICHES

VEGGIE SANDWICH
CHEESE VEGGIE SANDWICH
GRILLED CHEESE
BLT

FRIES
FIVE GUYS STYLE or CAJUN STYLE

LITTLE
REGULAR
LARGE
Cooked in pure, no cholesterol, tasty peanut oil!

MILKSHAKES

FIVE GUYS SHAKE
with or without Whipped Cream

ALL MIX-INS FREE

CHOCOLATE   PEANUT BUTTER   COFFEE   MALTED MILK
CHERRY   SALTED CARAMEL   STRAWBERRY   BANANA
VANILLA   OREO® CRÈME   OREO® COOKIE PIECES
Add Bacon to Any Shake!

DRINKS

REGULAR
LARGE
BOTTLED WATER

ALL BURGERS AND DOGS ARE AVAILABLE BUNLESS

ALL TOPPINGS FREE
MAYO   LETTUCE   PICKLES   TOMATOES   GRILLED ONIONS   GRILLED MUSHROOMS   KETCHUP   MUSTARD
RELISH   ONIONS   JALAPENO PEPPERS   GREEN PEPPERS   A.1® STEAK SAUCE   BAR-B-Q SAUCE   HOT SAUCE
(EVERYTHING or ALL THE WAY receives only toppings in black)

ZAGAT Survey Rated - Since 2001

Voted Best Fries - Best of the Twin Cities
City Pages '13

Voted Readers' Favorite Burger Around Boston
Boston.com '12

Best Hamburger in St. Joe
KQTV StJoeChannel.com '14

Readers' Pick: Best Burger & Fries
Washingtonian Magazine '13 & '14

"High-class burgers at low-end prices"
San Jose Mercury News '12

Voted Best of the Best French Fries
Watauga Democrat People's Choice Awards '14

Winner: Cheap Eats Burger
KTVB Seven's Best of (Boise, ID) '13

Reminder: Consuming raw or undercooked poultry, meat, eggs, shellfish or seafood may increase your risk of foodborne illness.

For more area locations go to www.FIVEGUYS.com
© 2014 FIVE GUYS HOLDINGS
OREO is a registered trademark of Mondelēz International Group.

Above: Menu,
Five Guys, Lorton,
Virginia.

Right: U.S. President
Barack Obama orders
lunch, Five Guys,
southeast Washington
D.C., 2009.

Johnny Rockets

The Modern Burger

"Our Passion. Our Burger."

⬇

Ronn Teitelbaum

Opposite:
The Original.

Top right: Route 66.

Center right:
Smoke House Double.

Bottom right:
Bacon Cheddar Single.

First location:
Los Angeles, California, USA
1986

Ronn Teitelbaum, an award-winning men's fashion retailer, launched the first Johnny Rockets, a twenty-stool diner, on Melrose Avenue, in Los Angeles, California. He founded the concept on the belief that everyone deserves a place where they can escape from the complicated world and experience the uncomplicated goodness of classic Americana. The name originated by combining the timeless Johnny Appleseed story with the classic Oldsmobile Rocket 88. Together, they embody the concept of classic Americana and the promise of the future.

Johnny Rockets is an international restaurant franchise, now owned by Sun Capital Partners, with 340 locations in 26 countries that offers high-quality menu items with fresh, never frozen 100 percent beef cooked-to-order hamburgers, including The Original, Smoke House Double, Route 66, and Bacon Cheddar Double.

The Modern Burger

Far left: Exterior restaurant design and branding, Johnny Rockets, 2016.

Left: Interior restaurant design, Johnny Rockets, 2016.

Ed's Easy Diner

First location:
London, UK
1987

It has been over a quarter of a century since Ed's Easy Diner opened its doors in the Soho district of London, bringing the culture of 1950s America to the British capital. From day one Ed's added fun and nostalgia, and it now has thirty-five locations nationwide.

The shiny chrome fittings, red-and-white signature color scheme, and dazzling neon lighting quickly made the place popular with locals, tourists, and celebrity guests, as well as a hotspot choice for photo shoots and film and TV locations.

It's the story of all classic diners—a quick bite, reliable food, and sassy service that customers always remembered. Ed's has been loved from the start, proving that nothing works quite like listening to Elvis Presley while enjoying a great hamburger, a big bowl of fries (chips), and the best milkshake in town.

"Quality Forever."

→ Ed's ethos

Right: Jukebox, Ed's Easy Diner, Soho, London.

Left: Restaurant interior, Ed's Easy Diner, Covent Garden, London.

Planet Hollywood

First location: New York City, New York, USA 1991

Robert Earl's father was a pop singer, so creativity and performance are in his blood and it was natural that his restaurants would have a flamboyant quality to them and an innate association with celebrity culture. Earl studied hotel management in college and then went quickly into restaurants, opening his first business, a medieval-themed banqueting hall in the shadow of the Tower of London, in 1977.

In the world of hamburger restaurants, Earl first came to prominence with the acquisition of Hard Rock Cafe (see page 118), an American-style casual-eating chain born in London in the early '70s. As he explained to me, "In 1988, Hard Rock was a troubled public company heading toward bankruptcy and I acquired it and grew it dramatically, in its association principally with the music world."

Earl's success at the previously ailing Hard Rock attracted attention, as did its unique pairing of American cooking and celebrity culture. As he told me, "At that time, as the '90s began, some Hollywood producers came and spoke to me about the concept of celebrity burgers, moving the music idea across to film." In 1991, Planet Hollywood was born. In 1993, Earl sold his interest in Hard Rock Cafe with, as he says, "the growth achieved and strategy set."

While Hard Rock Cafe was the place for music and a burger, Planet Hollywood rapidly became a venue that married burgers and films. This was no accident of celebrity patronage, but a deliberate, thoughtful piece of branding. As Earl says, "Right from the outset, as well as the Hollywood producers, I had around thirty film stars in partnership with me." Stars like Bruce Willis, Sylvester Stallone, and Demi Moore backed the restaurant and, along with Mel Gibson, Johnny Depp, and many others, were present when the first Planet Hollywood opened in New York in October 1991. Burgers were chosen to be central to the brand because of their enormous popularity

Right: Planet Hollywood, South Coast Plaza, Orange County, California.

Next spread (left): Menu, Planet Hollywood.

Next spread (right): BBQ Bacon Cheeseburger.

★BURGERS★

The Planet Hollywood Burger   Our classic hamburger, homestyle bun with lettuce,
tomato, onion & pickle and served with french fries **£8.50**

Classic Cheeseburger   Our classic burger, homestyle bun with lettuce, tomato,
onion & pickle with your choice of cheese and served with a side of french fries **£8.95**

BBQ Bacon Cheddar Burger   Our classic burger finished with smoked bacon, tangy
sweet barbecue sauce and sharp cheddar cheese with a side of french fries **£9.95**

Mushroom Onion & Swiss Burger   Our classic burger with sautéed fresh mushrooms and onion
layered on top of our classic burger complete with Swiss cheese and a side of french fries **£9.95**

Veggie Burger   A meatless patty made from fresh mushrooms, onions, whole grains,
low-fat cheese, seasonings and spices and served on a homestyle sesame bun with french fries ... **£8.50**

Chicken Burger   Grilled chicken patty with lettuce, tomato and onion on a homestyle sesame
seed bun served with french fries **£8.50**

★GRILLE SPECIALITIES★

Prime Scottish Sirloin Steak   10 oz. premium centre cut sirloin steak chargrilled to order
and served with a creamy peppercorn sauce, mashed potatoes or french fries and
roasted vegetables **£16.95**

New Zealand Lamb Cutlets   Four prime New Zealand lamb cutlets glazed with herb
olive oil, chargrilled to perfection and served with mashed potatoes and roasted vegetables **£14.50**

Grilled Salmon   Grilled 8 oz. salmon filet glazed with maple butter. Served with mashed
potatoes and roasted vegetables **£13.50**

BBQ Ribs   A full rack of tender baby-back ribs smothered with our tangy sweet barbecue sauce.
Served with french fries, ranch beans and coleslaw **£13.95**

Roasted Half Chicken   Lemon pepper and rosemary glazed roasted half chicken.
Served with mashed potatoes and roasted vegetables **£12.95**

Sizzling Fajitas   Your choice of chargrilled chicken, beef or vegetable served with sizzling
onions, red and green peppers, fresh guacamole, pico de gallo, sour cream, cheddar and
jack cheeses, flour tortillas and Mexican rice **£13.95**

★SIDE DISHES★

Baked Potato £2.50   **French Fries** £2.50   **Garden Salad** £2.50

Coleslaw £2.50   **Mashed Potatoes** £2.50

All beef and lamb dishes are cooked medium to well unless otherwise requested.

Steak weights are approximate, uncooked. Menu items may contain nuts.

*VAT is included at 17.5%. For your convenience a 12.5% discretionary service charge
is added to parties of 6 or more.*

PLANET HOLLYWOOD

and salability across the world. As Earl puts it, "The prevailing cuisine was the predominant idea, so we looked for ways to change the presentation and do something different. The idea was to create a new style of restaurant but with a type of food people were familiar with."

Burgers were the ideal fit for the brief. As Earl says, "Burgers are perceived as being safe, a good American export, and within a sensible price margin. For the masses, the grass roots, burgers are the staple diet." By taking that staple and setting it in a location filled with all manner of Hollywood glitz, Planet Hollywood created a restaurant that was at once familiar and utterly exciting. The vast array of film memorabilia, most of it unique and much of it donated by the original backers or their friends, gave customers direct access to things they had never seen before except on celluloid.

Right from the beginning, Earl saw the potential in the sort of word-of-mouth publicity that has since become a staple of how brands operate through social media. Positive association with the film industry drew enormous attention to Planet Hollywood. "Advertising was a small part of the budget and concept, but PR and word-of-mouth and premieres and so on were much more significant." The star power of Planet Hollywood's backers and their friends ensured a ready supply of beautiful people posing in front of the chain's venues, while regular hosting of film premieres and parties at various Planet Hollywood restaurants produced just the right blend of exclusivity and popularity to ensure its continued success.

Even though the burger business and, indeed, the whole hospitality sector have undergone enormous change over the years, Earl sees the trusty hamburger as a hugely reliable source of pleasure and something around which to build a business. "It'll never change. Regardless of all the changes, different meats, different fillings, and so on, the burger is fundamentally the same." Nonetheless, he continues, "You can go so many places with burgers." He thinks there are brands doing interesting things with gourmet burgers and flavor combinations but, ever the businessman, is quick to point out, "It's like a high-class actor who is still trying to sell tickets but tries it in a more

artistic way." Earl is very much involved in the business, and has a hand in even the most detailed aspects of the food: "I introduced Gordon Ramsay to a pig farmer in Connecticut and he then created the Hog Burger for the BurGR restaurant in Planet Hollywood casino."

Interestingly, Earl sees the future of burgers and fast food differently than many people I spoke to, telling me that, in the United States, "In the future, the burger may be edged out. Chipotle and other taco places could take over; they're more versatile than the burger." In the rest of the world, though, Earl sees the burger's hegemony continuing. For the cinema-inspired, burger-loving team at Planet Hollywood, that can only be a good thing.

Fergburger

First (and only) location: Queenstown, New Zealand 2001

Fergburger (known as Ferg's to its customers) is a hole-in-the-wall burger joint. Ferg's owner prefers to remain hidden from the public and management refuses to say anything about him/her. So who is Ferg? Steve Bradley, Fergburger's general manager, says, "There are so many stories I don't even remember what the real legend is—he may have been the first person to swim naked to Glenorchy or—my favorite—the first man to go down Shotover River in a barrel."

Since it first opened, Fergburger has become somewhat of a cult to both locals and tourists. Like visiting the Eiffel Tower in Paris, Ferg's has become the compulsory stop in Queenstown. Open 24/7, people often have to wait in line for up to an hour to be served its gourmet hamburgers. Ferg's serves up a variety of mouthwatering burgers including The Fergburger, Mr Big Stuff, and Bun Laden. "We're about the customer and the product, and providing great service and fresh, honest food. The staff has the philosophy that Ferg loves you—we treat others the way they want to be treated, and I think that's really the key to our success," says Bradley.

FERGBURGER

The Fergburger $11.50
Prime New Zealand beef, lettuce, tomato, red onion, aioli & tomato relish.

Fergburger w/ cheese
Cheddar	$12.50
Blue, Swiss, Brie	$12.90

Double Ferg w/cheese
Cheddar	$15.50
Blue, Swiss, Brie	$15.90

Southern Swine $13.00
Prime New Zealand beef, American streaky bacon, lettuce, tomato, red onion, avocado, aioli & tomato relish.

Tropical Swine $14.50
Prime New Zealand beef, American streaky bacon, cheddar cheese, pineapple, lettuce, tomato, red onion, aioli & tomato relish.

Mr Big Stuff $16.50
1/2 lb of prime New Zealand beef topped with melted cheddar cheese, American streaky bacon & bbq sauce, lettuce, tomato, red onion & aioli.

Little Lamby $12.90
Prime New Zealand lamb, mint jelly, lettuce, tomato, red onion, aioli & tomato relish.

Sweet Bambi $12.90
Wild Fiordland Deer with a Thai plum chutney, lettuce, tomato, red onion & aioli.

The Bulls Eye $18.50
Prime New Zealand Ribeye steak (200g). Grilled medium, topped with rings of white onion, swiss cheese, lettuce, tomato, aioli & tomato relish.

The Codfather $14.90
Fresh Blue Cod, beer battered with Ferg's dill tartare, lettuce, tomato, red onion, & aioli.

Chief Wiggum $14.90
Slow roasted New Zealand pork belly, lettuce, tomato, red onion, hash brown, with aioli and a delicious apricot seeded mustard.

Cockadoodle Oink $14.50
Butterflied & crumbed chicken breast, American streaky bacon, avocado, lettuce, tomato, red onion, aioli & tomato relish.

Bombay Chicken $13.50
Grilled chicken tenderloins marinated in a chilli, ginger & coriander yoghurt with cucumber raita, lettuce, tomato, red onion, aioli & mango chutney.

Cockadoodle Doo $13.50
Grilled chicken tenderloins with sundried tomato tapenade, lettuce, tomato, red onion & aioli.

Sweet Julie $13.50
Grilled chicken tenderloins marinated in a ginger soy sauce dressed with sweet chilli, lettuce, tomato, red onion & aioli.

Cock Cajun $13.50
Grilled chicken tenderloins rubbed with cajun spices, cooled with a lemon yoghurt, lettuce, tomato, red onion & aioli.

Holier than Thou $11.90
Tempured tofu with a spicy satay, coconut and coriander sauce, lettuce, tomato, red onion, cucumber, snowpea shoots & aioli.

Bun Laden $12.90
Falafel patties dressed with lemon yoghurt and chipotle chilli sauce, lettuce, tomato, red onion, cucumber, avocado & aioli.

The Morning Glory $10.00
With your choice of avocado or hash brown, American streaky bacon, egg, lettuce, tomato, red onion, tomato relish & Ferg's tarragon mayonnaise.

The Dawn Horn $12.50
American streaky bacon, egg, hash brown, cheddar cheese, avocado, lettuce, tomato, red onion, beetroot, tomato relish & Ferg's tarragon mayonnaise.

Gluten Free Bun $3.00

BIG AL $17.90
Al delivers a double serving of prime New Zealand beef (1/2lb), lashings of bacon, a whole lotta cheese, 2 eggs, beetroot, lettuce, tomato, red onion, relish & a big wad of aioli.

Gourmet Burger Kitchen (GBK)

The Modern Burger

First location:
London, UK
2001

In 2001, three guys from New Zealand, Greg Driscoll, Andy Wills, and Brandon Allen, set up the first Gourmet Burger Kitchen (GBK) in Battersea, South London. Their philosophy was simple—to create a fresh, quality burger reminiscent of what they were used to at home. They were the first to introduce gourmet burgers to the London market and still pride themselves on serving up the freshest burgers, combining 100 percent prime beef, hand selected and traditionally reared on independent farms across the Southwest counties, with the freshest ingredients and sauces made from scratch every day in each GBK kitchen.

Now owned by South African company Famous Brands, GBK has over seventy restaurants throughout the UK and has plans to expand.

Left: Kitchen service counter at GBK, Waterloo, London.

Below: External restaurant signage at GBK, Bayswater, London.

157

Burger Joint

First location: New York City, New York, USA 2003

Burger Joint opened in New York City at Le Parker Meridien in 2003 and, as Marisa Zafran, Director of Public Relations and Marketing, explains, "When we first opened it was the first of its kind because at that point, at least in the landscape in New York, you could go get burgers at a fast-food place or you could go to a restaurant where they have a million other things on the menu, but there weren't places that specialized in just doing really good burgers."

The Parker Meridien, a well-known luxury hotel in Midtown, had a space in the lobby that served as a bar, but Zafran said the thought occurred, "Why don't we have this hidden, hole-in-the-wall type place that just serves burgers?" In a vein often associated with diners and less with upscale hotels, "You go behind a curtain and see a neon sign and find a space that is very different to the rest of the hotel, and quite dive-y and people love that."

The success of the Burger Joint led to expansion, first in New York in Greenwich Village, where they serve 1,200 burgers a day, and then abroad—there are now several international locations including the United Arab Emirates, South Korea, and Brazil.

Zafran says that Burger Joint believes in doing one thing and doing it really well: "When you come in, the menu isn't turkey burger, veggie burger, toppings, foie gras, truffle, or any of that, it's just one beef-burger patty." The beef is freshly ground and left unseasoned, so the cooking speaks for itself. The signature item is a cheeseburger with the works—radish, tomato, pickles (gherkins) and onions, ketchup, mustard, and mayo: "We have all of that or whatever you want of that as everything is customized, you decide. We believe in the simplicity of really good beef."

There's also a vegetarian option called the Grilled Cheese with all the toppings, as well as fries (chips), brownies

and milkshakes, beer, wine, and soda (soft drinks). The Greenwich Village outlet offers bacon cheeseburgers and milkshakes, but otherwise simplicity reigns supreme, as Zafran points out: "We're so accessible and the burger is so good; there's nothing fancy about it, so it appeals to everybody. We do everything fresh and take it seriously, and the hidden, fun atmosphere here adds to it too."

Zafran says, "Those coming from overseas think of the burger as being particularly 'Americana.'" Add to that the burger's democratic allure, and you have a winning combination: "It's tasty food and it's not super-expensive. People love burgers and I don't see that going away any time soon."

"Our customers are a huge mix because who doesn't love a burger?"

↓

Marisa Zafran

Opposite:
Cheeseburger.

Right: Neon sign,
Burger Joint,
Le Parker Meridien,
New York City.

Haché Burger Connoisseurs

First location:
London, UK
2004

Haché Burger Connoisseurs, winners of *Time Out*'s 2005 Best Burger in London award, started out in the grungy confines of Inverness Street in Camden, a stone's throw from the bustling and vibrant Camden Lock Market. The business was co-founded by Berry and Suzie Casey. Having fallen in love with the burger while traveling in the United States, particularly those offered by Miller's in Chicago, Berry Casey was keen to bring the relaxed atmosphere he experienced back to England, providing quality burgers in a casual, family-friendly setting.

Haché produced a Chef's Special every month, and some were so popular that they have migrated to the main menu; these have included a Flambé burger and the Louisiana peanut-butter burger. Such inventive options aside, Haché's most popular item is still the ever-reliable cheeseburger, crammed with melting aged cheddar, often ordered with a side of sweet potato fries (chips).

Nonetheless, it's that playful aspect of the burger that most appeals to Berry Casey, who describes the burger as "a great basic food concept waiting for an original approach." The basics do still matter, though, and Berry Casey stresses that the core strength of a burger is always the quality of its ingredients; he also says that its versatility comes from the fact that if you get those right, the rest is pretty straightforward! Berry Casey is always on the lookout for exciting, innovative burger approaches himself and describes with relish a recent discovery in the smart London shopping and eating district of Knightsbridge: a scallop and shrimp (prawn) burger that was "amazingly special." This type of luxury burger is indicative of the trend that Berry sees toward "upscale concepts" in the burger market, as businesses wrestle with increased competition. This impetus will, he believes, ensure that burgers are continually improving as well as being shaped with greater imagination, something that can only be good for the customer.

Haché now has five sites around London, with plans in the works for more. The restaurants receive regular visits from musical luminaries like singer-songwriter Paul Weller and rapper Tinie Tempah, but Berry Casey says the person he'd most love to sit down with for a burger is Roger Federer, who seems like "one of the coolest guys on the planet." Haché Burger Connoisseurs are doing great things with their laid-back, welcoming style, and were judged the best burger in London by the *Daily Telegraph*.

Opposite (clockwise from top left): Steak Bavarian, Steak Blue Cheese, Steak Milano, Steak Canadien.

Shake Shack

First location: New York City, New York, USA 2004

Shake Shack was born as a hot dog stand in Madison Square Park in New York City, and was created by Danny Meyer's Union Square Hospitality Group, which brought its thirty years of experience to the project. Begun, in the words of CEO Randy Garutti, "to support an art project and raise some money across the street from two of our fine-dining restaurants," Shake Shack now has over one hundred restaurants and employs more than two thousand people in the United States alone. Its humble origins were in 400 square feet (37 square meters) of temporary space, then Shake Shack took off at an extraordinary rate and Garutti said, "the rest is history."

The hot dog stand was certainly popular and became, said Garutti, "an iconic thing to see and do in New York: the money went to the park and we thought we'd sell a few hot dogs and burgers." The success wasn't planned: "We never thought or dreamed that we would be sitting here talking to you." The Union Square Hospitality Group was known for fine dining, not perfecting burgers, but the skills and experience it brought to the kiosk quickly made it a must-visit location.

Interestingly, for Garutti, who wanted to evoke "the old roadside burger stand," Shake Shack was conceived as a place "more about communities gathering together than it was about feeding people." The location was ideal for both, though, in its public aspect and its centrality, and word about the venue traveled fast. Garutti cites the growth of social media as a way by which word was spread and as an incentive to do better: "When there's this instant audience, you care that little bit more about what you do." He also believes that there is a trend in food for customers to seek out restaurants "whose ethos they share," and Shake Shack's sense of community spirit, as evidenced by their support of the Madison Square Park art project, was part of that.

"Shake Shack is a marriage of fine dining and community."

→ **Randy Garutti**

Right: First and flagship location, Madison Square Park, Shake Shack, New York City.

Shake Shack quickly set about working out how to build on its success and viral reputation. It wanted to challenge the core ideas of fast food: "Whoever wrote the rule that the burger business has to act like this, with bad design, poor ingredients, the drive-thru ... well, we wanted to knock down those rules," says Garutti. The company took a fine-dining approach to every item on the menu, using fresh beef from Pat LaFrieda (see page 310) for its burgers, each cooked to order. It teamed up with local chefs and sourced, where possible, local ingredients, a practice still followed as the brand has spread globally. In Covent Garden, London, for example, the restaurant serves baked goods from nearby St. John Bakery, and buys its pork sausages from Jimmy's Farm, based only 80 miles (130 kilometers) away in East Anglia.

There was also something revolutionary about the way the Shake Shack team sought to renovate an American icon, as Garutti told me: "The old diner was great for decades, but then it went the wrong way. So we brought it back." By recognizing what its customers wanted and cared about, the company rode the wave of greater concern about, for example, food sustainability: "People want to share their money with brands who share their views ... it says something about me when I walk out with a Shake Shack bag." Garutti believes that Shake Shack "helped to redefine the fast-food industry, even if accidentally."

He also thinks that the idea that becoming a bigger chain leads to a drop-off in quality is a myth: "Our food and our supply chain have gotten better because we've grown, not in spite of it; our people and our leadership have improved, and we use growth for the purpose of improvement these days." It's a spur that drives the brand on: "You can't open another Shake Shack unless every other one gets better, unless every link in the chain makes the others stronger."

In order to retain a sense of place and individuality, each restaurant is designed to fit its location. As Garutti says, "We don't just parachute a design in: it feels like Shake Shack but it tastes like London or Connecticut or wherever you are."

Shake Shack made the news in 2015 when it went public, but Garutti insists that the brand will grow with "energy, compassion, and commitment" rather than purely for profit: "We're not going to grow for the sake of Wall Street; we're going to grow when we know it's good for our brand." Garutti is also very upbeat about Shake Shack's future, saying, "We're just getting better. We just want to share what we do and do it more often."

Above: Vanilla, strawberry, and chocolate milkshakes.

Opposite: SmokeShack (left) and ShackBurger (right).

Barracuda Diner

The Modern Burger

"A burger can turn an average day into a really great one."

⬇ Andrés Anhalt

First (and only) location: Mexico City, Mexico
2004

Barracuda Diner is based in the Colonia Condesa district of Mexico City and started with an aim to rectify the sense that "real diners in the city were a rare calamity" by "recreating the complete diner style and becoming a true pioneer," according to Operations Manager Andrés Anhalt. The restaurant is now well established and is hugely popular in Mexico's teeming capital, especially with "a fair share of foodies who enjoy our delicious milkshakes and decadent hamburgers."

The restaurant aims to "execute and serve delicious food made with the best-quality local produce available," explains Anhalt. It keeps as much as possible of the food production in house, baking its own breads, pickling its own cucumbers, and aging and processing its own cuts of meat to be turned into hamburgers and sausages. Its signature items have a distinctly Mexican twist, of course. The Nuevo León Hamburger is Mexican beef from the northwestern state of Sonora, hand-reared and steroid- and antibiotic-free, topped with Oaxaca cheese, guacamole, bacon, fried onion, and the restaurant's own special chili salsa. La Gringa burger is also beef-based, topped with a paste made from guajillo and ancho chilis, Manchego cheese, avocado, pineapple, cilantro (coriander), and chopped onion. The most popular sides are the fries (chips), sweet potato fries, and onion rings.

Anhalt sees burgers becoming one of the most popular food items on any restaurant menu and puts this surge in demand down to the versatility of the product, and the fact it can gather so much flavor up in one simple package: "I believe it is the real love and appreciation of food in every sense of the word. A hamburger, executed properly, gathers all the ingredients to deliver a great culinary experience." The inventiveness of Barracuda, given a local twist, bears witness to just how much variety can go into the humble burger: "I guess it has to do with the amount of different ingredients and toppings you can play with to turn a burger always into a delicious and unique item.

Hamburgers can be very similar all around the world, but it's all the different possibilities you add to it that make the burger such a spectacular sandwich."

Anhalt also loves the pleasure that the burger can bring to anyone, especially his own children: "Just the look on their faces when they take their first bite into a burger gives you the joy and satisfaction of how easy and wonderful it is to make someone really happy.... For me, that's probably the reason why I love working in the restaurant business."

Opposite: Barracuda Diner, Mexico City, Mexico.

Elevation Burger

The Modern Burger

"People already demand better, cleaner food."

↓

Jay Wisse

First location: Falls Church, Virginia, USA 2005

Hans and April Hess, young parents who wanted to offer healthier alternatives to traditional burgers and fries (chips) to other young families, founded Elevation Burger in 2005. They concentrated on sourcing organic, grass-fed, free-range beef, free of chemicals, to complement their hand-cut, olive-oil-cooked fries (chips), to create a lighter style of hamburger meal. Hans was a physics student at the University of California, Berkeley, who used his science background to work out how to get crisp fries from olive oil. He also researched and put together a network of over a hundred organic farms to provide the brand with all its meat and produce. Elevation's first restaurant opened in Falls Church, Virginia, and proved so popular that the company expanded, then went into franchising in 2008. There are currently thirty-three Elevation Burgers across the United States, plus one in Mexico and a further twenty in the Middle East.

The brand's philosophy extends beyond healthy burgers into an environmentally conscious infrastructure and a focus on sourcing produce that encourages and supports sustainable, humane animal husbandry. This, added to a desire to produce a healthier way to make burgers and fries, is what drives Elevation to make "arguably the [most] popular food in the world" into "a delicious indulgence that doesn't have to be unhealthy," according to Marketing Vice President Jay Wisse.

Elevation's signature item is the Elevation Burger, a double-patty burger made with organic beef, covered in aged, unprocessed cheddar and a range of toppings. The company also produces the epic Vertigo 10, a ten-patty monster that Wisse has never actually seen anyone finish.

Wisse believes that Elevation's choice of beef is what makes it stand out: "There are a couple of restaurants that serve organic burgers but no other major chains. We have made organic affordable—even though organic beef costs two or three times as much as non-organic at grocery stores, our burgers are no more expensive than our competitors in the better burger category." This marriage of sustainability and price attracts a loyal customer base, whom Wisse describes as "smart, informed, environmentally aware, and caring." Indeed, he sees consumer pressure as crucial to helping create a market for better, more sustainably sourced meat that will, in turn, lead the farming industry toward meeting that demand and allow for a greater availability of high-quality beef and chicken at lower prices.

With this ethos at the core of what Elevation does, and its belief that changes in the way burgers are crafted can lead to real change, perhaps it's not a surprise that the team would most like to share a (vegan) burger with Mahatma Gandhi: "He would have one of our veggie burgers but would appreciate that we treated our livestock with respect and humanity and allowed them to live free as nature intended." To the folks at Elevation, the burger is more than just food; it's part of a movement of change.

Opposite: Elevation Burger wrapped in lettuce.

The Oinkster

First location:
Los Angeles, California, USA
2006

The Oinkster, with two branches in Los Angeles, is the brainchild of Andre Guerrero, who was born in the Philippines and grew up in a foodie family in LA. He majored in fine arts in college but moved into food as a fine-dining chef. After twenty-five years of professional cooking, he "longed to do something simpler and familiar" and The Oinkster was born.

Guerrero describes the restaurant as "Slow Fast Food" and he says this really defines the whole Oinkster concept. "Everything is made from scratch, so while our concept is formatted as a traditional fast-food joint, the higher quality we offer is dictated by a much more involved process. For example, we are building a bakery in order to produce a better organic burger bun."

The Oinkster's classic cheeseburgers are their biggest seller, but the three-day-aged Carolina Pulled Pork Sandwich is another big winner; the pork is cured and smoked in house. Guerrero is also very proud of his French fries (chips), or, to be precise, Belgian fries: "They are the closest thing I have had to a true Belgian fry. We use Kennebec potatoes, which are cooked twice in two different types of oil. They also pair perfectly with our ketchup, which is made in house as well."

Guerrero thinks the secret to his success is taking "the most iconic food in America" that "covers all the major food groups" and cooking it the way a chef would cook it "for his friends," with a lot of skill but also with heart. The relaxed feel is very important to him, too: "There is a primal quality in the act of eating seared meat between two pieces of bread that one holds in their bare hands. It is very informal and unpretentious." This attitude is reflected in the restaurant's customer base: "The Oinkster is an 'everyman's restaurant.' If you were to sit in the dining area to observe for a few hours, you would see a cross-section of every ethnic group, age group, religion, and lifestyle from every economic level represented."

Doing the simple well is a kind of mantra at The Oinkster, too. Guerrero thinks that in the future "you will see some of the established burger places jockey for market share by creating weird, overwrought burgers." Not that that is necessarily a bad thing, as he says, speaking from the heart about why the burger is so versatile: "A burger can be simple. It can be elevated to a lofty, chef-driven gourmet meal. It can be a healthy option, vegetarian, or vegan. It can be a very inexpensive meal. It can be fast. It can be a soulful experience." But as long as Guerrero and The Oinkster keep the focus on doing the simple burger really well, they will continue to succeed regardless of where else the market goes: "I take the food and the service seriously, but always maintain a sense of humor about everything else."

"We have a customer who orders a veggie burger and adds bacon. He calls it the Paradox Burger."

⬇

Andre Guerrero

BURGER WEEK

"A TRIBUTE TO CLASSIC AMERICAN BURGERS"

JUNE 4TH – JUNE 10TH

The Oinkster is proud to announce our Second Annual Burger Week celebration! Please join us June 4th-10th as we pay tribute to some of America's Classic Hamburgers...

MONDAY
JUNE 4TH

WHITE CASTLE

TUESDAY
JUNE 5TH

ANIMAL STYLE
DOUBLE-DOUBLE

WEDNESDAY
JUNE 6TH

BACON WESTERN
CHEESEBURGER

THURSDAY
JUNE 7TH

GRILL EM' ALL

FRIDAY
JUNE 8TH

SOURDOUGH JACK

SATURDAY
JUNE 9TH

PORK ADOBO
BURGER

SUNDAY
JUNE 10TH

THE BIG MAC

For more info log onto: www.facebook.com/theoinkster

Previous spread (left): The Royale.

Previous spread (right): The Oinkster Burgerlords t-shirt.

Left: The Oinkster Burger Week media advertisement.

Opposite: The Oinkster, Hollywood, California.

Byron

First location:
London, UK
2007

Tom Byng loves a burger. Having spent four years in the United States eating, as he says, "enough hamburgers to sink the Titanic," he returned to London and found nowhere that served burgers as he had enjoyed them across the pond. In 2007, he set about rectifying what was, in his eyes, a distinct paucity of good, simple hamburgers in London. The outcome of his efforts was Byron, a restaurant group that prides itself on "serving proper hamburgers the way they should be."

Byng wanted, as he says, "simple, tasty things, a bit messy, but made with good-quality meat and only classic adornments: some lettuce, tomato, red onion, and maybe a slice of cheese or bacon." His primary inspiration for this pared-down approach was the legendary Silver Top diner, located in Providence, Rhode Island. As Byron has expanded, the challenge for Byng and his team has been to design restaurants that work within the group's aesthetic framework and brand identity, but eschew the sort of homogeneity often associated with fast-food restaurants.

Byron's approach to design is fluid. The company now has over sixty locations in the United Kingdom and is opening and developing more. As the business grows, the availability of appropriate sites presents various challenges. The Camden restaurant opened in a converted office block on a single floor for seating diners, with additional facilities on the floor above. The St. Giles site, on the ground floor of the vibrant towers that have housed tech companies, as well as residential properties, showcases a gleaming metallic open kitchen and bar area, and has adapted the exposed piping of the building's fabric into the overall aesthetic. The restaurant on The Cut, a street near Waterloo train station, occupies three separate stores knocked into one: each facade has a sign over its front with a different typeface saying "Byron," retaining the feel of a row of cafés while skillfully weaving the property into one place.

Left: Byron, Salisbury, UK.

The Modern Burger

The interior design plays with the same idea of difference. Using an array of distinctive typefaces, for example, distinguishes each venue in the chain, while suggesting a single visual approach of inventive playfulness; the brand's identity is to be different, to avoid the homogenous appearance common to many restaurant chains. In Byron's Soho venue, the typeface used for the window sign writing is based on a 1960s-style font called Turnpike, reworked to be thinner and more stretched on the horizontal. The Cowcross Street brand, in contrast, uses what looks like Plaza, but thinned, evocative of East German store signs.

The art direction on menus and the restaurant's interiors are similarly varied, but with an emphasis on less being more. For example, there's no overt advertising of the quality of the food, which should speak for itself.

These twin approaches to interior design and art direction dovetail neatly, giving rise to the sense that each restaurant should be tackled as if it were the only Byron restaurant, the brand's ethos and menu being the constants across the chain, with layout, visual identity, and interior design and architecture all up for grabs. This has resulted in the unusual pleasure of each venue feeling familiar, but looking different: crucial as the brand has expanded.

Byron has also extended its range of burgers away from the core menu of diner-style classics. A fine example of this is the B-Rex, created by head chef Fred Smith and born of his nostalgia for his first-ever hamburger. The B-Rex heaps an onion ring, American cheese, lean (streaky) bacon, jalapeños, pickles (gherkins), onion, mayonnaise, and barbecue sauce onto a 6-ounce (175-gram) patty. Formerly a special item only, the burger's popularity saw it brought onto the main menu in early 2015. Other permanently adopted specials include the Chilli, a punchy combination of green chiles, chipotle mayonnaise, and American cheese, which began life as the Chilli Queen and was created in honor of the Golden Jubilee of Queen Elizabeth II in 2002.

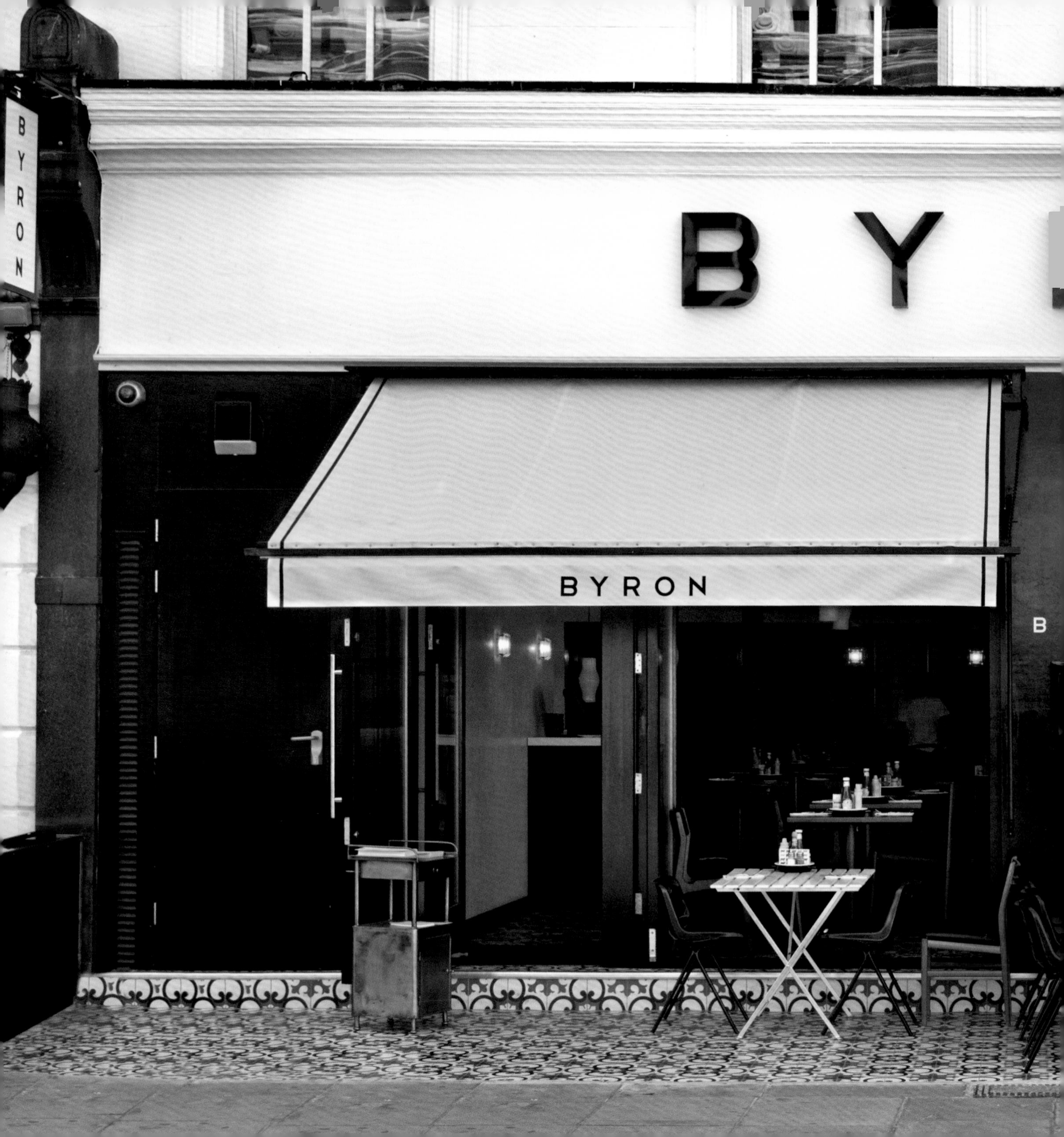
BYRON
BY
BYRON
B

With an innovative approach to branding and a menu that is at once malleable and consistently true to Tom Byng's initial vision, Byron is able to show dynamism and creativity in the brand's approach to design, while focusing on keeping the food simple and tasty.

The Modern Burger

Opposite (top):
The Classic.

Opposite (bottom):
Interior, Byron, Old
Brompton Road, London.

Left: Byron,
West London.

5 Napkin Burger

First location:
New York City,
New York, USA
2008

5 Napkin Burger, an upscale casual brand, was founded by partners Andy D'Amico, Simon Oren, and Robert Guarino. D'Amico, the executive chef, explains that "With roots in fine dining and a roster of innovative eateries under us, including L'Express, Nice Matin, Sushi Samba, and Marseille, we brought our skills to the creative, bustling streets of Hell's Kitchen in New York City. We now have five locations in New York, one in Boston, and we're looking to expand."

The 5 Napkin gourmet burgers are just like their name. They say you will need five napkins because they're so juicy. The signature Original 5 Napkin Burger is a 10-ounce (280-gram) chuck beef patty, made with rosemary aioli, Gruyère cheese, and caramelized onions. They also serve a range of other fantastic burgers including the Double Cheese, Ahi Tuna, and Korean BBQ.

"At 5 Napkin, we haven't forgotten why you love an old-school burger – we just think you should define the rest."

⬇ Simon Oren

Burgerim

First location: Tel Aviv, Israel 2008

Burgerim was founded in 2008 by Oren Loni and Donna Tuchner. The name translates to "multiple burgers" in Hebrew. In 2013, Ashley Gershoony opened the first North American offshoot on Santa Monica Boulevard in West Hollywood, California.

The restaurant serves mini burgers (not sliders) and has custom-made sesame seed, brioche-like buns. With their slogan, "always more than one," customers can choose from a box of two mini burgers (a duo), a box of three mini burgers (a trio), or a party box containing sixteen mini burgers. Each burger is the customer's to build. There are three buns, six sauces, and eleven patties to choose from, including beef, Wagyu, merguez, lamb, and a vegetarian option. In an interview Gershoony said, "There really is no other concept like this in the States, where you can choose such a variety of different meats, have smaller options, and mix and match them."

Burgerim now has 168 locations worldwide with 30 more locations expected to open in the United States in 2017.

Opposite: Mini Burger Party Box.

"We'd share a burger with Colonel Sanders— to show him where he went wrong."

⬇

Ashley Gershoony

Umami Burger

The Modern Burger

First location:
Los Angeles, California, USA
2009

Self-taught chef and wine expert Adam Fleischman founded Umami Burger in 2009, opening a small restaurant on La Brea Avenue in Los Angeles. He had been intrigued by a discovery he made when traveling in Europe—a French cookbook that examined the fifth flavor, "umami," a pleasant savory taste imparted by glutamate, a type of amino acid, that occurs naturally in food such as beef, certain mushrooms, and Parmesan cheese, This flavor seemed to resonate with the American love for hamburgers, a food crammed with umami.

Fleischman figured that if he could work out how to build the most umami burger ever, he might be onto a winner, and so he sought out ways of heightening the umami quality in burgers he experimented with at home. He developed a sauce, based on East Asian hoisin, kombu, and soy sauces, and worked out that a dust made from dehydrated mushrooms would amp up the umami too. He added roasted tomato, shiitake mushrooms, onions sautéed in star anise, a homemade Parmesan frico (a sort of crispy wafer), and a Portuguese bun that contains a little milk. This was the first Umami Burger burger, every component selected and refined to maximize the savory experience. Fleischman was ready to launch his brand.

By 2010, the venture had grown into four venues, as Fleischman pushed his experimentations further, basing his approach around "culinary trends, taking flavor profiles that might be found in *haute cuisine* and applying them to the burger," as a spokesperson for the company says. It received a boost when GQ magazine named Umami Burger the best burger of 2010, and by 2016 there were more than twenty restaurants across the United States.

Umami describes its typical customers as people on the lookout for an "interesting culinary experience, the adventurous who are into trying new things." Fleischman's approach was based in asking not what the burger was, but what it could be, moving it away from

traditional approaches of cooking and trying to reinvent it by unlocking the flavor potential of blends and balances of savory. An example of this innovative approach was the famous pumpkin-spiced latté burger, which sought to ape the taste of a certain coffee shop's creation. The taste of the drink was dissected and the flavor combinations worked out, before the Umami team conjured ways of mimicking them using ingredients that would suit a burger. Japanese pumpkin, or kabocha, was fried tempura-style and combined with the American Wagyu beef patty, garlic aioli, mascarpone, and coffee glaze. The team has also created a bacon-wrapped Scallop Burger with spicy Yuzu Koshu; a Kimchi Burger featuring Korean-style fermented vegetables; and a Baja Burger, which was inspired by fish tacos. It seems as if, by taking a thoroughly scientific approach to taste, Fleischman and Umami Burger have managed to fuse science and imagination to draw maximum flavor from the burger.

Opposite: Umami Burger restaurant, Santa Monica, California.

Above: Throwback Burger.

新しい料理の発見は人類の幸福
がある。　誰かを招待するとい
その人の幸福を引き受けるとい
調和する愉しみは良き仲間との
は星　秋に満月　冬には雪

Honest Burgers

First location:
London, UK
2010

Right: Cheeseburger.

When Tom Barton and Phil Eeles started their business as Honest Food Company in 2010, they had a small tent and were working friends' weddings, fireworks parties, and birthdays. Six years later, they had sixteen restaurants, with an experienced restaurateur, Dorian Waite, as a partner, and had raised seven million pounds using a private equity firm. As Barton told me, "If you said to me when I was sitting in a field in the pissing rain with Phil six years ago we'd be doing this, I wouldn't have believed you." It's not hard to see why, but the growth and development of Honest Burgers are a testament to the popularity of good hamburgers and the principles of running and expanding a business by staying close to your core ideas.

Barton and Eeles worked in hospitality together in Brighton, but decided to be their own bosses and initially started with sensibly limited ideas of what they might achieve. As Barton told me, "We didn't have any money, so getting a restaurant was never our goal to start with. We had two and a half thousand pounds and much of that was loans from friends and family." But their ad-hoc open-air catering worked so well that after only a short while and having met Waite, a friend of a friend, they decided to take the chance. A small space became available in Brixton, South London, and Honest Burgers was born.

Barton describes himself at that time as "a passionate amateur" when it came to cooking, but thought he "could do a burger justice ... and who doesn't like a decent, chunky homemade burger?" The restaurant and the brand grew, in the simplest terms, from that idea: get the burgers right, create the right atmosphere, friendly and low-key, and the rest will follow. Barton says, "I wish there was more of a eureka impulse to do burgers," but the team quickly found that, as a food, it suited exactly what they were trying to achieve within the means they had at the time. Central to the brand's development, according to Barton, were the name Honest and the

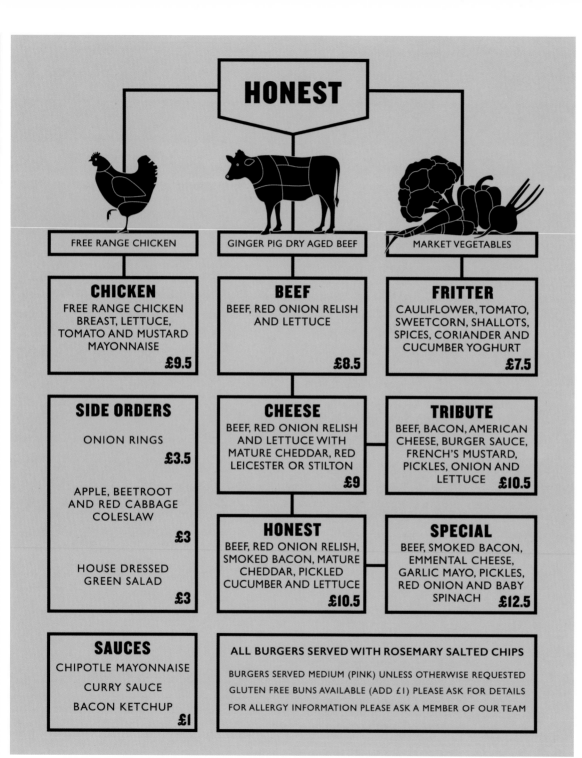

HONEST

FREE RANGE CHICKEN

GINGER PIG DRY AGED BEEF

MARKET VEGETABLES

CHICKEN
FREE RANGE CHICKEN BREAST, LETTUCE, TOMATO AND MUSTARD MAYONNAISE

£9.5

BEEF
BEEF, RED ONION RELISH AND LETTUCE

£8.5

FRITTER
CAULIFLOWER, TOMATO, SWEETCORN, SHALLOTS, SPICES, CORIANDER AND CUCUMBER YOGHURT

£7.5

SIDE ORDERS
ONION RINGS

£3.5

APPLE, BEETROOT AND RED CABBAGE COLESLAW

£3

HOUSE DRESSED GREEN SALAD

£3

CHEESE
BEEF, RED ONION RELISH AND LETTUCE WITH MATURE CHEDDAR, RED LEICESTER OR STILTON

£9

TRIBUTE
BEEF, BACON, AMERICAN CHEESE, BURGER SAUCE, FRENCH'S MUSTARD, PICKLES, ONION AND LETTUCE

£10.5

HONEST
BEEF, RED ONION RELISH, SMOKED BACON, MATURE CHEDDAR, PICKLED CUCUMBER AND LETTUCE

£10.5

SPECIAL
BEEF, SMOKED BACON, EMMENTAL CHEESE, GARLIC MAYO, PICKLES, RED ONION AND BABY SPINACH

£12.5

SAUCES
CHIPOTLE MAYONNAISE

CURRY SAUCE

BACON KETCHUP

£1

ALL BURGERS SERVED WITH ROSEMARY SALTED CHIPS

BURGERS SERVED MEDIUM (PINK) UNLESS OTHERWISE REQUESTED

GLUTEN FREE BUNS AVAILABLE (ADD £1) PLEASE ASK FOR DETAILS

FOR ALLERGY INFORMATION PLEASE ASK A MEMBER OF OUR TEAM

Left: Menu, Honest Burgers.

Opposite: Honest Burger.

constraints the team encountered while building the Brixton location up: both would shape everything Honest Burgers has done since.

"Honest" as a term conjures up everything that is key to Barton, Eeles, and Waite: "simplicity and transparency; it's a benchmark for our whole decision-making process." Early conversations about brand development, "all very opinionated, very discursive," were held around the kitchen table, and Barton's girlfriend Connie Dickson, a graphic designer by trade, was instrumental in the process. This use of a close network, incidentally, has been a feature of the brand: Barton's stepfather is a carpenter who outfitted the Brixton restaurant and lots of the initial hands-on work was done by family and friends.

Dickson took the word "honest" and devised a simple, rustic color palate, focusing on a warm, deep green that evokes the British countryside, natural ingredients, and a sense of welcome. Natural colors and woods formed the basis of the interior design of the Brixton location and have stayed the hallmark of the brand's style.

As Barton told me, Brixton was something of a crucible for Honest: "So much of our character was crafted in that atmosphere and by those challenges; Brixton had real limitations of space, size, and budget." Simplicity was key, and this was the idea behind the blocky, flow diagram-style menu boards, which then translated onto the menu: "We're never going to have fifty things on it; we like to stick close to our core stuff."

For a burger restaurant, meat is obviously the most crucial item, and Barton spent a great deal of time researching the options, looking at restaurants that he, Eeles, and Waite admired and seeing where they sourced their produce. Barton also spoke to butchers, and quickly realized that he had found a like-minded individual in Tim Wilson of acclaimed butchery The Ginger Pig: "Tim was really helpful, serious but not condescending, and he gave us loads of advice." Tom initially cycled about 6 miles (10 kilometers) every day from Brixton to Marylebone to collect meat from The Ginger Pig, but after word got out and Honest Burgers started flying off the grill, a delivery system was promptly arranged.

Success came quickly, but bred its own challenges: "We had people queuing out the door, people loving the food but complaining about having to wait." Waite's nous was crucial when it came to expanding, because, as Barton says, "He's been a real mentor and he knows the market so well." Premises were found in Camden, Soho, Portobello and more, until in 2016 the company opened its fifteenth restaurant, making that the biggest year of expansion so far. Each location brings new challenges, and restaurants are tweaked and amended based on those, but with the Honest philosophy at the heart of each one. Part of that is an investment in people. Barton is very proud of the fact that six of the first nine managers of Honest's venues started waiting tables for the company before progressing, saying, "It's all about the dynamic, getting the right managers in and committing time to people—that's Phil's big thing." It allows the brand to stay close to the ideals from which it grew, because the company takes the time to instill those ideals in the people trusted to run each branch.

Honest intends to grow more, but without losing those values. Barton is adamant on that point: "We take each restaurant as it comes. We've chosen a path and we're committed to it. We just want loads of people to try our food, try our customer service." He doesn't see becoming a chain as a bad thing, either, providing that there is a philosophy at the core of what it does: "We are a group, but we don't see why that means we have to become expensive or use cheap produce." The important thing is keeping things as close to what happened in Brixton as possible, but learning all the time as well; as Barton says, "We aren't the finished article; there's still so much to learn. But we know our market and our customers really well." As he sees it, that's the key to growing a great burger brand. Find out what you stand for and make sure you don't forget it. At Honest, they've even put their name to it.

Fat Hippo

The Modern Burger

First location: Newcastle upon Tyne, Tyne and Wear, UK 2010

Fat Hippo's burger philosophy is simple: "good food and messy fingers." Born in northeastern England from a love of burgers and an observation that the city was lacking in good burger joints, it was the brainchild of Mike Phillips, Managing Director and self-titled burger wizard. He assembled a team of "borderline burger obsessives" and set out to change the landscape. Fast-forward six years and Fat Hippo has three restaurants and more in the pipeline.

From the outset, Phillips and his team have focused on "honing our burger skills and experimenting with quirky toppings." As he says, "We're not about fine dining and fancy cuisine. We serve the ultimate comfort food and we do it in a relaxed friendly environment, serving good old dirty burgers and filling them with high-quality, gourmet ingredients." Fat Hippo's core group of customers is "a cult following of students, young professionals, and families," but as its reputation has grown, so has its popularity.

The Fat Hippo signature item is the Fat Hippo Burger, a double 4-ounce (120-gram) beef burger with cheese; lean (streaky) bacon; chorizo; the company's very own, top-secret Fat Hippo sauce; and onion rings; all crammed into a brioche bun. Also popular is the PB & J Burger, which combines bacon, jam, and peanut butter in a cheeseburger. Fat Hippo serves an array of sides, including deep-fried mac and cheese balls and buffalo chicken strips, delicious with a spot of Alabama white barbecue sauce.

Phillips sees the popularity of the burger as having grown as perceptions have changed: "If you travel back five years, I think the humble burger was one of the most underrated foods, shunned by many as an unhealthy, lazy option and neglected by restaurants and fast-food joints alike." The rise of the gourmet burger and the emphasis on quality ingredients have changed all this. Fat Hippo makes all its patties from scratch daily; the idea is to treat a burger patty as you would a prime cut of steak and reap the benefits. Indeed, as Phillips says, a patty can blend various cuts of meat to create the perfect balance of fat and lean, giving a good patty even greater depth of flavor than a straight cut.

With this intensity of passion, it's not a surprise that asking Phillips to explain what the burger means to him prompts an outpouring of love in the form of a quote from *How I Met Your Mother*:

JUST A BURGER? IT'S SO MUCH MORE THAN "JUST A BURGER." I MEAN ... THAT FIRST BITE—OH, WHAT HEAVEN THAT FIRST BITE IS. THE BUN, LIKE A SESAME-FRECKLED BREAST OF AN ANGEL, RESTING GENTLY ON THE KETCHUP AND MUSTARD BELOW, FLAVORS MINGLING IN A SEDUCTIVE PAS DE DEUX.... THIS IS NO MERE SANDWICH OF GRILLED MEAT AND TOASTED BREAD, ROBIN. THIS IS GOD, SPEAKING TO US IN FOOD.

"Our burgers are the type to make you loosen your belt buckle before you've even started."

⬇ Mike Phillips

Opposite:
The Fat Hippo.

Left: Fat Hippo logo.

The Modern Burger

Left: Selection of burgers and hand-cut fries (chips) at Fat Hippo, Newcastle, UK.

Right: Menu, Fat Hippo.

EST. 2010

FAT HIPPO

TAKEAWAY

TAKEAWAY AVAILABLE FOR COLLECTION ONLY
0191 340 8949

ALL BURGERS £6
SERVED IN BRIOCHE BUNS AND WITH
HANDCUT CHIPS

* * *

LITTLE AMERICAN
SINGLE 4OZ BEEF PATTY TOPPED WITH CHEESE, GHERKINS, KETCHUP AND MUSTARD

LITTLE TEXAS
SINGLE 4OZ BEEF PATTY TOPPED WITH BACON, CHEESE AND BBQ SAUCE

LITTLE HIPPO
SINGLE 4OZ BEEF PATTY TOPPED WITH CHORIZO, CHEESE AND FAT HIPPO SAUCE

LITTLE PB&J
SINGLE 4OZ BEEF PATTY TOPPED WITH CHEESE, CRUNCHY
PEANUT BUTTER AND BACON JAM

* * *

LITTLE WHITE BUFFALO
BUTTERMILK CHICKEN FINGERS, BUFFALO HOT SAUCE AND HOUSE SLAW

LITTLE SPICY BEAN (v)
OUR HOMEMADE RECIPE WITH A KICK! TOPPED WITH SWEET CHILLI SAUCE

* * *

Hard Times Sundaes

The Modern Burger

First (and only) location: New York City, New York, USA
2010

Hard Times Sundaes is a burger truck in Brooklyn, New York, which also has a spin-off location at the Urbanspace Vanderbilt indoor food hall near Grand Central Terminal in Manhattan. It is run by chef and owner Andrew Zurica, a one-man band producing burgers described as "worth the schlep." As the *New York Times* wrote about Hard Times Sundaes in 2014, "In the end, the greatness of a burger lies not in the quality or provenance of its ingredients, but in the touch, care, and God-given talent of its maker."

Zurica says he's been "cooking and working in food my whole life, but I've never been wowed by a burger, so that's what put me on this journey." He has been covered in the *New York Times*, *Zagat*, and *New York* magazine, and been nominated for the street food Vendy awards.

Zurica's philosophy is "Keep It Simple, Stupid—nothing fancy, no secret blends or special sauces, just great, simple, quality products." His signature item is the Hard Times Burger, with American cheese, caramelized onions, and bacon on a potato roll. He serves this with thin-cut fries (chips), cooked in peanut (groundnut) oil and sour pickle (gherkins). In the summer, he grows his own lettuce and tomatoes in his backyard. He describes his customers as "burger enthusiasts" and the same could very much be said of him.

Zurica admires Danny Meyer, the CEO of Union Square Hospitality Group, which owns and runs Shake Shack (see page 162), for his business acumen and the way he has created such a successful brand. He tells me mischievously, "One day, I'll open up across the road from them."

Zurica describes the burger as "a go-to meal for all mankind, it doesn't matter where you are in the world." He believes its greatness lies in simplicity, though, and feels that some people are trying to do too much with it:

"I can only hope and pray that people stop trying to re-create the wheel. I hate gourmet burgers. I wish that over the next ten years they disappear." He likes to keep what Hard Times Sundaes produces to what's on the menu, telling me, "I do not accept weird orders." This is as much a reflection of his philosophy of simplicity as it is a practical matter since he's doing everything himself in a small burger truck.

Zurica is also adamant that there are many wonderful burgers out there, and that it's all a matter of personal taste; as he says, "There is no correct answer to 'Who makes the best burger?' There will never be someone to point a finger at and say, 'He or she makes the best burger in the world.'"

"Done correctly, the burger can appeal to any palate."

➡ Andrew Zurica

Opposite: Bacon Cheeseburgers in front of the Hard Times Sundaes burger truck.

Burger Theory

First location: Adelaide, South Australia, Australia 2010

Given that the restaurant's name is Burger Theory, it's perhaps not a shock that co-founders Rob Dean and Dan Mendelson met while doing postgraduate studies. It was at Flinders University in Adelaide: Dean was studying sociology and Mendelson had embarked on a Ph.D., but, as Dean says, "Our grades were okay, but where we really excelled was in the discussion of food." Mendelson had a preternatural ability to craft a good burger, so the pair left academia and hit the road in an old catering truck. Now employing over thirty people using a profit-sharing scheme and taking on family and friends where possible, Burger Theory has three restaurants in Adelaide, one in Melbourne, and a truck for events and catering.

The "theory" at Burger Theory is "to keep the length of time between grinding [mincing] a burger and grilling it as short as possible. For this reason we do the meat grinding ourselves," Dean explains. "Touching is caring, and loosely packed patties sear better and stay juicier than those formed by machine."

Their most popular item is the #1, a freshly ground patty seared to medium, doused in gooey American cheese and topped with iceberg lettuce, tomato, and a dollop of homemade tangy mayonnaise, all inside a toasted brioche bun. The tang is important, as Dean says: "Pickle [gherkins]. Or tang from somewhere else. The tang is the key."

It's not all about burgers though. Burger Theory also has an item on the menu that is unique for South Australia: frozen custard. Frozen custard is a very creamy, buttery form of ice cream that has much less air than typical ice cream and sounds divine. Nevertheless, Dean is blunt about what the burger means to him: "We are now inseparable. I'm not even kidding. I spend all day around them, all night thinking about them, no doubt dream about them, and have come to be defined by them—

whenever I'm introduced to people, a burger reference is never far away."

While Dean reckons there's no limit to where the burger can go, he places a strong emphasis on the importance of tradition and quality: "I think we'll see it all, but whatever happens it'll always return to its roots—the best cut of beef, seasoned and seared hot and fast, then balanced appropriately against the chosen bun, toppings, and sauce, wins!" He also has a strong message for people thinking of further education: "Study hard, and you'll end up flipping burgers."

THOUGHTFUL FAST FOOD

BURGER
Theory

LA TROBE	BURGER *Theory*	LA TROBE

BEEF BURGERS

We cook our beef **medium**. Please ask if you would prefer **well done** (no pink). Seasoning is to order and can be adjusted to your liking.

#1   10
With lettuce, tomato, cheese and truck sauce

#2   12
With bacon, onion confit and blue cheese sauce

PEARL'S CHEESEBURGER   11
With cheese, pickles, onion, ketchup and mustard

KID'S BURGER   8
Cooked well done with cheese and ketchup

BURGER OF THE MONTH
See specials board...

FRIED CHICKEN BURGERS

Our patties are hand-battered with seasoned flour and fried to order, for extra succulence and crunch.

ORIGINAL   11
With pickles and special sauce

CAESAR   13
With lettuce, Caesar sauce and bacon

SPICY   14
With kimchi, gochujang sauce, bacon and cheese

FALAFEL BURGERS

Dried chickpeas and parsley, ground together and hand-formed, then cooked to order in a dedicated vegan deep-fryer.

ORIGINAL   11
With lettuce, tomato, pickles and special sauce

MEDITERRANEAN   11
With lettuce, pickled red onions and tahini sauce

FRIES & DRINKS

FRIES   4
With choice of tomato sauce, truck sauce or special sauce

SOFT DRINKS   3.5

WATER   3.5

JUICE   3.5

SHAKES   7
Vanilla, chocolate or strawberry

MAKE IT A MEAL
Choose your burger and...
Add fries & a soft drink, water or juice   6
Add fries & a shake   9

LOADED FRIES

A larger serve of fries with your choice of toppings

CLASSIC   7
With spring onion, sour cream and bacon bits

CHICKEN   8
With pickles, special sauce and fried chicken skin

SPICY   9
With kimchi, gochujang sauce, sour cream and bacon bits

HOT FRUIT PIES

Pastry dough filled with fruit and then deep fried

APPLE PIE   4

BLUEBERRY PIE   4

Add a scoop of vanilla ice cream   2

BURGER *Theory*

293 LA TROBE ST. MELBOURNE
OPEN MON - FRI: 11:00 - 2:30
AND FRIDAY 5:30 - 9:00
CLOSED WEEKENDS & PUBLIC HOLIDAYS

BURGERTHEORY.COM
@BURGERTHEORY

"The burger is round. That's a good start. People like round things."

➡

Rob Dean

Opposite: Burger Theory food truck, Adelaide, Australia.

Far left: Burger Theory logo.

Left: Menu, Burger Theory.

Big Fernand

First location: Paris, France
2011

Big Fernand was born in a tiny street in Paris's trendy ninth *arrondissement*. Its burger epiphany came when its founders realized that the French are celebrated for their great beef, bread, and cheese: all the things you need to make a great burger. The company now has a dozen outlets, including its own bakery, across Paris and the rest of France, as well as in London and Hong Kong.

Despite this international expansion, Big Fernand remains rooted in French culinary traditions: as the company's "UK Ambassador" Mathieu Durand explains, "We select the best-grade meat in France and grind [mince] it ourselves, we have our own bakery in France and make our own sesame-topped bun, and our cheese is French and unpasteurized; it comes from the countryside, not the supermarket." The challenge, as Durand admits, is not to let the simplicity of the hamburger lull a chef into complacency: "Just because it's a sandwich, a hand-held snack that can be eaten quickly, that's no reason not to do it well."

The company's signature item is Le Big Fernand, a beef burger dripping with Tomme de Savoie cheese, topped with sun-dried tomatoes and flat-leaf parsley, and finished off with its own homemade cocktail sauce, Tata Fernande. As Durand says, "If you're coming to Big Fernand for the first time, it's a good place to start: the cheese is subtle; the flavors well balanced; it's simple, not too complex." The next most popular burger, says Durand, is probably Le Bartholomé, a rich mountain of ripe Raclette cheese, caramelized onion, lean (streaky) bacon, and barbecue sauce and Tata Fernande. The restaurant also offers customers the chance to exercise their creativity and build their own burger from scratch from the enormous array of items on the menu.

This wide variety and the universal appeal of the burger mean that Big Fernand's customer base is similarly broad: "Local workers, tourists, suits, families, older people looking to eat pre-theater, young people starting a night out...." One group of customers made quite an impression, a stag party that ordered the groom a burger with every single one of the items from the build-your-own option: that's a burger containing beef, veal, lamb, chicken, Portobello mushrooms, herbs, each of the many homemade sauces, four different types of cheese, eggplants (aubergines), and sun-dried tomatoes.

Durand believes that despite France's reputation as the center of world gastronomy, the country has fallen hard for the simple hamburger: "London has had a thriving burger industry for the last decade, from the very traditional to the gourmet. I think Paris will follow suit and the burger will become a more common product, but with more influences and international ingredients, as people put their own twist on things."

> **"At its heart, it's meat, bun, cheese. It's beautifully simple."**
>
> ➜ **Mathieu Durand**

Above: Bacon Cheeseburger.

Left: Big Fernand logo.

The French Burger Workshop

BIG FERNAND

Burger & Lobster

First location:
London, UK
2011

Created by George Bukhov-Weinstein, a director of the Goodman steak restaurant in Moscow, Burger & Lobster is what happens when you want to open a burger joint, or a lobster restaurant, and then realize you can combine them. Having experienced success in Russia, Bukhov-Weinstein decided to move into the London market and brought the first Burger & Lobster to a former tiny old Irish pub in Mayfair. His mission was to create the best burgers in the world and make the joy of lobster accessible to everyone. The company now has ten sites in the UK, one each in New York, Dubai, Kuwait City, and Jeddah, and a franchise partner in Stockholm, a first for the group.

The premise is simple, but rendered effective by the quality of the food. There are only three items on the menu: the Burger, the Lobster, and the Lobster Roll, each refined by knowledge and testing. James Warrillow, Operations Manager, says: "We believe that to do it well it must be done simply but perfectly, and we've worked for years to craft the best burger, the best lobster, and the best lobster roll around." The company is also hugely proud of its secret-recipe burger sauce, describing it as "basically a side dish in itself."

Burger & Lobster doesn't have printed menus; as Warrillow says, "We believe if it's too long to say then it shouldn't be there." This leaves the restaurant open, despite being quite obviously a burger and lobster joint, to "some left-field requests: top of the list are pizza, turkey burgers, crab ... you name it, we've been asked!" According to Warrillow, Burger & Lobster doesn't have a usual customer. "Anyone is welcome in our businesses as long as they have three things in common: they love lobster, they love burgers, and they love having fun." Sometimes putting what you do out there front and center is the best way to go and, for Burger & Lobster, it doesn't get any better than, well, burgers and lobster.

"It's pretty clear what we specialize in."

↓
James Warrillow

Opposite: Advertisement photograph, Burger & Lobster.

Next spread: Burger & Lobster, Threadneedle Street, London.

Wahlburgers

First location: Hingham, Massachusetts, USA 2011

Founded by Executive Chef Paul Wahlberg and his celebrity brothers Mark and Donnie, Wahlburgers debuted in October 2011 and now has ten locations across the United States, with plans for a further fifteen.

The subject of a TV reality show on A&E in the U.S., Wahlburgers offers a fun, casual, music-filled atmosphere where it hopes that guests share great food, laughs, and lots of love. While its walls celebrate the story through photos and words of the Wahlberg brothers' life journeys from Dorchester, Massachusetts, neighborhood kids to rising chef and international singing and acting stars, it's the food at Wahlburgers that takes center stage.

Crafted by Chef Paul and served with heartfelt hospitality, the menu features a variety of fresh burgers including The Our Burger, The Beast, and The Double and Triple Deckers, all accompanied by housemade condiments.

Right: The Our Burger with fries (chips) and milkshake.

Next spread: Wahlburgers, Boston, Massachusetts.

MEAT IS NEAT!

Lucky CHIP BURGERS

www.luckychipuk.com

BURGERS ↓

no.1	CHEESEBURGER	7.95
	AGED BEEF PATTY, AMERICAN CHEESE, KETCHUP, MUSTARD & PICKLES	
no.2	KEVIN BACON	8.50
	SAME AS THE CHEESEBURGER BUT WITH APPLEWOOD SMOKED BACON	
no.3	ROYALE WIT CHEESE	8.95
	AGED BEEF PATTY, BACON, AMERICAN CHEESE, TOMATO, ONION, LETTUCE, KETCHUP, MUSTARD & SPECIAL SAUCE	
no.4	EL CHAPPO	9.50
	AGED BEEF PATTY, SMOKED BACON, BLUE CHEESE, ROASTED JALAPENOS & AIOLI	
no.5	JOHN BELUSHI	16.50
	DUCK, VEAL & MARROW PATTY, FOIE GRAS, TRUFFLE AIOLI, CHEDDAR, TARRAGON BUTTER & PEDRO XIMENEZ ONIONS	
no.6	CHICKEN BURGER	8.95
	FRIED CHICKEN, CHEESE, CREAM SODA B.B.Q. SAUCE AND LETTUCE	
no.7	WOODY HARRELSON (V)	7.50
	PORTOBELLO MUSHROOM, AUBERGINE, ROASTED PEPPER, CHEDDAR, GINGER SWEET CHILLI & AIOLI	

SIDES ↓

★ FRENCH FRIES	3
★ CHEESE FRIES	4
CHILI CHEESE FRIES	6.95
BEEF & PORK	
★ SPICY MAYO CHEESE FRIES	4.5
★ WASABI MAYO & GINGER SWEET CHILLI FRIES	4
★ JALAPENO COLESLAW	3.5

SPECIALS ↓

★ HOT WINGS!	6.5
WITH BLUE CHEESE DRESSING	
★ HOT DOG	5.5
PORK DOG, KETCHUP & MUSTARD	
★ UNDER DOG	7
PORK DOG, FRIED ONION, CHEESE, KETCHUP & MUSTARD	

BURGER of the WEEK

JOHN CANDY

TWO AGED BEEF PATTIES, SECIAL SAUCE, LETTUCE, CHEESE, PICKLES, ONION ALL ON A SESAME SEED BUN   £10.95

SAUCE & DIPS ↓

★ GINGER SWEET CHILLI
★ GARLIC AIOLI
★ WASABI MAYO
★ SPICY MAYO
★ MAYONAISSE
★ CREAM SODA B.B.Q SAUCE

ONE POUND! Each

🐦 @Lucky_Chip   f Lucky chip

First location: London, UK
2011

Lucky Chip was founded by Ben Denner, who started his career as a DJ before becoming the manager at the Cobden private members club in Notting Hill in London. After the club closed, Ben realized his dream to open Lucky Chip, which had been in his sights for many years. It started trading from a burger van in a church parking lot of Kensal Rise. Then it moved to Netil Market in Hackney, before taking up residence in the Sebright Arms in Bethnal Green. In January 2016, Lucky Chip opened its first permanent location in Hackney.

When Ben first launched Lucky Chip he caused a sensation; burger lovers and aficionados would travel across London to try his burgers that include the Kevin Bacon, Royale Wit Cheese, and El Chappo. Ben worked tirelessly to create the best burger he could, testing up to seventy bakeries before finding the perfect bun and sourcing the very best beef for the patty, a fifty-day dry-aged Galician Beef. But it isn't just about the burger; no burger is complete without a side portion of "lucky chips." The French fries are hand-cut, triple cooked, and covered with cheese, garlic, and fresh herbs or truffle and Gorgonzola.

Lucky Chip has plans to expand to further locations throughout London.

Above: Royale
Wit Cheese.

Au Cheval

First (and only) location: Chicago, Illinois, USA
2012

Chicago-based Au Cheval, part of Hogsalt Hospitality, has a simple philosophy: make high-quality burgers and respect what you're doing: "simple dishes executed very well, every single time."

The diner's location was previously a Greek restaurant but, as Director of Marketing and Communications Rachel Gillman Rischall told me, "The owner knew it would be a diner from the second he walked in." The restaurant now serves about seven hundred customers a day and as many as six hundred burgers each weekend.

The mission from the beginning was to create good food with wide appeal: "It's comfortable American fare that we can stand behind. We genuinely love every dish on our menu and feel excited telling guests about it. We're trying to get you to order a dish because it will make your life better if you put it in your mouth."

The restaurant's signature item is a Cheeseburger, a single, not a double, though one regular customer orders a triple with four patties. Au Cheval even once served a guest who ordered three double burgers with bacon and eggs and ate all three. It offers a huge array of sides as well, including crispy fries (chips) with eggs and Mornay sauce, and hash browns with duck-heart gravy.

Au Cheval appeals to a wide range of customers, not just those with extraordinarily capacious stomachs. Rischall explains, "We attract every shape, size, color, and creed. Everyone loves cheeseburgers. You can come to Au Cheval and see grandmas, ten-year-olds, a guys' night out, a girls' night out, parents with kids, and people who decided not to be vegetarians any more." The popularity of the restaurant, as Rischall sees it, is doing the most democratic food in the world very well: "Burgers are a national staple in America—they unify people. At Au Cheval, we serve approachable food in an unforgettable way."

Au Cheval sees the burger as being flexible and responding to prevailing tastes; as Rischall puts it, "I think the burger will remain the same—a classic American staple. It will go through the fad of gourmet-style back to classic, but will remain true to itself. Burgers won't go anywhere, but will alter based on what's popular at the time." This flexibility is inherent in the very make-up of the burger: "A burger can be anything you want it to be. A veggie burger, turkey burger, or beef burger. A brioche bun, white bun, or pretzel bun. You can add fancy cheese, bacon, avocado—mold it into any style you want."

But the basic appeal of the burger, as Au Cheval sees it, is comfort: "A burger signifies home. It's relaxing like a bubble bath. You don't have to think about it. You can enjoy yourself and not analyze it." And when a burger is so good it improves your life, what's to think about?

"The respect for a burger goes to the cow."

➡ **Rachel Gillman Rischall**

Left: Double Cheeseburger with bacon.

Dirty Burger

The Modern Burger

First location: London, UK 2012

"The idea for Dirty Burger came about because although we always had burgers on our menus, what I really wanted was a burger shack ... not a restaurant,' says Nick Jones, founder of the hip London club and restaurant group Soho House. "We became obsessed with getting the burger right. My operations director and myself tried so many versions that we both must have put on two stones [28 pounds] in weight."

The first shack came about in 2012. Jones and his colleagues found a site in Kentish Town, in North London that was too big for just a Pizza East, another of their operations. So they decided to do a Chicken Shop with a Dirty Burger shack around the back in a parking lot. Then came Vauxhall, Whitechapel, and Shoreditch. "Location isn't everything. I like a pretty terrible site! I believe if you are serving anything halfway decent, people will find out about it. You don't need a prime spot any more."

Nick Jones's burger tips

The Modern Burger

THE BEEF SHOULD BE MEDIUM-GROUND (MINCED): "You want it to have some air in there, and a bit of bite."

DON'T SQUASH IT: "People make the mistake of pressing down on the burger. You need to get the balance right between tight meat and loose meat. It's an art."

MUSTARD: "We cook the burger in mustard on the griddle. That way, it melts and infuses the meat to keep it extra moist and flavorsome."

IT HAS TO BE COOKED MEDIUM:

"As prescribed by Westminster Council, of course."

SAUCE: "We don't add sauces. We leave that to the customer. Keep it simple."

WAX PAPER: "That was an important part for us. The beauty of the Dirty Burger is that it is messy and greasy, so the wax paper acts almost like a napkin."

SOME LIKE IT HOT: "We always steam the burger after cooking, melting all the flavors together."

ONION FRIES: "I love anything out of the fryer and these fries are delicious. They are fried to perfection."

FRENCH FRIES: "Our chips are cooked three times: steamed, blanched, and fried. Why crinkle cut? So that they have a greater surface area and are crispier."

Gordon Ramsay BurGR

First (and only) location: Las Vegas, Nevada, USA 2012

Gordon Ramsay BurGR launched to rave reviews at Planet Hollywood Resort & Casino in Las Vegas. Its name is a play on celebrity chef and restaurateur Gordon's initials. The restaurant focuses on traditional burgers, fries (chips), and milkshakes.

Ramsay's third restaurant in Vegas is an incredibly popular and cool eatery that offers a simple but exciting menu with unique flavors. Gourmet items including The Hog Burger, Hell's Kitchen Burger, and Truffle Burger are favorites in this two-hundred-seat restaurant. Patties are cooked over an open flame using prime cuts of meat made of beef short ribs and brisket, then basted in Devonshire butter. Only a talent as qualified, experienced, and tenacious as Ramsay could have found a way to add duck breast, English cheddar, and a fried egg to a burger.

Executive chef Christina Wilson says, "We're orchestrating 1,400 covers a day here. The Strip is so competitive, and Vegas is probably unlike any other place on the planet with so many decorated chefs. I think there were sixty openings on the Strip in the past year. But we are still doing some of the highest numbers."

In September 2016, Gordon Ramsay BurGR sold its two-millionth burger.

Right:
American Burger.

Bleecker Burger

First location:
London, UK
2012

Bleecker Burger was founded by corporate lawyer Zan Kaufman, named after her favorite street in Manhattan. While working in New York City, she tasted the best burger she had ever eaten, at East Village burger joint Zaitzeff. She was so impressed with the taste that she started moonlighting there in her free time. "I wanted to know everything about this burger: How it was made. Where the ingredients were sourced. And how it tasted so amazing." Kaufman knew then and there what she was going to do. Leaving her previous career behind, she moved to London, bought an old van, and converted it into a food truck. She started grilling burgers for hungry Londoners.

Bleecker Burger serves a variety of burgers including the Blue Burger, Bacon Double Cheeseburger, and the Bleecker Black (see recipe on page 288). Kaufman says, "There is zero compromise with our ingredients. Burgers are all about the beef. We use rare-breed, pasture-fed beef from small farms in the UK. It comes to us from the geniuses at The Butchery in Bermondsey, where it's dry-aged for about forty to fifty days, giving it an intense, beefy flavor. The finishing touches: a sesame seed bun, scratch burger sauce, and good old American cheese."

In addition to the food truck there are locations in Victoria, Old Spitalfields Market, and Canary Wharf. The business also has plans to expand throughout London during 2017.

Its burgers have twice been voted best burger in London by *Time Out London*: the Bacon Double Cheeseburger in 2015 and the Bleecker Black in 2016.

"We aim to serve the best burger in London, heck, the world."

⬇

Zan Kaufman

Opposite: Bleecker Black.

Chur Burger

First location: Sydney, New South Wales, Australia 2013

Warren Turnbull, the owner of Chur Burger, is by training a fine-dining chef who used to run a well-known restaurant in Sydney. When a fire destroyed it, Turnbull went back to basics and created Chur Burger, initially as a pop-up to fill a gap in the market; however, "from day one it just went crazy and hasn't stopped." There are now three restaurants in Sydney, two in Brisbane, and one in Melbourne. Turnbull's approach was to showcase great ingredients and to use classically trained chefs, balanced with "a super-chilled-vibe dining room with old-school hip-hop tunes."

Chur Burger's signature dish is a crispy pork side (belly) burger with a chili caramel, served with Asian slaw. Turnbull says, "It started as a special when we opened and now we have trouble keeping up with demand." As a side, the classic fries (chips) with aioli and tomato sauce or sweet potato fries are hugely popular. Unafraid to push the envelope, Chur Burger is also happy to satisfy one odd, regular order: "A gentleman comes in and gets a beef patty with fish on top; it's totally weird but he loves it!"

While Turnbull's reasons for getting into burgers were perhaps unusual, as he says, "I don't think there's a person out there who doesn't love a burger from time to time." The burger's significance as a shared meal, as an echo of family time, is not lost on him either: "When we were kids our favorite dinner was Mum's burgers. She would cook the patties and toast the buns and serve with at least twelve different accompaniments that we would go on and construct ourselves." If you want to know the inspiration for Turnbull's own creativity, you need look no further.

"Burgers will always be a massive part of our lives."

⬇ **Warren Turnbull**

Opposite: Chur Burger.

Despite his upscale culinary background, Turnbull retains a healthy respect for the Big Mac as a forerunner of much that is good in the burger world. But he also celebrates the vision of the more "foodie" chefs who are imaginatively moving the burger into new and exciting areas.

Nonetheless, whether it's basic or gourmet, for Turnbull the burger is more than just food: "For me, the burger means a sense of family or hanging with mates for a simple and fun meal.... I would love to sit around one of the restaurants with my whole family and eat burgers and have a bloody good laugh."

The Butchers Club Burger

First location:
Hong Kong Island, China
2013

The Butchers Club Burger started in Tin Wan, Hong Kong, as a private kitchen and butchery that specialized in dry-aged beef. The company now has five restaurants across Hong Kong, as well as a retail outlet and online store, and a restaurant in Bali. Its focus is on "high-quality ingredients, prepared and presented simply," as Executive Chef Aarik Persaud explains: "Our entire company is built around the practice of dry-aging beef. We treat our ingredients with the utmost respect and like to do as little as possible to them." The chain's signature item is a dry-aged Angus beef burger with maple-glazed bacon, aged cheddar, and a homemade caramelized onion burger sauce, but the Double Happiness is also huge, and hugely popular: it's a double patty burger, with double cheese and double bacon, all encased in two grilled cheese sandwiches.

Persaud, from Canada originally, explains that "hamburgers are something you grow up eating in North America," but that the Butchers Club's development into burgers was more of a necessity: "We began to import our own beef for our steakhouses and were forced to buy the whole animal. We used the primary cuts for these restaurants, but needed something to do with all of the lovely secondary cuts such as chuck, rump, and brisket. Opening a burger place seemed only natural."

For Persaud, the burger is "one of the simplest and most basic meals, yet one of the most comforting ... it reminds me of family barbecues, road trips, and camping." Despite this echo of childhood, he thinks there has been a genuine movement toward a more gourmet style of cooking burgers, explaining that "we've seen a shift in popularity from fast-food burgers toward burgers like ours, prepared with love and top-quality ingredients." If you get the base of a burger right, you can then take it in any direction: "It's easily customizable to any taste. If you don't like tomatoes, take them off. If you prefer blue cheese to cheddar, it's easy to swap."

Persaud's favorite non-Butchers Club burger clearly shows his love of customization: it's the In-N-Out Double Double Animal Style (see page 63), "hands down the greatest burger of all time. Apart from ours, of course!" His ideal person to share a burger with would be acerbic comedian Larry David or any of the founders of Five Guys (see page 138), and he strongly advocates pickles (gherkins). With several pristine, secret burgers having recently made their debut, and further restaurants planned in Singapore, London, Manila, Jakarta, and Bangkok, the Butchers Club is definitely open to new members.

"Our typical
customer:
hungry,
salivating,
and not
afraid
of being
judged."

↓

Aarik
Persaud

Opposite: The
Butchers Club Burger,
Hong Kong Island.

Left: The Burger.

THE MENU

All of our burgers are served on a freshly baked floured scotch bap and topped with mature cheddar cheese, glazed bacon, tomatoes, pickles and onion spread.

THE HOGTOWN

DRY-AGED BEEF PATTY TOPPED WITH CLASSIC PULLED PORK, CANADIAN PEAMEAL-STYLE BACON, PICKLED SHALLOTS WITH THYME, SHARP HONEY MUSTARD AND SMOKED CHEESE

THE BURGER
$100

Listed in the 2015 MICHELIN GUIDE

BACON, CHEESE, TOMATO, PICKLE, SPECIAL SAUCE

CAPTAIN AHAB
$130

PANKO-BREADED SUSTAINABLE NZ LING FILLET WITH HOMEMADE TARTAR SAUCE AND SPICY COLESLAW

THE GAMBLER
$140

DOUBLE-FRIED BUTTERMILK CHICKEN, TOSSED IN FRANK'S HOT SAUCE & BUTTER, WITH BLUE CHEESE SAUCE, SPICY COLESLAW & PICKLES

DOUBLE HAPPINESS
$180

DOUBLE PATTY, DOUBLE CHEESE AND ALL THE FIXINS BETWEEN TWO GRILLED CHEESE SAMMYS

WU TANG Style
$120

FRIED IN SRIRACHA AND TOPPED WITH CHEESE, KIMCHI, KEWPIE MAYO AND TEMPURA SWEET POTATO

What Food EATS
$120

CHICKPEA PATTY WITH FRIED HALLOUMI, LETTUCE, TOMATO AND SPICY GREEK YOGHURT

SECRET MENU

S1 — **THE GAMBLER** **140**
DOUBLE-FRIED BUTTERMILK CHICKEN, TOSSED IN FRANK'S HOT SAUCE AND BUTTER, WITH BLUE CHEESE SAUCE, SPICY COLESLAW AND PICKLES

S2 — **DOUBLE HAPPINESS** **180**
DOUBLE PATTY, DOUBLE CHEESE AND ALL THE FIXINS BETWEEN TWO GRILLED CHEESE SAMMYS

S3 — **WU TANG STYLE** **120**
FRIED IN SRIRACHA AND TOPPED WITH CHEESE, KIMCHI, KEWPIE MAYO AND TEMPURA SWEET POTATO

S4 — **THE HOGTOWN** **160**
DRY-AGED BEEF PATTY TOPPED WITH CLASSIC PULLED PORK, CANADIAN PEAMEAL-STYLE BACON, PICKLED SHALLOTS WITH THYME, SHARP HONEY MUSTARD AND SMOKED GOUDA.

S5 — **WHAT FOOD EATS** (VEGETARIAN) **120**
CHICKPEA PATTY WITH FRIED HALLOUMI, LETTUCE, TOMATO AND SPICY GREEK YOGHURT

S6 — **CAPTAIN AHAB** **130**
PANKO-BREADED SUSTAINABLE NZ LING FILLET WITH HOMEMADE TARTAR SAUCE AND SPICY COLESLAW

THE GAMBLER

DOUBLE HAPPINESS

WU TANG STYLE

THE HOGTOWN

WHAT FOOD EATS

CAPTAIN AHAB

Opposite: Menu, The Butchers Club Burger.

Left: Secret Menu, The Butchers Club Burger.

Pono Burger

The Modern Burger

> **"I wouldn't feed our guests anything I wouldn't feed my family."**
>
> ↓
> **Makani Geradi**

First location: Santa Monica, California, USA 2013

Pono Burger was founded by Hawaiian chef and restaurateur Makani Geradi. "Pono" means "to do things the right way." That translates to fresh, never frozen organic beef from pasture-raised, grass-fed cows. Organic ingredients from local farmers' markets and great-tasting burgers are served with fresh-cut organic French fries. Chef Makani says, "I wouldn't feed our guests anything I wouldn't feed my family. So eat better, feel better, and live better."

"I chose burgers because I love them the most," Geradi says. "I love the versatility of a cheeseburger when I feel like a particular cuisine or I'm in a certain mood. Maybe it's a Japanese twist with the Sassy Wahine—pickled ginger, avocado, pea sprouts, ponzu dressing, and crispy wonton chips. Or if I'm feeling spicy, a habanero guava rum sauce, aged cheddar, Niman Ranch bacon, and Russet potato chips (crisps). The possibilities are endless. The cheeseburger is my favorite canvas to build upon."

Pono serves signature burgers that include the Piku "Fig" Burger, Kuawa Crunch, and Paniolo, all charbroiled (chargrilled) over an oak fire.

With California locations in Santa Monica, Venice, and West Hollywood, Pono Burger has plans to expand.

Opposite: Paniolo.

Top right: Kuawa Crunch.

Bottom right: Mahana.

Burger Burger

The Modern Burger

First location:
Auckland, New Zealand
2014

Burger Burger, so good they named it twice, was founded in Ponsonby, a suburb of Auckland, in 2014 by Mimi Gilmour, a photographer turned events manager, and Adrian Chilton, a chef and restaurateur. This perfect partnership of skills quickly saw the brand take off, and in 2015 they expanded, opening further sites in two more Auckland suburbs, Newmarket and Takapuna. Using fresh produce from local suppliers, "because veggies don't like road trips," their ethos is to "make simple, honest hamburgers, and a few things besides," including old-fashioned shakes. Their signature item is a straight-up beef burger, dressed with homemade pickles (gherkins), tomato jam, mustard, and mayonnaise, with the ever-popular charred broccoli with garlic butter and almonds as a side.

Sides are, in fact, something of a fetish for Burger Burger, which also makes delicious crispy shoestring fries (chips), kumara (New Zealand sweet potato) fries with aioli, and honey-glazed carrots. Gilmour and Chilton describe burgers as "the perfect comfort food," but they also clearly enjoy injecting a bit of glamor into the mix: they created the restaurant because "there was nowhere you could go and have a decent burger with a glass of bubbly or wine!"

A bit of booze aside, Gilmour and Chilton stress that "the burger is such a versatile food because all age groups can enjoy one at a reasonable price." They also, perhaps a little tongue-in-cheek, say that burgers "could be a superfood … they provide carbs, protein, good fats, dairy, and vegetables all in one." It's a convincing argument, but one customer who felt his fish burger didn't have quite enough balance decided to add a beef patty and pineapple to create Burger Burger's oddest ever order; there's just no pleasing some people. Gilmour, who told me she doesn't like sharing food much, nonetheless said she'd most like to share a burger with her Mama, perhaps because she cooks what is apparently an astonishing homemade, spiced burger with sauerkraut.

Burger Burger reckons that its insistence on good-quality ingredients, especially meat, is going to be a growing trend in the hamburger market "as people are now more conscious about where their food is coming from and how it is prepared." Gilmour and Chilton's mission is to have fun and eat great burgers made from great produce: "We play music all night long, because silence is boring. We'll never tell anybody to keep it down and we'll never stop anybody from taking their burger home with them."

Opposite: Burger
Burger, Auckland,
New Zealand.

Below: Beef Burger.

"We don't keep hungry people waiting."

⬇

Mimi Gilmour and Adrian Chilton

Burger Liquor

First (and only) location: Wellington, New Zealand 2014

Burger Liquor has one restaurant in Wellington, but its relaxed style and consistent delivery are winning many friends in a busy market. Burger Liquor was founded, says General Manager Dan Haydock, when "a group of well-established Wellington restaurateurs had an opportunity to bring to fruition a concept that was simple, fun, and different from what they had succeeded in before." That simple concept was delicious burgers and booze, delivered fast and with enjoyment. The team realized that people loved burgers, that they loved burgers, and the rest was easy.

Burger Liquor's signature item is the Standard Burger, a 4-ounce (120-gram) chuck and sirloin beef patty, covered with cheddar, pickle (gherkins), house ketchup, and a mustard-infused mayonnaise, crammed into a brioche bun; Haydock describes it as "just a f**king great cheeseburger." Also hugely popular is the Smokey, which features the same patty and cheddar, but is augmented with lean (streaky) free-range bacon, double-crumbed onion rings, nam jim (Thai dipping sauce), and mayonnaise in a brioche bun. The onion rings make a crisp, exciting side as well, but the blow-out side is jalapeño poppers—pickled bell peppers stuffed with cream cheese and mozzarella, then crumbed and fried, and served with sour cream.

Despite the wide variety of burgers, which Haydock says is the crux of the idea—"a fantastic everyday way to eat any number of flavors, styles, or cuisines from around the world"—Burger Liquor appreciates the simplicity of "just good ingredients in a tasty bun." This approach draws in a variety of customers, "from hungry and cash-strapped students to corporate types, families, couples, friends, and solo diners. Basically, just lovers of good burgers and good hospitality." It's not hard to see why Burger Liquor, despite its youth, is making its mark on the Wellington scene.

> "The humble burger can be a vessel for almost any cuisine from around the world. The world is your burger, really."
>
> ⬇ **Dan Haydock**

Above: Smokey Burger.

Opposite: Burger Liquor logo.

Dirty Bones

First location:
London, UK
2014

Dirty Bones was founded in London in 2014 with its first restaurant in Kensington. Following its success, the company now has two more London locations, in Soho and Shoreditch. Founded by Dipak Panchal and Cokey Sulkin, Dirty Bones celebrates New York-style comfort food and cocktails at their finest. The stylish but laid-back approach to dining is complemented by cool, vintage interiors and a soundtrack of old-school hip-hop, soul, and funk, described by the Dirty Bones team as "high fives, good vibes."

One of Dirty Bones' signature items is the Mac Daddy, a 6-ounce (175-gram) burger served with pulled beef short rib, gooey mac and cheese, house barbecue sauce, and pickles (gherkins). Also in demand are the Double Dirty Fries (chips), which come with the house barbecue sauce, cactus salsa, and pulled pork to almost make a meal in themselves. The Dirty Bones chefs are prepared to innovate, too: they once produced a burger smeared with Welsh Rarebit and melted under the broiler (grill) for a customer, then realized it was so good that it became a signature dish.

Sulkin and Panchal have always loved burgers. They see the burger as one of the ultimate comfort foods. "The burger is seemingly timeless. It transcends all menu snobbery," says Panchal, who recently added Cheeseburger Dumplings to the appetizer menu for those who agree that one burger course just isn't enough. As for Sulkin's thoughts on the burger, "I'm not into sharing. It's a crime to cut a burger in half."

LUNCH & DINNER
Available Monday to Friday from 12pm and Saturday from 5pm

New York comfort food and cocktails. Everything you'd expect just twisted a little to make it more fun and more fine. Then there's the music – the greatest old school hip hop, soul and funk. Beats you just can't ignore. Good times.

INTRO

CHARRED PADRÓN PEPPERS — 4
Sprinkled with Maldon salt

HOT WINGS — 6.5
Free range chicken wings tossed in chef's own Louisiana style hot sauce

SALT & PEPPER SQUID — 8
Deep fried salt & pepper squid with chipotle aioli

DEEP FRIED MAC BALLS — 5.5
With Dirty Bones sweet chilli sauce

CHEESEBURGER DUMPLINGS — 6.5
Homemade gyoza dumplings stuffed with our burger mince and melting cheese. Served on pickled green chilli & bone marrow sauce

BURGERS

CLASSIC — 8.5
6oz aged burger mince, ketchup, mustard, baby gem, pickles and burger cheese

THE BURGER — 9
6oz aged beef burger, black treacle bacon, gorgonzola sauce, pickled jalapeño, baby spinach and garlic aioli

THE MAC DADDY — 10
6oz house burger topped with pulled beef short rib, mac & cheese and homemade BBQ sauce

SPICY CHICKEN BURGER — 8.5
Free range crispy fried chicken burger with charred lettuce, homemade hot sauce and Dirty Bones smoked chilli mayo. Served with pickles

ADD ANOTHER PATTY FOR — 4.5

DOGS
All our dogs are available in pork, beef & veggie

YANKEE — 7
Sauerkraut, spring onion, French's mustard and tomato ketchup

THE ASIAN — 8
Kimchi ketchup, wasabi mayo, crispy seaweed, pickled sushi ginger and sesame seed

DIRTY DOG — 8
BBQ pulled pork, crispy bacon, jalapeño cheese sauce and crispy shallots

BONES

CRISPY FRIED CHICKEN (½ PILE / FULL PILE) — 8.75 / 14
Free range crispy fried chicken in spiced buttermilk coating. 6 hour brined and 6 hour sous-vide cooked for extra tenderness and flavour. Slightly pink when fully cooked

CHICKEN & WAFFLES — 10
½ pile of crispy fried chicken with freshly baked waffles and a shot of maple syrup

BABY BACK RIBS — 10
Crispy pork ribs, sweet miso & pomegranate glaze

BEEF SHORT RIB — 15
Salted caramel & burnt onion BBQ sauce, crispy shallots and spring onions

FLAT IRON STEAK — 13
Dry aged steak & burnt rosemary served with our homemade steak glaze

SHOREDITCH SIGNATURE — 14
Our East London house dish. Crispy, long cut lamb ribs slow-cooked for 15 hours served with tangy chimichurri

SALADS

CRISPY SHORT RIB — 12
Cajun short rib, blackened sweet potato, béarnaise salsa verde, quinoa and spinach

SPICED ROAST VEG — 10.5
Aubergine marinated in garlicky yoghurt and slow-roasted, with blackened sweet potato, Ras El Hanout spiced fregola and charred radicchio

SIDES

DIRTY MARY SALAD — 5
Charred baby gem lettuce, smoked and cured cherry tomatoes, wild black rice. Virgin Mary & smoked tomato dressing

SPICY SLAW — 3.5
Crunchy slaw with sweet chilli and lime

COLLARD GREENS — 4
Sautéed greens, garlic, red chilli and soy

GRILLED AUBERGINE & GRUYERE — 5.5
Robata grilled aubergine layered with gruyere, dressed in garlic and basil

MAC & CHEESE — 6.5
Macaroni, taleggio & smoked cheddar sauce and parmesan crumbs

SKINNY FRIES — 4
With onion & garlic salt

CHEESY TRUFFLE FRIES — 5.5
Cheese sauce, cheddar, taleggio cheese and white truffle oil

CRISPY LAMB FRIES — 6.5
Skinny fries topped with crispy lamb, sweet miso, red chilli and jalapeño

LUNCH 10
Your choice of main below served with never ending classic fries. Monday to Friday noon to 3pm

CRISPY FRIED CHICKEN
Free range crispy fried chicken in spiced buttermilk coating. 6 hour brined and 6 hour sous-vide cooked for extra tenderness and flavour. Slightly pink when fully cooked

30 DAY AGED STEAK
4oz of our chargrilled flat iron steak and burnt rosemary. Served medium rare with our homemade steak glaze

SPICED ROAST VEG SALAD
Aubergine marinated in garlicky yoghurt and slow-roasted, with blackened sweet potato, Ras el hanout spiced fregola and spinach

Allergies? Ask our server for all allergen information. An optional service charge of 12.5% will be added to your bill.

INSTAGRAM *@dirtyboneslondon*
TWITTER *@dirtybonesLDN*

Above: Menu, Dirty Bones.

Opposite: The Burger.

Next spread: Dirty Bones, Kensington, London.

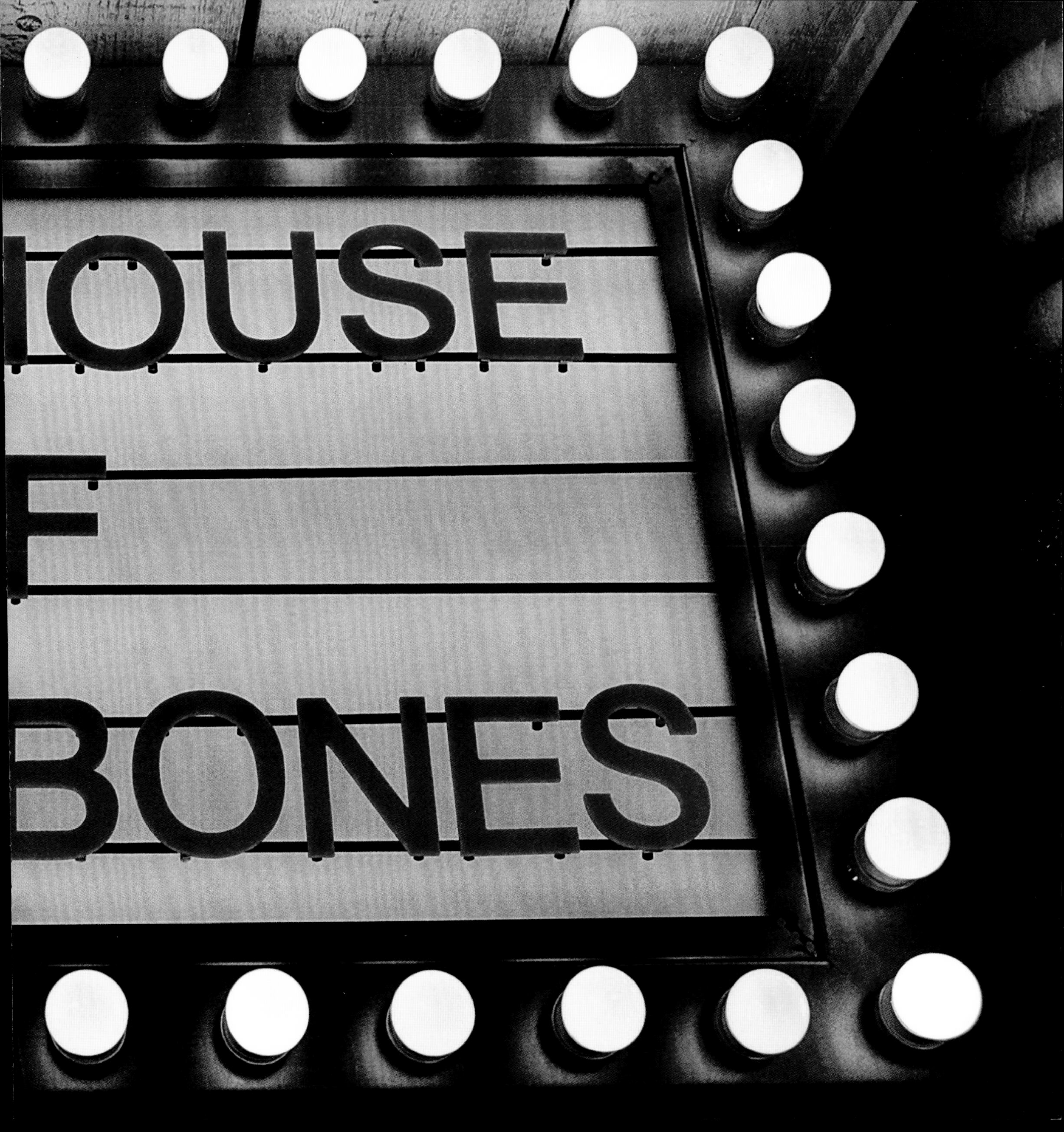
OUSE
F
BONES

Patty & Bun

The Modern Burger

First location: London, UK 2014

Patty & Bun started as a series of pop-up stints around London after its founder, Joe Grossman, decided he wanted to get into burgers and embarked on a relentless quest to find the perfect recipe. As Tom Monaghan, Operations Manager, says, "Eventually it was time to open the first Patty & Bun restaurant, and we ended up on James Street in Central London. The pop-up following was enough to give us a running start, and we soon gained more and more popularity as time went by at the store.... We were simply lovers of burgers. We had ideas of our own that needed to be shared with the world."

A focus on "good, honest, delicious food, banging tunes, and great service" has led to Patty & Bun quickly becoming a clear favorite in London, with frequent long lines of people outside its locations. There are now five Patty & Buns, with a sixth "coming soon," backed up by a prep kitchen and augmented by Shirley, an old walk-in truck (an American Grumman Olson Kurbmaster) fitted out as a mobile burger truck.

The menu's signature item is the Ari Gold Cheeseburger, an aged-beef patty with Red Leicester and cheddar, pickled onions, smoky Patty & Bun mayonnaise, ketchup, lettuce, and tomato, served in a brioche bun. Sides include double-cooked hand-cut fries (chips) with rosemary salt, confit barbecue wings, and fresh coleslaw. The wings are so popular that people apparently "go bonkers" for them, and often order them as a main dish, forgoing even a burger!

There's no such thing as a usual Patty & Bun customer, although Monaghan says that each restaurant has its own core group: "At James Street there's a real blend of office workers and shoppers and regulars, while at Liverpool Street the City workers hit it for their lunchtime fix. London Fields has a real neighborhood vibe—quite a Brooklyn feel to it."

According to Monaghan, the burger is "massively symbolic, it's something that people find comfort in and in most cases is their go-to meal." Nevertheless, he acknowledges that "at the end of the day, everyone has their own opinion on what's 'the' best burger, 'the' best combo of ingredients ... it comes down to personal preferences. The versatility comes as a result of people trying to push the boundaries." But that's the great joy of the burger: "It's subjective ... there's no right or wrong, just different tastes."

This wide range of flavors and possibilities is one of the reasons Monaghan and the crew at Patty & Bun feel very positive about their, and the burger's, future: "I think it will continue to grow and grow, as long as people continue to focus on delivering a great product consistently!" Patty & Bun is definitely setting a burger benchmark.

Patty & Bun now has six locations in London, with plans for further expansion.

"If someone had a gun to my head, I'd say no pickle."

⬇ Tom Monaghan

Opposite: Portobello "Dig It" Mushroom Burger.

Above: Artwork on cardboard box, Patty & Bun, James Street, London.

247

The Modern Burger

Art Burger Sushi Bar

The Modern Burger

First (and only) location: Myrtle Beach, South Carolina, USA 2014

In 2014, Larry and Fabiana Bond opened Art Burger Sushi Bar, beside the Myrtle Beach Boardwalk on Ocean Boulevard. Having traveled extensively to many different countries, they had learned about varied cooking techniques, and now blend those experiences with talented local chefs.

Art Burger specializes in gourmet burgers with grass-fed and hormone- and antibiotic-free beef, creatively tasty sushi, and liquid-nitrogen cocktails. The atmosphere is casual, friendly, and artistic, with digital monitors displaying hundreds of images created by Old Masters as well as accomplished local artists.

At Art Burger, burgers are treated as the name suggests: like art. Each is named after a different artist and each is unique. The Art Burger, for example, features a ground (minced) beef patty with bacon, onions, blue cheese, and walnut chutney.

Larry Bond attributes his success to working hard, surrounding himself with talented and passionate people, and staying humble. He works with his team, not above them, and together they aim to open more interesting concepts and help transform historic downtown Myrtle Beach into a fantastic dining destination.

Left: The Art Burger.

251

Original Patty Men

First (and only) location: Birmingham, West Midlands, UK
2015

The Original Patty Men (Scott O'Byrne and Tom Maher) are based in Birmingham. They were inspired to get into burgers after scoping the scene in the Midlands and finding it lacking. With a background in design rather than cookery, they had to start from scratch in their quest to make "something a bit special that felt naughty in the mouth … a top-quality, filthy burger," as they put it. They have certainly succeeded in creating something suitably naughty, winning the 2014 British Street Food award for Best Burger and coming third against pan-European competition at the Burgers & Hip-Hop awards in Berlin.

Their signature item is the killer Big Vern's Krispy Ring, a five-week-aged beef patty topped with American cheese, maple-soaked bacon, smeared with ketchup and mustard, all squeezed together inside a grilled, glazed Krispy Kreme donut. The Bean Bean King, a special that is offered at regular times throughout the year, is also hugely popular, a beef burger topped with slow-cooked barbecue pork and beans, Red Leicester and Double Gloucester cheese, pickles (gherkins), mustard, and lashings of barbecue sauce. Interestingly, the Original Patty Men only do sides for special events, but when they do, it's an event in itself: their barbecue-sauce-flavored pork scratchings, beer-battered pickles (gherkins) with a Cajun remoulade sauce, and triple-cooked seasoned fries (chips) are worth the wait.

There's a strong strain of creativity running through all their food, but even their skills were stretched to fulfill the oddest order they ever received: a burger topped with mac and cheese using two waffles as a bun. And there's no such thing as a typical Original Patty Men customer—just people who love food and appreciate their iconoclastic attitude. The great thing about the burger, O'Byrne and Maher say, is that it is "a blank canvas; as long as you have the basics nailed, the possibilities of toppings are endless." Love for the burger, which they see as "ingrained from childhood," is what motivates them—hardly

surprising when they say that the burger is "life itself!" And perhaps because their cooking is rooted in both tradition and innovation, they celebrate the variety and difference in the current burger scene but say that it's hard to beat the classic cheeseburger and their burger hero, Mr. Wimpy. The Original Patty Men will continue to produce their idiosyncratic take on the burger, pushing it into undiscovered flavor territories, but mindful that a burger "always has to be filthy!" It's hard to disagree.

Opposite: Bacon Cheese with yogurt.

Left: Original Patty Men stall at an outdoor market in Birmingham, UK.

253

Burger Table

The Modern Burger

First location:
São Paulo, Brazil
2015

The first Burger Table opened in March 2015. São Paulo is a huge city with chaotic traffic, but people would cross town to taste this special burger. A second location in a downtown neighborhood opened in 2016.

Founder and chef Manuel Coelho's passion for burgers started in childhood, in parallel with his love for cooking. For years he tried innumerable blends, production processes, and cooking methods to achieve what he believed was the perfect burger: the ideally balanced blend, juicy and soft and grilled on charcoal. He decided to share his "perfect recipe" with other burger lovers in a private room within his Italian restaurant—one big common table with only twenty-six seats. His guests loved it and opening a dedicated burger restaurant was the obvious next move.

His philosophy was to keep it simple: only one blend, only beef, and guests can choose a range of toppings at a fixed price. All ingredients are the best available and everything from bread to ketchup is prepared in house, assuring the unique taste and quality. The bread is a brioche-based recipe, with or without almonds on top.

Coelho is so passionate about his burgers that he has even developed his own "Ten Burger Table Commandments" (see page 292).

Left: Two "Eater" burgers and the Crispy Pork Burger, a monthly special (right).

Next spread (left): Graffiti by Magoo Felix on restaurant wall.

Next spread (right): Burger Table interior.

Mick Adams Burger Bar

The Modern Burger

"I honestly think we have the best beef patties in Melbourne!"

⬇

Declan Keogh

First (and only) location: Melbourne, Victoria, Australia
2015

Mick Adams was founded by Michael Koutroulis and Theo Raptis and is located in Oakleigh in Melbourne. The name is a tribute to a Greek immigrant who opened Australia's first Milk Bar, known to its patrons as the Black and White, in Sydney in 1932. Mick Adams has rolled with this design theme throughout, with white tiles with black accents paying homage to the old days of diner eating.

The restaurant serves a variety of burgers including Dirty Dion, The Big T, and Cheeky Charlie. Mick Adams's operations manager, Declan Keogh, says "Our burgers are based on the highest quality of ingredients with no compromise. Our head chef, Dominic Pipicelli, worked tirelessly to perfect his patties—the way he grinds (minces) them, the quantities of fat to meat, sourcing our Tasmanian grass-fed Australian beef, not overworking them so they don't become too dense or too firm, and cooking to a perfect medium every time."

Left: Petey Sweetie.

LocoL

First location: Los Angeles, California, USA 2016

LocoL was founded by chefs and restaurateurs Roy Choi and Daniel Patterson. They joined forces with the mission to bring fresh, affordable, and healthy food to local neighborhoods that have long been underserved and, by doing so, transform what they consider to be fast food in the United States.

Patterson is best known for his San Francisco restaurant Coi, which has two Michelin stars. In 2013, he co-founded The Cooking Project, a non-profit organization that offers free cooking classes to young people in the San Francisco Bay Area and aims to teach individuals how to cook simple, tasty, nutritious food at home. Choi is the co-owner and co-founder of several restaurants, and is the man behind Kogi BBQ Trucks.

LocoL opened its first restaurant in Watts, a neighborhood in south Los Angeles, in January 2016. This was quickly followed by another branch in Oakland, and the company now also operates a food truck that travels throughout Los Angeles. LocoL aspires to keep the appeal of fast food but also features chef-driven flavors. Its take on the traditional cheeseburger, called the LocoLCheeseburg, includes a bun created by Chad Robertson of San Francisco's Tartine Bakery and a beef patty with sprouted grains and tofu to provide a healthier alternative to processed ingredients. Adding grains and tofu to the patty also offsets the price of meat, allowing the Cheeseburg to be available for four dollars.

"The long-term vision is not one or three or five restaurants—we want to be the next fast food," said Hanson Li, the San Francisco restaurant financier who is also a LocoL partner.

YOTCHAYS $2

RICE

MESSY GREENS

BEEF AND ONION GRAVY

SPICY CORN CHIPS

SLAW

FLAT BREAD

FOLDIES $3

CARNITAS

BBQ TURKEY

BEAN-N-CHEESE

MACHACA

CRUNCHIES $4

CHICKEN NUGS

VEGGIE NUGS

BURGS $5

LOCOL CHEESEBURG
Jack, scallion relish, awesome sauce

FRIED CHICKEN
Slaw, buttermilk mayo, hot sauce

BBQ TURKEY
Buttermilk mayo

VEGGIE CHEESEBURG
Jack, scallion relish, awesome sauce

BOWLS $7

NOODLEMAN
Ginger, chile, lime

CRUSHED TOFU AND VEGGIE STEW

MESSY BEEF CHILI BOWL
Traditional, onions, cheese, crackers, hot sauce

BULGAR LANGUAGE
Green goddess creamy dressing and croutons

DULCES $5

SOFT SERVE SUNDAES

ICE CREAM

DRINKS $2

HOT OR ICED COFFEE
Black or sweet and creamy

AGUA FRESCAS

BREKKIE

EGG IN THE HOLE $5

Egg and cheese

Egg, bean and cheese

Machaca and cheese

Carnitas, egg, cheese

FRESH FRUIT $4

FRENCH TOAST HOLES $3

GREEN JUICE $3

YOGURT AND GRANOLA $4

"You can do anything in this world if you believe in it. We believe in LocoL. It's not just an idealistic dream. We have the knowledge and experience to make it happen."

➡ Roy Choi

Opposite:
LocoL Cheeseburg.

Left: Menu, LocoL.

Salvation Burger

First (and only) location: New York City, New York, USA 2016

April Bloomfield is a New York-based British chef best known for the Michelin-starred The Spotted Pig and The Breslin Bar & Dining Room at The Ace Hotel. In February 2016, Bloomfield and restaurateur Ken Friedman opened Salvation Burger, a casual spot in the Pod51 Hotel on East 51st Street in Midtown.

Bloomfield's burgers have earned a devoted following over the years, and this restaurant is dedicated to her take on the American classic. Most everything at Salvation Burger is made in house, from the patties to the mustard to the cheese. Wood-fired and plancha-seared burgers are served on housemade potato buns with a variety of homemade toppings.

The burgers play with tradition, from the Classic Burger—made with two smashed patties, American cheese, pickles (gherkins), and special sauce—to the Salvation Burger, a wood-fired 8-ounce (225-gram) patty topped with a rotating selection of seasonal toppings.

The vibrant space, designed by Friedman, features pops of color and wood, along with plenty of cow-inspired objects that contribute to the fun, lively atmosphere.

"You get treated like a millionaire when you walk through the door."

⬇

April Bloomfield

Right:
Salvation Burger.

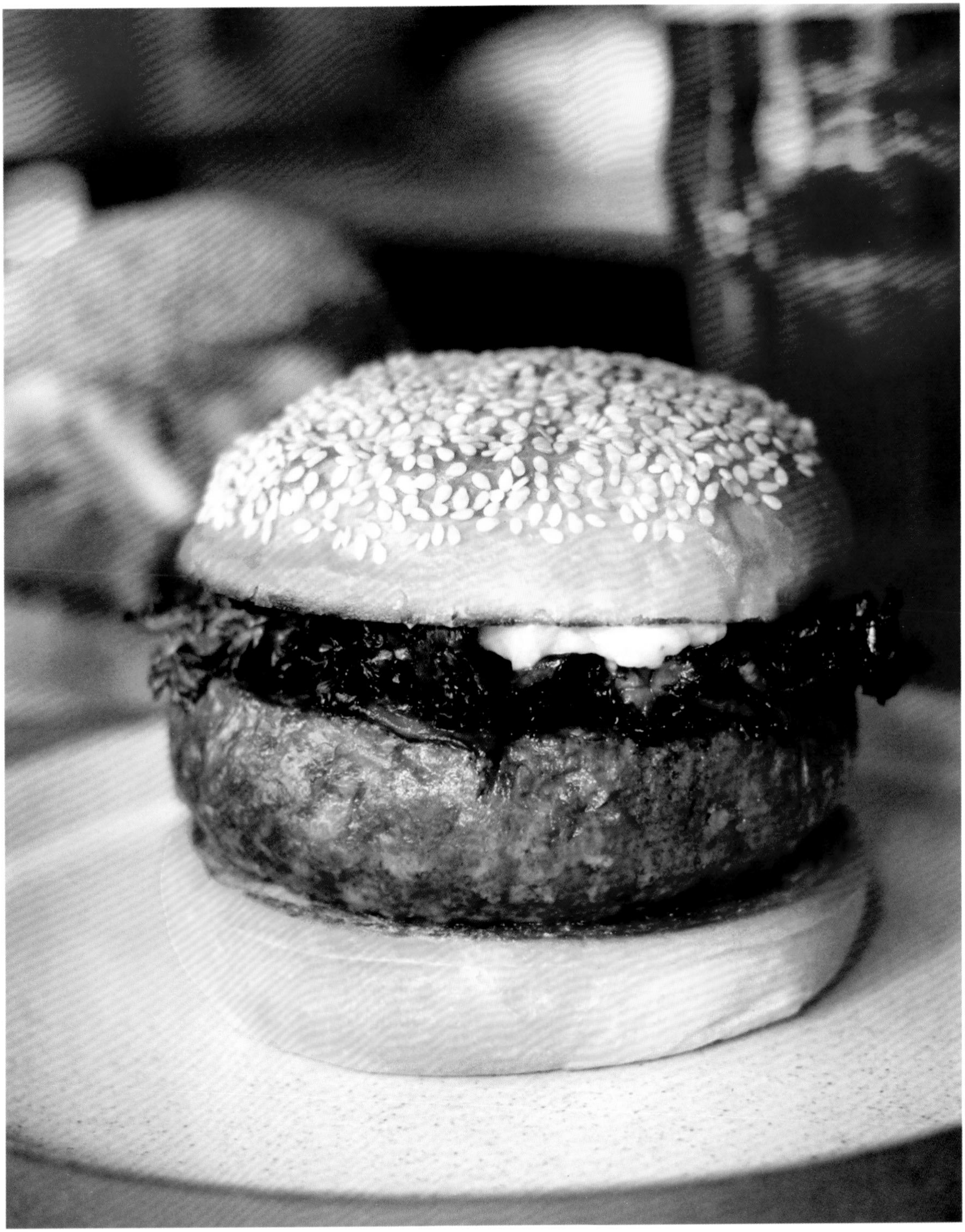

3

Recipes

Angie Mar

Chef and restaurateur

Angie Mar is a chef and restaurateur who owns and operates The Beatrice Inn in New York City. She has a fixation: meat. "I wake up thinking about meat and I go to sleep thinking about meat," she says. "It's a primal obsession. I might be one of the only chefs to say I hate vegetables." Angie's carnivore imagination is a boon for lovers of the burger. In May 2015, The Beatrice Inn celebrated National Burger Month by adding three new burgers to its two tried and tested creations. Though the menu is supposedly a secret, you can't keep burgers that good off the radar for long, especially at such a popular and talked-about spot as The Beatrice Inn.

The three burgers Mar devised were a dry-aged lamb burger, a black truffle burger with duck egg, and an "Animal Style" burger, a homage to In-N-Out, whose burgers are served at the annual Oscars party thrown by former Beatrice owner Graydon Carter (see page 64).

Mar bought The Beatrice Inn from Carter in April 2016, having previously worked there as Head Chef. She remains indebted to him for her start in the frenetic New York restaurant scene, saying, "Graydon gave me my first kitchen to cook out of and I'm so grateful to him and his wife Anna for giving me this opportunity and passing on the torch. Being a young chef, it's everyone's dream to have their own restaurant." Under her ownership The Beatrice Inn has stayed close to what Carter set up, but she's also made changes: "My flavor profiles will always be my flavor profiles, but in the fall [autumn] we want to make this the best iteration of the Beatrice, a bit more rock 'n' roll, a bit more New York, but with great service."

Burgers will still be front and center: Mar is hugely proud of the two regular burgers on the menu, especially the forty-five-day dry-aged burger: "That's my baby," she tells me. "Only three people have the recipe; it's a secret." Nonetheless, the opportunity to experiment was very welcome—Mar likes thinking outside the box: "No one dry-ages lamb and I love lamb, so I thought I would try it."

All the food at The Beatrice Inn is based around meat, fruit, and herbs. These parameters allowed Mar to explore her passion for meat and for burgers within a framework that lets her stay true to what she feels is most important in cooking, blending extraordinarily good components to create dishes whose simple appearance belies their complexity of flavor.

Mar describes her food as "comfort food, reimagined, taking elements of masculine and feminine and combining them on the plate." It's an interesting idiom to use for food, and she explains what she means: "You have the beef, ribeye and short rib, which is robust and funky and masculine, combined with, say, a d'Affinois cheese, which is light and nutty and floral and feminine." So too the onions caramelized in red wine, which Mar says remind her of her father's home cooking. "In the secret-menu lamb burger, the meat provides the masculine flavors, while the higher notes of the cherry mustard, which is light and sweet, lend a feminine accent to the dish," explains Mar.

"I take really beautiful ingredients and showcase that. I don't care where it comes from, I just want the best," Mar continues. She describes the burger, with its simplicity and form, as "the perfect vehicle to showcase the best products possible." For her, the burger should never stray too far from the basic foursome: meat, cheese, onions, and bread. While she recognizes that other chefs are doing interesting things with flavor combinations, for her there is more than enough in those core ingredients, especially if they are of the best quality, to make the burger a sensuous and complex experience.

> **"Food should be sexy and sensual, every mouthful the perfect bite."**
>
>
>
> **Angie Mar**

Below: Beatrice
Burger, a forty-five-
day dry-aged patty
with duck egg and
shaved truffle from
the secret menu.

This philosophy of the essential extends into all her cooking, as she says: "There's that old Chanel adage that before women go out, they should look in the mirror and take one thing off. Our plates are the same: there's a beauty in simplicity." She is keen to stress, though, that simplicity in presentation and ingredients does not equate to food being boring. "There's a complexity there, too. The richness of the beef, the textures and temperatures, the crusted outside of the patty contrasting with the creamy melted cheese...." When listening to Mar describe food, it's hard not to drift into a reverie of one's own and dream of burgers.

Mar honed her skills at restaurants like The Spotted Pig in Manhattan and Marlow & Sons in Brooklyn, both well admired for their cuisine, but her roots in the kitchen go back further. "So much of my cooking centers around what I ate as a child and what my father cooked," she says. This marriage of simple home cooking with culinary technique and an appreciation for flavors finds its apogee in Mar's burger creations. The burger's roots lie in the blending of meat and seasoning, the flavors heightened with onion and thickened with cheese, and then encased in a fluffy, pillowy bun.

To hear Mar talk about food is to understand why she says that "food should be sexy and sensual, every mouthful the perfect bite." And what could provide a more perfect bite than the perfect burger?

Below: Beatrice
Burger.

Recipes

Wolfgang Puck

Chef and restaurateur

Wolfgang Puck is an Austrian-born American celebrity chef and restaurateur. His restaurants include the world-famous Spago in Hollywood, Chinois in Santa Monica, and CUT in Beverly Hills and London. He is also the author of several cookbooks.

Chef Puck was born in Sankt Veit an der Glan. He learned to cook from his mother, a part-time pastry chef, but quickly developed an interest in a variety of culinary approaches. Having trained in several French restaurants, he moved in 1973 to the United States, where he spent two years honing his skills at La Tour in Indianapolis before moving to the bright lights and glitz of Los Angeles. His first restaurant, Ma Maison, served a take on modern French cuisine, which he then carried over into his next venture, Spago, combining it with other styles to create a very Californian fusion form of cooking. Opened on the Sunset Strip in 1982 by Puck and designer Barbara Lazaroff, Spago quickly became a hotspot for the Hollywood elite, as did its sister restaurant, Spago Beverly Hills, opened in 1997.

In 1994, Chef Puck's celebrity fan base and long-term association with Los Angeles saw him installed as Chef in Residence for the Governors Ball, the official post-Academy Awards bash—a position he has held ever since. He almost always serves his signature starter of Mini Prime Burgers with aged cheddar and remoulade, a French sauce traditionally made with an aioli or mayonnaise base. He uses heavy (double) cream, garlic, rosemary, paprika, bell peppers, red onion, and peanut (groundnut) oil to create a thick, rich sauce, which is spooned onto a Wagyu beef patty, with sliced, aged cheddar, arugula (rocket) leaves, and cornichons, all crammed into a brioche bun. On the 2015 menu this mini burger featured alongside a lobster BLT with bacon, chive aioli, and tomato in a brioche bun, and a smoked salmon matzo. Puck has also created a spicy Asian burger, peppering a beef patty with cilantro (coriander), garlic, cumin, and chili, and topping it with shiitake mushrooms, scallions (spring onions), and a teriyaki sauce.

Chef Puck now owns over one hundred eating establishments worldwide, produces soup and frozen organic pizzas for supermarket sale, and in 2012 received a James Beard Foundation Lifetime Achievement Award, one of the highest accolades in the food world.

> **"The hamburger is the perfect comfort food."**
>
> ↓
>
> **Wolfgang Puck**

Below: Cheeseburger
and seasoned fries
(chips).

Daniel Boulud

Chef and restaurateur

Daniel Boulud is an award-winning French chef and restaurateur with many international restaurants including Daniel, Café Boulud, and db Bistro Moderne in New York City, and Bar Boulud at the Mandarin Oriental Hotel in London. Boulud is also the author of a number of books.

Boulud never intended to create a burger, let alone one of the most celebrated burgers ever made. The bombing by Breton separatists of a McDonald's restaurant in France in April 2000, which killed a female employee, changed that. There was speculation about why the group had targeted McDonald's, including the possibly spurious suggestion that it was because the French do not like burgers, and so Boulud decided to assert in the clearest possible way that his nationality and background in *haute cuisine* did not preclude him from enjoying, even admiring, the hamburger.

Boulud trained in France with noted chefs such as Roger Vergé and Georges Blanc, before moving to the United States and becoming the private chef to the European Commission in Washington, D.C. From 1986 to 1992, he was in New York as Executive Chef at the renowned Le Cirque, before setting up his own restaurant, Daniel, in 1993. With his background and training in classic French *haute cuisine*, as well as his early successes in restaurants that served such fare, burgers were not part of his culinary upbringing. Nonetheless, he told me, "I've always had a passion for burgers. I didn't really learn about them in France, more in America. Every casual occasion I had with friends in America, we had burgers." Boulud's roots may have been in France, but his tastes were changed and his culinary horizons enlarged by his experience of the United States.

After the bombing, he was interviewed by the *New York Times* about why the bombing might have occurred. "I didn't know," he says. "But I felt maybe the French were jealous of not inventing the burger." The journalist's question spurred him to start thinking about burgers more and he decided to make one for him: "I wanted to create a gourmet burger that I could be proud of, maybe the greatest burger on Earth."

He considered how he could fashion a burger that reflected his background in food, a burger that would not compromise his beliefs, but would also stay true to the sense of what a burger should be; thus, the first db burger was born. And it was the first of many, as Boulud explains: "It was an instant classic, an instant success. I made it for some customers that I knew really well and I wanted to surprise." We can only assume they loved it, as the db burger was soon on the menu and flying off the grill.

The burger, now a modern culinary classic, combines traditional French flavors (Boulud tells me that he had the beef dish Tournedos Rossini in mind when devising it) with invention: "I wanted to stay close to cuisine cooking, where the flavor was beyond plain ground [minced] beef, more a braised beef flavor. And I don't like burgers with all kinds of junk on them. I was not trying to take the flavor of the meat away, more elevating the preparation of the meat with something delicate."

The delicacy was added by truffle and foie gras, both elements of the Tournedos Rossini, being cooked into the burger, as well as short rib for extra beefiness, and the sharpness of horseradish sauce, all encased in a Parmesan bun. The db quickly became the cognoscenti's burger of choice, as well as one of the world's most expensive. That expense reflected the complexity of its creation: "It's a very labor-intensive preparation for a burger. It took three days to make it: three days to braise the beef, shred it, create the fois gras, reduce the sauce, find the right cuts of meat, and so on. It was not something you could whip up on a whim."

Boulud's background certainly gave him the skill set to devise and make such an extraordinary burger and have it reflect the traditions within which he worked: "I wanted the burger to be very French, that was my goal. For that, it had to consist of a great combination of flavors that were reminiscent of French cuisine. It was never going to be a burger to eat with a beer or a Coke, but with good wine."

Growing up on a farm outside Lyons, Boulud enjoyed beef, though "we didn't put it in a bun, we had steak haché, except it was always overcooked. And we used to have it with mashed potato." Beef is the key to a good burger, and Boulud's team still ensures that his restaurants source the best cuts. "It's very important to trust the source of the beef," he told me.

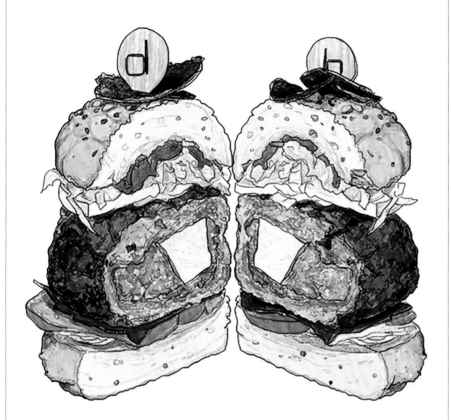

Below: Illustration
from *New York*
magazine of the
original db burger.

"In DBGB we do burgers and we make sure that
we buy in the best beef and grind [mince] it in the
restaurant ourselves."

Boulud's many venues still create and serve an array of
burgers: "We created the burger in London [the BB] that
is like the db burger but more simple. It's more casual and
it's a different way of preparing the burger. The Piggie
burger is a more American burger, but instead of braised
beef we have pulled pork and jalapeño mayonnaise in a
cheddar bun. The Frenchie has rillon—a slab of poached
pork belly [pork side]—which is then slightly roasted,
with a slice of Morbier, a blue-veined cheese. The burgers
are all very distinctive but very me, me the Frenchie, me
the American."

This French Michelin-starred chef, who came to love
American food and culture, has produced one of the most
thoughtful responses to the burger, a celebration of its
most endearing qualities, given fresh verve and delicacy
with an *haute-cuisine* palate. As Boulud told me, "The db
had the basic flavor and expectation of a burger, but there
was so much more to it." In challenging himself to create
"the greatest burger on Earth," Daniel Boulud changed the
face of hamburgers, creating an environment in which
gourmet techniques and flavors could sit at ease alongside
America's most popular and perhaps simplest food.

273

George Motz

Author, filmmaker, and burger expert

George Motz is an American filmmaker, hamburger expert, and author of the book *Hamburger America*. He is the Alan Lomax of hamburgers, delving into the folklore of the food the way Lomax researched music. Part epicure, part archivist, Motz's quest to locate the essence of the traditional hamburger has taken him all across the United States as he documents the nation's quintessential food.

Motz, who makes TV commercials for a living, never meant to become the great chronicler of burgers: "It was completely by accident—about fifteen years ago, I decided to make a documentary. I love food, so I decided to make a short piece that I could pitch and sell to the Food Network. No one had made a documentary about hamburgers. Hot dogs were kitschy, but no one really understood the burger."

So the tv show *Hamburger America* was born. What Motz discovered, alongside the fast-food chains and outside the culinary capitals of the country, was a food as rich in narrative as it was tasty: "I realized there was a big story there with all the small places, the Mom and Pop places. I asked friends if they had a local place they'd want to talk about. They were great stories as well as great burgers. It was about trying to get people to understand how hamburgers fit into the gastronomic fabric of America. I wanted people to get out of New York and L.A. and see the middle of the country."

Though Motz started with only eight burger joints, the project quickly spiraled and became a book. As he explained, "The first book had one hundred restaurants, so I expanded, changed the criteria, and the floodgates opened. I would ask truck drivers, the receptionists at hotels, and so on: people understood my mission and loads of people had places they loved. Then I also had this fan base, spread out all over America, the 'expert burger tasters,' a legion of first responders to great hamburger discoveries—in Seattle, Los Angeles, Miami, all over."

Motz was looking for stories as much as for the tastiest burgers. He wanted to find burger joints that were woven into the fabric of their communities: "Remember the experience and look for the places that have served burgers for a long time. Restaurants I feature have to have had a burger on the menu for over twenty years: continuity and longevity are really important." So is taste, of course. Motz is all about simplicity when it comes to the burger's build: "It has to be made with fresh-ground [minced] beef. Don't look for burgers with stuff in them; the best are just made with fresh-ground beef without spices or whatever added." As he says, a burger is basically "meat that's been chopped up somehow, cooked somehow, and put on bread somehow."

Hamburger America came out at a time—2008—when the burger was undergoing a surge in popularity, something that Motz sees as being rooted both in a sense of history and in a change in the way we share information. As he says, "Americans are intensely proud of their hamburger heritage; when they bite into a hamburger they're biting into America. Americans also know about the history of the hamburger, so they appreciate how it's changed. I wanted to make sure that in twenty years' time we don't think of a burger as just fast food." But the information age has also changed how people can talk about food and, crucially, share their local knowledge of where the best burgers can be found: "I think the internet, the rapid dissemination of information across the world in the last few years, has really accelerated the interest in burgers. People can learn a lot about whatever they're interested in, and people want to know where their food comes from."

"Americans are intensely proud of their hamburger heritage; when they bite into a hamburger they're biting into America."

George Motz

The great achievement of Motz and the increasingly thorough versions of *Hamburger America* and its companion cookbook, *The Great American Burger Book*, is the seeking out and finding of the places that survived and carried with them a sense of the culinary history, even the cultural history, of the United States. Just as Alan Lomax sought out and recorded the country's folk music, cataloging it for future generations, so Motz has used his network and his own assiduous research to catalog America's greatest food item. As he says, "Being an expert is a combination of passion and knowledge." And it's hard not to be passionate about the burger because, first and foremost, burgers are tasty and fun, a treat. As Motz says of the burger's renaissance, "People were tired of not being indulgent—hamburgers are healthy in the sense that they make you happy. Happiness is the first step to healthiness." It's hard not to admire Motz's achievement, but it's even harder not to envy him.

The Oklahoma Fried-Onion Burger

**GEORGE MOTZ
AUTHOR, FILMMAKER,
AND BURGER EXPERT**

Oklahoma is one of my favorite places to immerse myself in burger culture. It sits in the center of what I like to call the American Burger Belt, an invisible line that can be drawn from Texas north to Wisconsin. This is where the majority of America's primary-source hamburgers can be found; the burgers that are unaffected by time or trend; the ones that have been made the same way for, in some cases, a hundred years. One of those burgers is the fried-onion burger of Oklahoma.

El Reno, Oklahoma is the epicenter of the fried-onion burger universe. At one point there were more than nine joints in town that served this regional treat. Today only a handful of places remain, but they are preserving an important piece of American food history.

An entrepreneurial burger man in the 1920s used a handful of thinly sliced onions in his burger and a legend was born. Sid's Diner in El Reno, one of the greatest guardians of this unique hamburger tradition, continues that legacy by taking a gob of onions and smashing it into a ball of beef on the flat top. The contents fuse, creating a caramelized, onion-beef mess that tastes incredible. The griddle masters that smash hundreds of these burgers daily at lunch are not shy about the amount of sliced onion they use, and the onion-to-beef ratio at Sid's is close to 50/50.

This method goes against everything you've been taught about how to treat a burger on a cooking surface. Pressing the life out of a burger seems wrong until you try it. And there's no other way to make this burger.

The trick to retain the juiciness here is to press the patty only once at the beginning and allow the burger to cook in its own grease, a sort of burger confit, if you will. Behold the Oklahoma fried-onion burger.

GEORGE MOTZ

peanut (groundnut) or other neutral oil, for oiling
2 lb (**900** g) ground (minced) **80/20** chuck beef
2 large Vidalia onions, sliced super-thin (this is best done with a mandoline slicer set to its thinnest setting—the onions should be translucent and thinner than paper)
8 slices American cheese
salt

ASSEMBLY

8 soft white buns, halved and toasted
sliced pickles (gherkins) (optional)

STEP 1

Preheat a large cast-iron skillet (frying pan) over medium heat (or preheat a flat top to medium) and add a drop or two of oil. Spread the oil with the flat side of a stiff spatula (fish slice) to coat the surface.

STEP 2

Put the ground (minced) beef into a bowl. Form **8** balls of beef, gently releasing them into the hot skillet with **2** to **3** inches (**5** to **7** cm) of space surrounding each. (You may only be able to cook **2** or **3** burgers at a time.)

STEP 3

Grab a golf-ball-size pile of the sliced onion and push it onto the center of each ball of beef so it sticks, for the most part. (Smashing requires more force than you'd think. Don't worry about pressing the patties too thin—they'll shrink up to the size of your buns as they cook. The onions should fuse nicely with the raw beef.) Season each beef ball with salt. Once the patties are smashed, don't touch them again until ready to flip—**4** to **5** minutes or until red moisture begins to form on top of the patties. Flip the glorious beef-and-onion-fused patties and slide a slice of American cheese on top of each. Cook for an additional **2** minutes.

STEP 4

To assemble each burger, transfer the patties with the melted cheese to the toasted buns. Serve immediately, with sliced pickles (gherkins), if desired.

The Infamous Balans Burger

BALANS SOHO SOCIETY
LONDON, UK

8 oz (**225** g) ground (minced) beef
olive oil, for drizzling
4 slices cheddar cheese
8 slices (rashers) smoked lean
   (streaky) bacon
salt and pepper

ASSEMBLY
4 slider or brioche buns, halved
   and toasted
mayonnaise
sliced beefsteak (beef) tomatoes
butter lettuce, such as Bibb, Boston,
   or Little Gem
sliced dill pickles
thinly sliced red onion

STEP 1
Preheat a charbroiler (chargrill) to
high heat or heat a dry griddle pan
over high heat.

STEP 2
Shape the ground (minced) beef into
4 patties, each about **1** inch (**2.5** cm) thick.
Drizzle each patty with a little oil.

STEP 3
Place the patties on the charbroiler or
griddle pan and cook for **6** to **8** minutes
until nicely charred. Sprinkle the patties
with a pinch of salt and pepper. Flip the
patties, place a slice of cheddar on top of
each patty so that it starts to slowly melt,
and cook for another **6** to **8** minutes.

STEP 4
Meanwhile, add the bacon to the
charbroiler or griddle pan and cook
until crispy.

STEP 5
To assemble each burger, spread the
bottom of a toasted bun with mayonnaise.
Onto the bottom bun, place slices of
tomato and some pieces of lettuce, then
a patty with the melted cheese, followed
by **2** slices (rashers) of crispy bacon, some
sliced dill pickle, and some onion. Finish
with the top half of the bun.

Piggie Burger

DANIEL BOULUD
CHEF AND RESTAURATEUR

BRINE

1-1/2 cups (**11** oz/**300** g) finely packed
dark brown sugar
1/2 cup (**3-3/4** oz/**115** g) kosher (coarse)
salt
3 tablespoons Worcestershire sauce
1 pork butt (shoulder of pork, bone-in)

PORK RUB

2-3/4 cups (**11** oz/**300** g) Spanish paprika
2-1/2 cups (**1** lb **2** oz/**500** g) firmly packed
dark brown sugar
2-1/2 cups (**9** oz/**250** g) ground
black pepper
3/4 cup (**3** oz/**80** g) ground white pepper
2 tablespoons salt
1/3 cup (**1-1/4** oz/**35** g) dry mustard powder
1/3 cup (**1** oz/**30** g) cayenne pepper
3 tablespoons granulated garlic
2 teaspoons allspice powder

CABBAGE VINEGAR SLAW

1 head red cabbage, thinly sliced
(use a mandoline slicer if you have one)
1 tablespoon salt
1/2 cup (**4** fl oz/**120** ml) apple cider vinegar
1/2 cup (**3-1/2** oz/**100** g) granulated sugar
1/4 cup (**2-1/4** oz/**60** g) yellow mustard
1/4 cup (**2** fl oz/**60** ml) mustard oil
1 clove garlic, grated
pepper

BARBECUE SAUCE

1 cup (**8** fl oz/**250** ml) olive oil
10 cloves garlic, minced
2 onions, chopped
2 red bell peppers, cored, seeded,
and chopped
2 tablespoons salt

1/2 cup (**4** fl oz/**120** ml) bourbon
3/4 cup (**6** oz/**175** g) firmly packed
brown sugar
4 cups (**2-1/4** lb/**1** kg) ketchup
1/2 cup (**5-3/4** oz/**170** g) molasses (treacle)
1/2 cup (**4-1/4** oz/**125** g) Dijon mustard
1 cup (**8** fl oz/**250** ml) apple cider vinegar
4 teaspoons Tabasco sauce
1/2 cup (**1-1/2** oz/**40** g) English dry
mustard powder, mixed with **2** cups
(**16** fl oz/**475** ml) water

JALAPEÑO MAYONNAISE

1 tablespoon olive oil
6 jalapeño peppers, seeded and
finely diced
2 tablespoons white wine vinegar
2 egg yolks
1 tablespoon Dijon mustard
2 cups (**16** fl oz/**475** ml) grapeseed
or canola (rapeseed) oil
salt

PATTIES

5 lb (**2.25** kg) diced chuck beef, chilled
1 lb **4** oz (**570** g) raw beef fat (or substitute
ground/minced chuck meat with about
30 percent fat), chilled

ASSEMBLY

14 cheddar cheese buns, halved
and toasted
28 pieces butter lettuce such as Bibb,
Boston or Little Gem
7 pickled jalapeño peppers,
halved lengthwise

STEP 1

To make the brine, heat **5** cups (**40** fl oz/
1.2 liters) water in a very large pan, add the
dark brown sugar and kosher (coarse) salt
and stir until they have dissolved. Remove
from the heat, add the Worcestershire
sauce and **4-3/4** gallons (**17.8** liters) water,
and mix well.

STEP 2

Using a meat injector, inject the brine
solution into both sides of the pork butt
(shoulder of pork) at about **2**-inch (**5**-cm)
by **2**-inch (**5**-cm) intervals. Place the pork
butt in the remaining brine solution,
cover, and let stand for **6** hours.

STEP 3

To make the pork rub, mix together all the
ingredients in a bowl.

STEP 4

Remove the pork butt from the brine
solution and rub it generously with the
pork rub, reserving **1/2** cup (**2-3/4** oz/**75** g)
of the pork rub for the barbecue sauce.
Place the pork butt on a rack, uncovered,
and let dry in the refrigerator for **24** hours.

STEP 5

Preheat a smoker to **200**°F (**95**°C). Fill
the woodchip box with soaked mesquite
wood. Cook the pork butt in the smoker
for **10** hours, refreshing the soaked
mesquite wood with **1/2** to **3/4** cup (**4** to
6 fl oz/**120** to **175** ml) water every **3** hours
or so.

STEP 6

Remove the pork butt from the smoker
and wrap it tightly in plastic wrap
(clingfilm). Let rest at room temperature
until cool enough to handle. Remove the
plastic wrap and coarsely chop the pork
butt. Let cool completely and then
refrigerate until you are ready to use.

STEP 7

To make the cabbage vinegar slaw, put the
cabbage and salt into a colander set over a
bowl, toss them together, and let drain for
3 hours. Pour the apple cider vinegar into
a pan, add the granulated sugar, yellow
mustard, mustard oil, and garlic, and bring

to a boil. Then remove from the heat and season with salt and pepper. Put the drained cabbage into a separate bowl and pour over the vinegar mixture. Chill in the refrigerator for at least **3** hours. Just before serving, drain off any excess liquid.

STEP 8

Meanwhile, make the barbecue sauce. Heat the olive oil in a sauté pan and add the garlic, onions, and red bell peppers. Cook over low heat until softened. Add the salt, bourbon, and reserved pork rub and stir well to deglaze the pan, scraping up any bits from the bottom of the pan. Add **4** cups (**32** fl oz/**950** ml) water and the remaining ingredients, except for the English mustard mixture, and simmer over low heat for **30** to **45** minutes, until the sauce has thickened. Whisk in the English mustard mixture, then transfer the sauce to a blender or food processor and blend until smooth.

STEP 9

Next, make the jalapeño mayonnaise. Heat the olive oil in a sauté pan over medium-high heat, then add the jalapeño peppers and cook for **3** to **4** minutes, until just starting to soften. Add the white wine vinegar and cook until the liquid has reduced completely. Using a slotted spoon, remove the jalapeño peppers, transfer them to a plate, and let cool in the refrigerator. Put the egg yolks, Dijon mustard, and **2** teaspoons water into a blender and blend on low. With the motor still running, gradually add the grapeseed or canola (rapeseed) oil in a thin stream until you have a thick mayonnaise. (If the mayonnaise becomes too thick, add an extra drop of water or white wine vinegar.) Transfer the mayonnaise to a bowl, season with salt, and stir in the cooled jalapeño peppers. Refrigerate until ready to use.

STEP 10

Now make the patties. You will need a meat grinder (mincer) fitted with a grinder plate with **1/4**-inch (**5**-mm) diameter holes. The grinder attachments should be chilled before you grind (mince) the meat. When well chilled, grind the meat, alternating pieces of chuck beef and beef fat, into a shallow tray. Divide the ground (minced) meat into **14** portions. On a stainless steel surface, using a metal ring or cookie cutter that is **4-1/2** inches (**11.5** cm) in diameter and **1-1/2** inches (**4** cm) high, gently press each portion of meat inside the ring or cutter. While pressing, twist the meat two or three times to be sure it is packed tightly. Do not squeeze the meat too hard or you will overwork the meat.

STEP 11

Preheat the grill (barbecue) for two-temperature cooking, with one area for medium-high heat and the other for medium heat. Cook the patties over medium-high heat, without moving them, for **2** minutes, or until they are well marked. Rotate the patties **90** degrees to make a crosshatch pattern and grill for another **2** minutes. Flip the patties, move to the medium heat, and cook, without moving them, for **3** minutes. Rotate the patties **90** degrees and cook for another **3** minutes. Transfer the patties to a platter and let rest in a warm spot for about **10** minutes for medium-rare.

STEP 12

Meanwhile, put the barbecue sauce and pulled pork into a pan and cook over medium heat until heated through.

STEP 13

To assemble each burger, spread both the top and bottom of a toasted bun with a thin layer of the jalapeño mayonnaise. Onto the bottom bun, place a couple pieces of lettuce and then some of the cabbage vinegar slaw, and top with a patty. Then add some more cabbage vinegar slaw, followed by some pulled pork, and finish with the top half of the bun. Thread a halved pickled jalapeño onto a small wooden skewer and insert the skewer into the middle of the bun to hold the burger together.

Avocado Bacon Burger

**GOURMET BURGER KITCHEN (GBK)
LONDON, UK**

two **6**-oz (**175**-g) beef patties
4 slices (rashers) lean (streaky) bacon
2 slices Red Leicester or aged
  cheddar cheese

AVOCADO MIX

2 ripe avocados
squeeze of lemon juice
squeeze of lime juice
1/4 teaspoon chili flakes
salt and pepper

ASSEMBLY

2 sesame seed buns, halved and toasted
4 tablespoons GBK Smoked Chill Mayo
  or GBK Harissa Mayo
4 tablespoons GBK House Relish
butter lettuce, such as Bibb, Boston,
  or Little Gem
sliced beefsteak (beef) tomatoes
finely sliced red onion rings (optional)

STEP 1

First make the avocado mix. Cut the avocados in half, remove the pits (stones), and scoop the flesh into a bowl. Add the lemon and lime juices and the chili flakes. Using a table knife, coarsely chop the avocado flesh into bite-size pieces. Season to taste with salt and pepper, then mix until the avocado flesh starts to break down—be careful not to over-mix, you want to keep the avocado quite chunky! If you're not using the avocado mix immediately, press a piece of plastic wrap (clingfilm) onto the surface of the avocado mix to stop it from going brown.

STEP 2

Preheat the grill (barbecue) to medium or heat a dry griddle pan over medium heat.

STEP 3

Place the patties on the grill or in the griddle pan and cook for **11** to **15** minutes, turning halfway through the cooking time, until the juices run clear and there is no pink meat.

STEP 4

Meanwhile, preheat a broiler (grill) to high and cook the bacon until crispy. Alternatively, if you are using a griddle pan, cook the bacon in the griddle pan with the patties.

STEP 5

Just before the patties have finished cooking, place a slice of cheese onto each patty. (If the grill has a lid, now is the time to close it so the cheese melts properly.)

STEP 6

To assemble each burger, spread the bottom of a toasted bun with half the mayonnaise and spread the top of the bun with half the relish. Onto the bottom bun, place a patty with cheese, then top with **2** tablespoons of the avocado mix, followed by 2 slices (rashers) of crispy bacon, some pieces of lettuce, slices of tomato, and onion rings, if using, and finish with the top half of the bun.

Bloody Mary Slider
BITE ME BURGER CO.
SYDNEY, NEW SOUTH WALES, AUSTRALIA

SAUCE
1 cup (**9** oz/**250** g) puréed
  canned tomatoes (passata)
1 tablespoon Worcestershire sauce
1 scant teaspoon Tabasco sauce
1 tablespoon vodka

PATTIES
2-1/4 lb (**1** kg) ground (minced) beef
1 large onion, finely diced
1-1/2 celery stalks, finely diced
1 tablespoon Worcestershire sauce
1 tablespoon grated fresh horseradish
1 tablespoon puréed canned
  tomatoes (passata)
1 tablespoon vodka
1 tablespoon chopped curly parsley
salt and pepper

ASSEMBLY
shredded romaine (cos) lettuce
12 Sonoma rolls (or you could
  substitute slider buns), halved
sliced pickles (gherkins)
diced onion

STEP 1
Preheat the grill (barbecue) to high or
heat a dry griddle pan over high heat.

STEP 2
To make the sauce, mix together all the
ingredients in a bowl.

STEP 3
To make the patties, mix together all the
ingredients in bowl. (Do not use a food
processor as you want to retain the
texture of the celery.) Shape the mixture
into **12** patties.

STEP 4
Place the patties on the grill or in the
griddle pan and cook for about **90** seconds
on each side for medium-rare, or longer
if you prefer your patties more well done.

STEP 5
To assemble each slider, arrange some
shredded lettuce on the bottom half of
a bun. Place a patty on top of the lettuce,
then add some of the sauce, followed by
some sliced pickles (gherkins) and diced
onion, and finish with the top of the bun.

"Making
the world
a burger
place."

↓

Bite Me
Burger Co.

The Bash Burger

JOSH CAPON

CHEF AND RESTAURATEUR

BACON JAM

12 thick slices (rashers) bacon,
   cut into **1/4** -inch (**5**-mm) lardons
1 tablespoon canola (rapeseed) oil
4 Spanish onions, cut into **1/2**-inch
   (**1**-cm) dice
1 tablespoon white wine vinegar
1 thyme sprig
salt and pepper

SPECIAL SAUCE

1 cup (**8** oz/**225** g) mayonnaise
3/4 cup (**7** oz/**200** g) ketchup
1 clove garlic
1 tablespoon sherry vinegar
1-1/2 teaspoons sriracha sauce
white pepper

PATTIES

six **6**-oz (**175**-g) beef patties, each about
   1/2 inch (**1** cm) thick
2 tablespoons Dijon mustard
6 slices American cheese

ASSEMBLY

6 slider or brioche buns, halved and
   toasted
2 kosher dill pickles, thinly sliced
12 deep-fried onion rings

STEP 1

To start the bacon jam, put the bacon into a skillet (frying pan) with **1/4** cup (**2** fl oz/**60** ml) water and cook over low heat for **20** to **25** minutes until the bacon is crispy. Using a slotted spoon, transfer the bacon to a paper-towel-lined plate to absorb any excess grease. Reserve the bacon fat.

STEP 2

Heat the oil and **2** tablespoons of the reserved bacon fat in a pan. Add the onions and cook over low heat for **20** to **25** minutes until the onions are translucent and lightly caramelized. Transfer to a bowl and set aside.

STEP 3

Put the bacon into a food processor and blitz until the bacon reaches a coarse consistency. Fold the bacon into the caramelized onions, then stir in the white wine vinegar and thyme. Season to taste with salt and black pepper—it will already by quite salty due to the bacon.

STEP 4

To make the special sauce, blend all the ingredients together in a food processor and season to taste with salt and white pepper. Set aside.

STEP 5

Season the patties generously with salt and black pepper. Heat a dry griddle pan over high heat. Add the patties and cook for **2** to **3** minutes, then flip the patties, add **1** teaspoon of Dijon mustard on top of each patty, and cook for another **2** to **3** minutes. Just before the patties have finished cooking, place a slice of cheese on top of each patty so it melts.

STEP 6

Meanwhile, put the bacon jam into a pan, remove the thyme, and reheat over low heat.

STEP 7

To assemble each burger, spread both the top and bottom of a toasted bun with **1** tablespoon of the special sauce. Onto the bottom of the bun, place a patty with cheese, then add a dollop of the bacon jam, followed by some dill pickles, and finish with the top half of the bun. Insert **2** wooden skewers into the middle of each bun to hold the burgers together. Slide **2** deep-fried onion rings over the skewers and serve.

Bleecker Black Burger

BLEECKER BURGER
LONDON, UK

8 oz (**225** g) ground (minced)
  dry-aged beef
2 oz (**50** g) ground (minced)
  blood sausage (black pudding)
2 slices American cheese
a few onion slices
salt and pepper

ASSEMBLY

1 sesame seed bun, halved and toasted
2 tablespoons burger sauce (our
  homemade burger sauce is a blend of
  ketchup, mayonnaise, and mustard, plus
  a few extra secret ingredients—we
  actually blitz up pickles [gherkins] in it)

STEP 1
Gently shape the ground (minced) beef
into **2** patties and season with salt and
pepper. Gently shape the ground blood
sausage (black pudding) into a patty.

STEP 2
Preheat a large, dry skillet (frying pan)
over high heat (or preheat a flat top
to high).

STEP 3
Smash a beef patty in the hot skillet and
cook for **1** to **2** minutes, then season with
salt and pepper and flip the patty. Cook for
1 to **2** minutes, then add a slice of cheese
and cook for another **1** to **2** minutes.
Remove from the skillet and set aside.
Now cook the remaining patties, adjusting
the timing if necessary to achieve
medium–rare, and excluding the cheese
from the blood sausage patty.

STEP 4
Add the onion to the skillet and cook for
a few seconds—just enough time to stop
the onion from being raw.

STEP 5
To assemble the burger, spread both the
top and bottom of a toasted bun with a
layer of burger sauce. Onto the bottom of
the bun, place a beef patty with cheese,
followed by the onions, the blood sausage
patty, another beef patty with cheese, and
finish with the top half of the bun.

Truffled Mayonnaise and Perfect Egg Burger

BURGER TABLE
SÃO PAULO, BRAZIL

SLOW-COOKED EGGS
4 eggs

MAYONNAISE
1/4 cup (2-1/2 oz/65 g) egg yolks
   (about 4 egg yolks)
2 teaspoons white wine vinegar
1 teaspoon salt
1 cup (8 fl oz/250 ml) sunflower oil
2 tablespoons Dijon mustard
1/10 oz (3 g) grated black truffle
grated zest of 1 Sicilian lemon
juice of 1/2 Sicilian lemon

PATTIES
1 lb 1 oz (480 g) beef shank (shin),
   ground (minced)
11-1/4 oz (320 g) beef brisket,
   ground (minced)
salt and pepper

ASSEMBLY
4 slider or brioche buns, halved
   and lightly toasted

STEP 1

First prepare the slow-cooked eggs. Preheat the water bath to **144.5**°F (**62.5**°C). Seal each whole egg in vacuum package, place them in the water bath, and cook for **1-1/4** hours. Carefully remove the shells. If you don't a vacuum sealer and a temperature-controlled water bath, you can substitute poached eggs for the slow-cooked eggs, poaching the eggs for **1-1/2** minutes just before you are ready to serve.

STEP 2

Meanwhile, to make the mayonnaise, put the egg yolks, vinegar, and salt into a blender and blend on low. With the motor still running, gradually add the oil in a thin stream until you have a thick mayonnaise. Transfer to a bowl and stir in the mustard, truffle, and lemon zest and juice. Refrigerate until ready to use.

STEP 3

To prepare the patties, mix together the ground (minced) meats in a bowl and let rest in the refrigerator for **30** minutes.

STEP 4

Preheat the grill (barbecue) to high heat.

STEP 5

Shape the beef mixture into **4** patties. Season with salt and pepper. Place the patties on the grill and cook for **3** to **4** minutes on each side.

STEP 6

To assemble each burger, spread the bottom half of a toasted bun with mayonnaise. Onto the bottom bun, place a patty, followed by a slow-cooked egg, and finish with the top half of the bun.

"Burger Table Commandments":

ONLY grill (barbecue) on charcoal
ONLY grind (mince) beef in house
ONLY serve buns fresh & soft
ONLY serve cheddar cheese from England
ONLY serve crispy bacon
ONLY use homemade ketchup & mayonnaise
ONLY cut & triple-cook French fries (chips)
    from locally sourced potatoes
ONLY use the secret burger recipe blend
ONLY season a burger with salt & pepper
ONLY eat a burger with your hands

Chicken Satay Burger with Pineapple Relish

DICKIE FITZ
LONDON, UK

SHREDDED CHICKEN

1/4 cup (**2-3/4** oz/**75** g) salt
1/4 cup (**2** oz/**50** g) superfine (caster)
   sugar
3 chicken legs, bone in and skin on
2-1/4 lb (**1** kg) duck fat, melted

SATAY SAUCE

1-1/3 cups (**7** oz/**200** g) roasted peanuts
5 teaspoons sesame oil
1 small onion, finely diced
3/4 teaspoon shrimp paste
1 teaspoon ground turmeric
1 lemongrass stalk, tough outer leaves
   removed and finely sliced
1 teaspoon chili flakes
3/4 cup (**6** fl oz/**175** ml) coconut milk
2 tablespoons tamarind paste
superfine (caster) or palm sugar, to taste

RELISH

1/3 cup (**2** oz/**50** g) diced fresh pineapple
1/3 cup (**2** oz/**50** g) diced cucumber
1-1/2 tablespoons diced red onion
scant **1/2** cup (**3-1/2** fl oz/**100** ml)
   pineapple juice
4 teaspoons Thai fish sauce
1 tablespoon lime juice
scant **1/4** cup (**1-3/4** fl oz/**50** ml)
   peanut (groundnut) oil
1 bunch cilantro (coriander), leaves only

ASSEMBLY

shredded iceburg lettuce
6 seeded buns, halved

STEP 1

To make the shredded chicken, put the
salt and sugar into a large pan with **3** cups
(**25** fl oz/**750** ml) water, bring to a boil,
and cook until the sugar and salt have
dissolved. Remove from the heat and let
cool. Once the liquid is cold, put the
chicken legs into the water and let soak
for **1** to **4** hours.

STEP 2

Preheat the oven to **325**°F (**160**°C/Gas
mark **3**).

STEP 3

To make the satay sauce, spread out the
peanuts on a baking sheet and roast in the
oven for **8** minutes, or until golden.
Transfer the peanuts to a bag and crush
with a rolling pin, until they are broken up
into medium-size pieces. Heat the sesame
oil in a small pan, then add the onion,
shrimp paste, turmeric, lemongrass, and
chili flakes, and cook over low heat until
very soft and fragrant. Add the coconut
milk, **3/4** cup (**6** fl oz/**175** ml) water, and
the tamarind paste and bring to a simmer.
Season to taste with sugar and salt, then
add the crushed peanuts and cook for
about **10** minutes until the sauce thickens.
Transfer to a bowl, let cool, and refrigerate
until ready to use.

STEP 4

Reduce the oven temperature to **250**°F
(**120**°C/Gas mark **1/2**).

STEP 5

Remove the chicken legs from the water
and pat dry with paper towels. Place the
chicken legs in a roasting pan and cover
them with the duck fat. Cook in the oven
for **3** hours. Remove from the oven and let
cool, uncovered.

STEP 6

Preheat a charbroiler (chargrill) to
high heat or heat a dry griddle pan over
high heat.

STEP 7

Remove the chicken legs from the fat.
Place the chicken legs on the charbroiler or
griddle pan and cook for **5** minutes, or until
the chicken is heated through. Remove
from the charbroiler or griddle pan, peel
off the skin, and shred the leg meat.

STEP 8

To make the relish, mix together the
pineapple, cucumber, and red onion in a
bowl. Add the pineapple juice, fish sauce,
lime juice, and peanut (groundnut) oil and
mix well. Stir in the cilantro (coriander).

STEP 9

To assemble each burger, arrange some
shredded lettuce on the bottom half of
a bun. Dip one-sixth of the shredded
chicken in the satay sauce and then place
it on top of the lettuce. Add some relish,
and finish with the top half of a bun. For
best results, insert a wooden skewer
into the middle of each bun to hold the
burgers together.

15-20
BURGERS

Spicy Beef Short Rib Bao Burger

CHA CHAAN TENG
LONDON, UK

CARROT AND CILANTRO PICKLE

scant **1/2** cup (**3-1/2** fl oz/**100** ml)
  rice vinegar
2-1/2 tablespoons superfine (caster) sugar
1 teaspoon salt
1 teaspoon sesame oil
1 carrot, peeled and cut into thin strips
1 small handful of cilantro (coriander),
  coarsely torn

BRAISING LIQUID

2 cloves garlic, chopped
one **1**-inch (**2.5**-cm) piece fresh ginger,
  peeled and chopped
5 to **6** scallions (spring onions), sliced
  into thin rounds
3 tablespoons oyster sauce
1/4 cup (**2** fl oz/**60** ml) Chinkiang black
  rice vinegar
1 tablespoon dark soy sauce
3 tablespoons superfine (caster) sugar
1 teaspoon chili flakes
1 tablespoon fermented black beans
1 to **2** tablespoons sambal chili paste

BRAISED BEEF

5 whole beef short ribs
generous **2** cups (**17** fl oz/**500** ml)
  beef broth (stock)

BAO BUNS

4-1/4 cups (**1** lb **2-3/4** oz/**530** g) Yellow
  Kirin steamed buns flour (or you can
  substitute all-purpose [plain] flour)
3-3/4 teaspoons baking powder
1/3 teaspoon salt
2-1/2 tablespoons superfine (caster) sugar

2-1/4 teaspoons active dry
  (fast-action) yeast
scant **1/4** cup (**1-3/4** fl oz/**50** ml) milk
3 tablespoons vegetable oil, plus extra
  for brushing

SAUCE

scant **1/4** cup (**1-3/4** fl oz/**50** ml)
  vegetable broth (stock)
scant **1/2** cup (**3-1/2** fl oz/**100** ml)
  sweet soy sauce (kecap manis)

ASSEMBLY

handful of watercress
thinly sliced red onion

STEP 1

First, make the carrot and cilantro
pickle—it will take overnight. Put the rice
vinegar, sugar, salt, sesame oil, and scant
1/2 cup (**3-1/2** fl oz/**100** ml) water into a
large glass jar. Stir until the sugar has
dissolved. Add the carrot, seal the jar with
the lid or cover with plastic wrap
(clingfilm), and refrigerate overnight.

STEP 2

The next day, make the braising liquid. Put
the garlic, ginger, and scallions (spring
onions) into a pan and quickly pan-fry
over medium heat until softened and
fragrant. Add the remaining ingredients
and bring to a boil.

STEP 3

Meanwhile, in a separate large pan over
high heat, make the braised beef. Sear the
ribs on all sides to seal in their flavor.
Preheat the oven to **275**°F (**140**°C/Gas
mark **1**).

STEP 4

Once the braising liquid is boiling, place
the ribs in the braising liquid and simmer
for **5** minutes, basting the ribs with the

braising liquid from time to time to keep
them well coated.

STEP 5

Transfer the ribs and braising liquid to a
large roasting pan. Pour over the beef
broth (stock)—the ribs need to be covered
completely by the broth—and cook in the
oven for **8** hours. (This will make the ribs
incredibly tender and intensely flavorful.)
Transfer the ribs to a cutting (chopping)
board and slice the meat off the bones.
Reserve the braising liquid—you will need
scant **1/2** cup (**3-1/2** fl oz/**100** ml) for the
sauce; any remaining liquid can be stored
in the refrigerator and used as a marinade
for pork or chicken.

STEP 6

Make the bao buns. Put the flour, baking
powder, salt, sugar, and yeast into a stand
mixer fitted with a dough hook and start
to combine on a low speed. Combine the
milk, **1-1/4** cups (**10** fl oz/**300** ml) warm
water, and **2** tablespoons of the vegetable
oil in a pitcher (jug). Slowly pour the milk
mixture into the mixer and knead on a
low-medium speed for **2** to **3** minutes until
all of the water is mixed into the flour.
Increase the speed to high and knead for
2 minutes, or until the dough has a
smooth-yet-tacky feel to it. Alternatively,
if you don't have a stand mixer, combine
the ingredients in a bowl as above, then
knead the dough on a lightly floured work
surface. Cover the dough with the
remaining vegetable oil, followed by a
damp dish towel, and let rest in a warm
place (preferably a moist, draft-free
location such as an oven) for **1** hour.

STEP 7

Once the dough has rested, separate the
dough into table-tennis-size balls (each
weighing about **3/4** oz/**20** g). Flatten half

of the balls with the palm of your hand and brush each bun lightly with vegetable oil. Place one of the remaining balls on top of each of the flattened and oiled balls, pressing down with a domed or cup-shaped palm to create height. Once all of the buns have been shaped, spritz them with cold water, cover with a damp dish towel, and let rise (prove) in a warm place for **20** minutes.

STEP 8

Meanwhile, make the sauce. Put all the ingredients into a pan with scant **1/4** cup (**1-3/4** fl oz/**50** ml) water and scant **1/2** cup (**3-1/2** fl oz/**100** ml) of the reserved braising liquid. Bring to a boil and cook until the sauce has reduced by half—the sauce should have a thick, syrupy texture.

STEP 9

To cook the bao buns, heat a large steamer over medium-high heat and steam the buns for **8** minutes, or until puffed up. Cut the bao buns in half.

STEP 10

Meanwhile, finish the overnight carrot and cilantro pickle by stirring in the cilantro (coriander).

STEP 11

To assemble each burger, spoon some of the carrot and cilantro pickle onto the bottom of a bun, top with some shredded beef and **1** tablespoon of the sauce. Then add some watercress and sliced red onion, and finish with the top half of the bun. For best results, insert a wooden skewer into the middle of each bun to hold the burgers together.

Reuben Burger

FOUNDRY 39
EDINBURGH, UK

PATTIES

14 oz (**400** g) dry-aged beef steak, ground
(minced)
11 oz (**300** g) chuck beef, ground (minced)
11 oz (**300** g) beef brisket, ground
(minced)
olive or other neutral oil, for brushing
salt and pepper

ASSEMBLY

5 seeded buns, halved
mayonnaise
1 oz (**25** g) sauerkraut
sliced pickles (gherkins)
5 slices Swiss cheese
2-1/2 oz (**65** g) corned beef (salt beef)

STEP 1

To make the patties, put the ground
(minced) meats into a bowl, season with
salt and pepper, and mix together. Shape
the mixture into **5** patties.

STEP 2

Heat a dry skillet (frying pan) over
medium heat. Brush the patties with
a little oil, then add them to the skillet
and cook for **4** minutes on each side.

STEP 3

To assemble each burger, spread the
bottom half of a bun with mayonnaise.
Onto the bottom bun, place some
sauerkraut, followed by some sliced
pickles (gherkins), a patty, a slice of
cheese, and some corned beef (salt beef).
Finish with the top half of the bun.

Global Traveler Burger

ADAM RAWSON
CHEF

BALSAMIC ONIONS
scant **1/2** cup (**3-1/2** fl oz/**100** ml) olive oil
6 red onions, sliced
2 teapoons salt
1/4 cup (**2** oz/**50** g) firmly packed
   brown sugar
2/3 cup (**5** fl oz/**150** ml) aged
   balsamic vinegar

AIOLI
scant **1/2** cup (**3-1/2** oz/**100** g) egg yolks
   (about **6** egg yolks)
1 tablespoon smoked salt
1 truffle, grated
1/3 cup (**2-1/2** fl oz/**75** ml) lemon juice
generous **2** cups (**17** fl oz/**500** ml)
   sunflower oil
scant **1/2** cup (**3-1/2** fl oz/**100** ml) truffle oil

PATTIES
4 lb (**1.8** kg) ground (minced) aged
   Galician beef (or substitute any
   good-quality beef)
12 slices Gorgonzola cheese,
   about **1** oz (**25** g) each
12 slices pancetta
salt and pepper

ASSEMBLY
12 burger buns (preferably potato buns),
   about **4-3/4** inches (**12** cm) in
   diameter, halved
handful of arugula (rocket)

STEP 1
First, make the balsamic onions. Heat the olive oil in a pan, then add the onions, salt, and sugar and cook over low heat, until the onions are translucent and lightly caramelized. Add the vinegar and cook until the onion mixture has thickened.

STEP 2
Meanwhile, prepare the aioli. Put the egg yolks, smoked salt, truffle, and lemon juice into a blender and blend on low. With the motor still running, gradually add the sunflower and truffle oils in a thin stream until you have a thick mayonnaise. Transfer to a bowl and refrigerate until ready to use.

STEP 3
To make the patties, shape the ground (minced) beef into **12** patties.

STEP 4
Preheat a large, dry skillet (frying pan) over high heat (or preheat a flat top to high).

STEP 5
Press the patties onto the skillet and season heavily with salt and pepper. Cook the patties until caramelized on the bottom, then turn over, place a slice of Gorgonzola on top of each patty, and continue to cook until the other sides of the patties are caramelized.

STEP 6
Meanwhile, heat a dry skillet, add the pancetta and pan-fry until crispy.

STEP 7
Just before the patties have finished cooking, put **1** tablespoon of the balsamic onions, **1** tablespoon of the aioli, and **1** slice of crispy pancetta on top of the cheese for each patty, then top with a bun lid.

STEP 8
To assemble each burger, spread the bottom half of a bun with **1** tablespoon of the aioli, then add a few arugula (rocket) leaves, and finish with an already-assembled top half of the burger.

4

Eating the Burger

The Basic Burger, Dissected & Explained

What is a burger? It might seem a curious question to ask, but given the recent surge in experimentation, the burger has seen so many departures from its basic identity that it's worth stating: the essentials are a beef patty and a bun. A patty on bread or toast is close to some of the burger's points of departure, but without the bun it doesn't achieve full "burgerness."

Of the variants that then go into this basic concept, cheese, bacon, onion, and a few sauces are truest to the ways in which the burger first manifested itself in the hot-food carts and roadside diners of early twentieth-century America. These days, the proliferation of options has taken the burger into wild and exciting new areas, and flavor combinations, but this is the basic burger, dissected and explained.

How We Taste

There are about 10,000 taste buds on the human tongue, throat, and the lining of the mouth, each containing between 50 and 150 chemoreceptors. When we chew, our saliva dissolves our food and creates different molecular bindings with these receptors; specialist cells called sensory neurons then transmit information about them along the thalamus in the brain to the primary gustatory cortex. In a nutshell, this information tells us what things taste like.

As writer Michael Pollan says in *Cooked*, "Strictly speaking, 'taste' is limited to one or more of the five senses perceptible to the tongue: sweet, salt, sour, bitter, and umami." These five "tastes" all correspond to different chemoreceptors, which is how we derive our ability to differentiate tastes. Flavor is, simply put, taste plus the input of the other senses, most importantly smell. Our ability to taste is hardwired and innate, but our ability to discern flavor, and to attribute flavor based on previous memories is learned. This combining effect, when referring to taste and flavor, is often called "synesthetic"; synesthesia is actually a neurological condition whereby someone perceives by substitution: for example, seeing sounds as colors, or smelling musical chords, or tasting coffee when tickled. But the term has become more generally used to describe perception achieved by more than one sense. Added to this mélange are the "trigeminal" qualities (so-called because they are perceived by the trigeminal nerve in the muscles of the jaw) of some foods, like heat from mustard, mint's cooling sensation, or the rasping quality of tannins in red wine.

Author Niki Segnit, in *The Flavor Thesaurus*, describes the taste of beef as "predominantly salty and umami-ish, with some sweetness and sourness…. Its flavor is clean, yeasty, and meaty, with a slight metallic edge." The tongue collects most of this information, and the fatty, gelatinous quality of the meat heavily stimulates the production of saliva in a way drier foods generally do not, thereby enhancing the chemoreceptors' ability to convey taste to the brain. Beef, due to its complexity of taste, tends to go well with everything, be it the sourness of pickles (gherkins), the heat of mustard, or the oily sweetness of ketchup.

While most flavor is actually perceived in the olfactory (scent) glands, the strong association between the gustatory (taste) glands and flavor is probably enforced by the physical act of chewing. Among other things, chewing seems to bind flavors in a way that can be beneficial, and there is strong evidence that salty flavors like bacon and umami flavors like beef are better grounded in the gustatory sensors when chewed with bread. This probably explains why a beef patty is more satisfying when encased in a fluffy bun than naked on the plate; the act of chewing the whole mouthful draws deeper levels of taste onto the tongue.

Chewing also creates a stirring up of the food and, because a burger contains many different tastes, the receptors in the mouth receive different levels of stimulation: in one mouthful, you might get a peppery cheddar, followed by some umami-ish beef, and then the saltiness of bacon. There is evidence that a multiplicity of tastes colliding and competing like this has an elevating effect on all of them.

Chewing has a further importance: the noise it makes. The crunch of the salad and pickles in a burger carries positive associations; we respond positively to the hard sounds we hear when we chew.

In effect, the burger, with its variety of tastes, its crunchiness, its saliva-stimulating fattiness, seems to have been created to set off a symphony of flavor in our mouths. Even the fact that we hold a burger up to our mouth, giving the nose ample time to draw in the flavor, not forgetting the tactile pleasure of the food in our hands, contributes to our synesthetic pleasure. Perhaps even the gooeyness of the sauce that runs over our fingers is a reminder of excess or the ferocious sating of hunger that echoes in the more primeval parts of our psyche. The hamburger is, truly, a feast for the senses.

Beef

Eating the Burger

A burger is made of beef. While there are now chicken burgers, vegetarian burgers using Portobello mushrooms or tofu, burgers created from bison or kangaroo, or even clams, the first and authentic burgers came from beef cattle. There is some debate about where the best beef comes from. Famously, Kobe beef, made from hand-reared Wagyu cattle of the Tajima strain in the prefecture of Hyogo in Japan, is often cited for its quality, the longer fattening period of the cattle that results in higher levels of unsaturated fat, and its beautiful marbling.

Kobe beef is like Champagne, in that it should come from only that one area in Japan and is subject to strict controls, but due to differing copyright laws between Japan and the rest of the world, much beef that is not strictly Kobe ends up being called by that name. Also, many culinary writers and chefs disagree as to whether Kobe beef, or any of the other Wagyu breeds in Japan, is actually the best for burgers. Aberdeen Angus, Italian Fassone beef from near Turin, and, of course, grass-fed Argentine cattle from the pampas all have their advocates too. Across the world there are also strains of cattle bred from Wagyu herds, including enormous, commercially reared herds in the United States.

The blend of meat cuts used in a burger is perhaps more important than where the beef actually comes from. Generally, grass-fed, hand-reared beef is best, and fattier breeds make for burgers with more moisture, which is, of course, critical in the cooking process. A blend of 70 percent lean cuts to 30 percent fatty cuts is generally considered the best ratio for a medium to medium-rare burger, though some advocate a 60/40 split for increased juiciness. Chuck, the slightly fatty musculature of the cow's shoulders, often forms the biggest proportion of the lean content, but brisket and round (rump, silverside, or topside) also add flavor. Navel (flank) is the creamiest fat provider, but short rib also works well; both add moisture, which helps balance out the drier but tastier lean element. Grinding (mincing), which allows anyone, even the very young and the old, to eat the patty meat, creates this meld of different cuts and facilitates the various ways of cooking the burger, too.

When cooking the patty, it is crucial to retain as much of the moisture as possible, while also allowing the juices that come out of the meat to add flavor. Pan-frying is a classic method, and probably closest to the way the first commercially available burgers would have been made. Compressing the patty in the skillet (frying pan) sears the meat and squeezes a little of the juice out to add flavor as the burger fries in its own fat. The more commercial variant of this requires a flat-top griddle, but the principles are the same. Flame-grilling over charcoal, the classic home method, gives a smokier taste to the meat, but the additional fatty flavor that comes from frying is lost. It's also possible to steam the patties, but although this keeps the burger moist, there is little in the way of additional flavoring, either of smoke or from the meat wallowing in its own fatty juices. Broiling (grilling) is another popular method, and, after steaming, the healthiest, but again, unless the meat is excellent and well seasoned, the flavor can be a little less complex.

Essentially, the classic beef patty needs little in the way of augmentation. Basic seasoning, and perhaps a little nutmeg or mustard for extra bite, are all that are generally added to the simplest variations. As just mentioned, some cooking methods will add more to flavor than others, but provided that the meat is of good quality and the blend of lean and fat is well balanced, it's difficult to go wrong. Obviously, the better the meat, the better the burger, but it's also true that the right blend of cuts can render even lesser quality meat tasty. The secret of the burger's accessibility lies in that truth, as much as it does in anything else.

Opposite: Raw beef patties.

Pat LaFrieda

Butcher and meat wholesaler

Pat LaFrieda is a fourth-generation meat wholesaler. Based in New Jersey, Pat LaFrieda Meat Purveyors makes 75,000 hamburgers a day, and provides meat and burger patties to 600 restaurants including Shake Shack, The Spotted Pig, and Union Square Cafe.

LaFrieda was never meant to be a butcher, let alone New York's finest and the one most synonymous with the "hamburger revolution" of the early twenty-first century. He comes from a family that has worked in the meat trade for generations and his fondest childhood memories are of watching his father at work:

BEING A BROOKLYN NATIVE, I WAS FORTUNATE ENOUGH TO GROW UP IN BENSONHURST, A PLACE WHERE THERE WERE PLENTY OF ITALIAN AMERICAN BAKERIES. IT IS THERE THAT I LEARNED THE LESSONS OF FRESHNESS BY EATING MY WAY THROUGH LOAVES AND LOAVES OF WARM, FRESH SEMOLINA BREAD. I EQUATE FRESH BREAD TO FRESHLY GROUND [MINCED] BEEF. THE FIRST DAY OF THE LIFE OF A LOAF OF BREAD IS ITS BEST. EVERY DAY AFTER THAT, IT LOSES JUST A LITTLE BIT OF QUALITY, TEXTURE AND FLAVOR, UNTIL DAYS LATER IT IS INEDIBLE. FRESH-GROUND BEEF HAS THE SAME PROPERTIES AND THAT IS REASON ENOUGH FOR YOU TO MAKE IT AT HOME.

MY FONDEST MEMORIES OF MY CHILDHOOD INVOLVE ME EATING RAW FRESH-GROUND BEEF OUT OF THE GRINDER [MINCER] IN MY DAD'S BUTCHER SHOP. HE WOULD GRIND [MINCE] FRESH DOMESTIC BEEF THROUGH HIS INDUSTRIAL-SIZE GRINDERS INTO THE PALM OF HIS HAND, THEN SPRINKLE A PINCH OF SALT OVER THE TOP AND SHARE A FEW OUNCES OF LOVE WITH ME. AT THE AGE OF TEN, I WAS EATING WHAT EVERY FINE RESTAURANT SERVED FOR STEAK TARTARE, BUT BETTER.

ON A LADDER, NEXT TO THE GRINDER, I WOULD CLIMB UP AND PEEK INTO THE MACHINE AS IT MIXED THE BEEF. THROUGH THE HOLES IN THE TOP, I WAS ABLE TO SNIFF THE SWEET AROMAS AND CHARACTERISTICS OF THE FRESH-GROUND BEEF. IT CAN BEST BE DESCRIBED AS SMELLING LIKE A CROSS BETWEEN THE CENTER, RARE PART OF A ROAST BEEF AND THE SWEETNESS OF FALL CORN. IF I HADN'T BEEN THERE TO EXPERIENCE IT FIRST HAND, I WOULD NEVER HAVE KNOWN WHAT I WAS MISSING.

Nevertheless, his father's sights were set elsewhere: "My dad's goal was to raise his four children and send them to the best schools he could afford. I was the generation that was afforded the chance to go and do that better thing." LaFrieda, Jr., graduated with a degree in finance and, despite having worked in and around the family butchery business all his life, went into stockbroking: "I thought wearing a suit to work was the coolest thing, but selling intangibles to strangers over the phone was the worst."

It was hardly a surprise when after a year on Wall Street, Pat LaFrieda, Jr. traded in his suit for an apron, and went back to the family business, albeit with new skills, as he explains: "Working in the family business was the only thing that ever made sense to me, but now I was doing it with an education. So I could bring the marketing aspect, the financial aspect, and some fresh blood to the business."

LaFrieda's career in meat has therefore been a meeting point—the old, traditional values and knife skills of his father and grandfather blended with his own take on marketing and business. That's not to say, of course, that he doesn't understand meat, but when the hamburger revolution occurred, Pat was in the perfect position to take advantage. That's why the LaFrieda meatpacking and butchery business is now seventy times the size it was when he rejoined.

As he explains, "My grandfather was renowned for making the most amazing ground beef—he ground this consistent grind of muscle, rather than trim, so he could control the quality, the flavor, the texture." Historically, burgers became mass-produced by taking a certain amount of

Eating the Burger

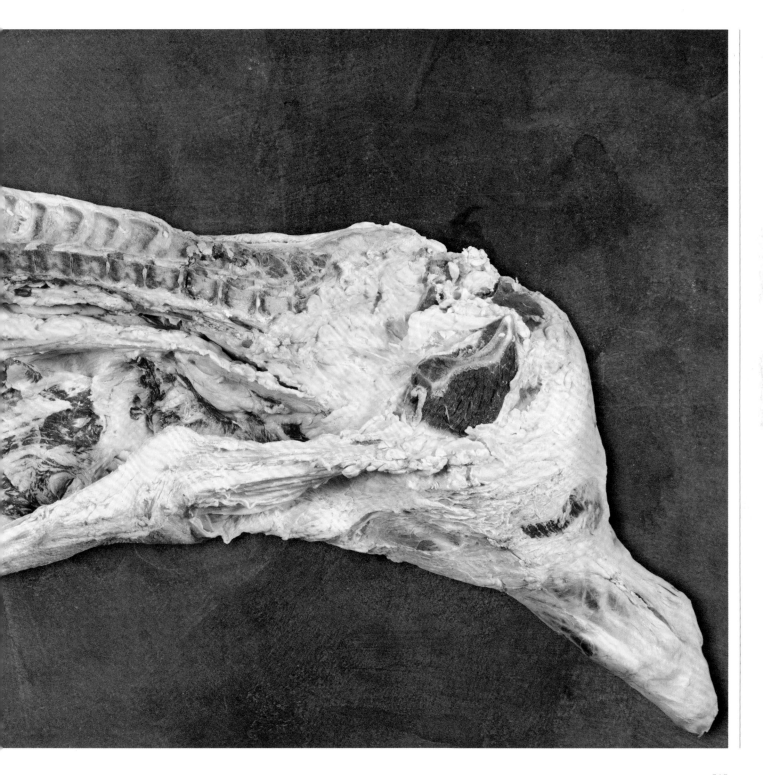

lean cow meat and mixing it with a certain amount of fat. The origin of those ingredients has changed over the life of the burger in the United States. As LaFrieda says, "In the '50s, it might have been 100 percent domestic, but now that might well be down to about 10 percent; the rest is imported trimmings. They use different breeds, different animals, being introduced to the blend. If you're on the commodities market for the cheapest stuff, there won't be any consistency."

For this reason, LaFrieda's take on creating the perfect patty doesn't reside in fat content, as many chefs and butchers advocate, but rather in choosing and blending the right cuts: "You're not getting the homogenous flavor because of how fat and protein cook out. So using cuts with whole muscle fat in them you get a better flavor, less chalky."

Because of this tried and tested method of making patties, when the burger's popularity surge happened, LaFrieda's meat already had a stellar reputation; now there was simply more demand. One of the first key vendors of his ground beef was Shake Shack. LaFrieda's already provided the meat for Union Square Cafe and so, when that company opened its now famous kiosk in the park, it came to the same source. LaFrieda was staggered by the shack's popularity, as he explains:

I took my dad down to see it because I wanted him to see how great a job we were doing. He couldn't conceive of waiting that long for a burger, like two hours! Up until that point, our policy was to make chopped beef and sell it in bulk 10-pound [4.5-kilogram] bags, and if restaurants wanted them formed they would form them in house. When I suggested to Dad that we do patties, he said, "What are we going to do next, go to the restaurant and cook for them?

With popularity and increased sales came the need for modernization, which in a traditional field like butchery, especially in a family company like LaFrieda's, can be a tough sell. As LaFrieda himself admits: "I remember breaking the news to my dad that we had ordered a shaping machine (costing $100,000)—we couldn't get the machine through the door. Dad gave me this look. I was on the phone to the translator in Germany to

disassemble the machine and break it up to get it through the door." Nonetheless, it meant that rather than forming patties by hand using a cookie cutter, the team could now rattle out 500 or 600 pounds (225 or 275 kilograms) in twenty minutes, a huge improvement.

There's no stopping LaFrieda or the burger. As he says, "The ultimate economy cut is a hamburger. Before, it was viewed as a family meal, but then owners like Danny Meyer or chefs like April Bloomfield came over and popularized it. It is a center-of-the-plate protein item now." With all the hard work comes the reward, not just of a flourishing business, but of being able to marry traditional skills with a fresh business outlook. It's taken LaFrieda to the very top of the game and, while it's a long way from a suit on Wall Street, it's exactly where he's supposed to be.

Previous spread: Facility cow.

Pat LaFrieda's tips on how to grind meat for burgers →

Whether you have a food processor, meat-grinder attachment or a hand grinder, the most common urban legend is that you need to chill the grinder knives and grinder plates before using them. This is false: it is the meat that should be chilled. Chilling the parts of the grinder could make them more brittle, increasing the risk of metal flakes and shavings falling into the meat. Spend the time you would have spent chilling the parts making sure they are sanitized.

Whatever apparatus you use, the meat should not be cubed; instead, it should be cut into strips, as wide as the hole of the feed neck and as long as possible. This is so that once you feed the meat into the machine, the "screw" will grab the tip of the strip and pull the rest of it in. You shouldn't have to force the meat in because the apparatus will already have a great grip on the strip.

Once you have your meat cut into strips, place them on a plate and put them in the freezer for a good five minutes. What you are looking for is not to freeze the meat, but to chill it so that it begins to get firm. This process will strengthen the integrity of the muscle cells and prevent them from emulsifying (separating the fat from the lean meat) under all the pressure of the grinder.

Always use two different-size grinder plates. Since it is best to grind the meat twice, a great way to reduce the coarseness is to do it in two stages. Regardless of what size you decide on as your final grind, use the coarser grind plate first. This again ensures the integrity of the muscles and prevents the meat from emulsifying.

My favorite cuts of meat to grind are chucks, clods with the flat irons still attached, briskets and boneless short ribs in equal parts. My favorite burger is an 8-ounce (225-gram) patty that is 1 inch (2.5 centimeters) tall and 4 inches (10 centimeters) in diameter, cooked rare with a heavy sear. I salt my burger before cooking and hold off on the black pepper until afterward to avoid the bitterness that comes with high heat. A dollop of mayo, melted American cheese, fresh baby arugula (rocket), sliced grape tomatoes on a potato roll is my comfort recipe.

Eating the Burger

> **"Round, puffed, a tempting golden brown with an eye-catching sprinkle of sesame seeds, it is the focus, the center, the treasure chest that holds the precious burger with its attendant savories."**
>
> ↓
> **Elizabeth Rozin**

The bun is what transforms the basic meat patty into a burger. Previous incarnations, proto-burgers if you will, saw the patty sitting alone on a plate, or atop a slice of bread or toast, but prior to the adoption of the bun, it's hard to make a case that what was being consumed was, in fact, a burger. The bun is the case for the patty, crucial to its being edible by hand: it protects the eater from the sticky squidge of juices and sauces, and it keeps all the potential fillings and toppings ensconced within the burger. Its round, soft, slightly golden appearance has a lure, too. And bread is one of mankind's first staples, the transformation of wheat into a carbohydrate one of the markers of the move from hunter-gatherer to agrarian society. Without bread, there would be no cities. Without bread, there would be no buns and, hence, no burgers. The discovery of how to leaven bread allowed for fluffier, lighter dough, and the addition of yeast refined the process further, enhancing its aesthetic and sensory appeal. The stage was set for the burger bun, but it took a while to reach its peak.

Culinary history traditionally credits the fourth Earl of Sandwich with the invention of the food form that bears his name: he is said, in the eighteenth century, to have devised a delivery method for meat that meant he could eat without leaving the card table. But the idea of putting meat or fish between bread has a longer history. Rooted in agricultural workers' need to carry their lunch into the fields with them, without having recourse to silverware (cutlery) or plates, the sandwich is really peasant food, despite its pretensions to an aristocratic origin. In medieval England, food was often served, either in grand halls or small farmsteads, on a hunk of slightly stale bread known as a trencher, rather than a plate. The trencher soaked up the juice of cooked meats and provided a heavier, filling base for meals that were otherwise rich in protein and not much else. This combination of portability, economy, and balance in the diet meant that the idea of using bread to form a house for meat carried on, even as society progressed. The men and women lining up at American hot-food carts in the 1920s were being served their food in a form that had its origins hundreds of years before.

The sandwich, of which the burger is obviously a derivative form that uses one specific type of hot food as its filling, works because it provides a housing into which all manner of ingredients can be stuffed, but it also has an immediacy, creating a tangible relationship between food and feeder, which adds to the pleasure. The soft give of a burger bun, the squeeze applied by the eater to compress and mingle and make it small enough to fit into the mouth, are physical sensations that do not normally accompany food and that increase the pleasure of the act of eating. The burger would not be the same without it.

And what are the best buns? A bun should be soft and stretchy enough to absorb the burger's juices and the sauces without disintegrating on the way to the mouth. Pillowy and sweet, it should also add texture and flavor. Brioche has its advocates, as do Portuguese buns, and some maintain that commercial brands like Martin's potato rolls make the best buns. In truth, as long as the dough is soft, with a hint of sugar, firm enough to hold its shape but giving enough for that glorious squeezing sensation, your patty will be in safe hands.

cheese

Not everyone likes cheese on their burgers, but since the cheeseburger was invented, either by Lionel Sternberger or at Kaelin's or Humpty Dumpty's in the 1930s, there is no doubt that it has become the most ubiquitous variant on the basic hamburger. The classic type of cheese to use is "American," a processed form traditionally made from a variety of white cheeses like cheddar; the yellow coloration comes from the addition of annatto, a peppery, slightly nutty natural flavoring and colorant. As American cheese is technically a combination of other cheeses and thus made differently to "natural" or unprocessed cheese, the product has to be referred to as "processed cheese" or sometimes simply American slices or singles.

The processed cheese comes in individual square sheets, which is one of the two reasons it is perfect for burgers. As it is draped over the rounded patty, which sits in a rounded bun, the squared edges melt and droop over the hot meat, creating an enticing splash of color. This melting property is the other reason that American cheese works so well: it has a much lower melting temperature than natural cheeses. Often added while the patty is still on the grill, it needs no more heat than that transferred from the piping-hot meat. Without the application of direct heat, other popular cheeses, such as natural cheddar, do not melt enough to create the right consistency.

Of course, other cheeses are popular, especially for those attempting a more gourmet style of burger, or because of the specific flavor combinations that can be achieved. Cheddar, for example, has a certain saltiness and a stronger taste that means it can hold up against flavorsome sauces. Brie, which also has a good, low melting temperature for burgers, is creamier, but with a tangy aroma that works well with salty bacon over savory beef. Daniel Boulud's Frenchie burger (see page 273) uses the rich blue-veined Morbier. His db burger adds Parmesan to flavor its bun, and many cooks seeking to enhance the umami quality of their burger also choose Parmesan for its deep, savory taste. Feta, which does not really melt, but rather softens to a crumble, is often found on lamb burgers to create a hint of the Mediterranean.

A good cheese can elevate a burger and provide a different texture and taste sensation, but sometimes, a basic, well-melted slice of processed American is the simplest way to guarantee the right result. Cheese, the result of a highly specialized form of food production, shows once again that the burger can play host to each and every type of nourishment available to us. Fatty, tasty, and rather indulgent, it also demonstrates the burger's enduring power to satisfy our desire to push food to its excess.

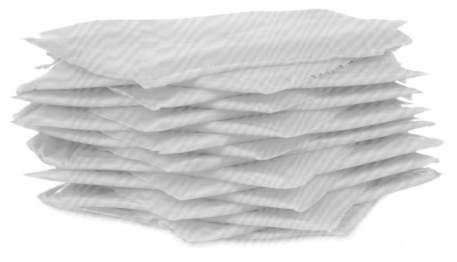

Bacon

The bacon cheeseburger is one of the most common and simplest variants of the hamburger. Bacon, usually smoked and in thin strips cut from pork side (belly) in the United States, and unsmoked and in thicker slices (rashers) in Europe, is made from salted, cured pork, which is sometimes air-dried for a period after curing. Bacon adds yet more meat to the hamburger, but its saltiness offsets the fatty, savory flavor of the cheese and beef. Bacon is very rarely found without cheese in a burger, perhaps because the additional creaminess of the cheese avoids the meal becoming too meat-heavy.

A & W Restaurants, which originated in Sacramento, California, but went nationwide after 1923, claim to have served the first commercially available bacon cheeseburger in 1963. Called a Teen Burger, it was one of four "family" burgers, along with Papa, Mama, and Baby, though only the Teen contained bacon. The standard McDonald's menu does not include a bacon cheeseburger, although regional variants exist, such as the Australian Double Beef 'n' Bacon Burger, as well as special menu items that crop up from time to time on promotion, such as the Bacon Clubhouse Burger. Burger King, on the other hand, serves a Bacon Cheeseburger, which also comes in Double and Ultimate versions, and a version of the Whopper that contains bacon and cheese, with all the salad garnish normally found in a Whopper.

Bacon sometimes has umami additives to make it even tastier, and its blend of sugars, fats, and salt make it extraordinarily addictive, especially when further flavored with sweeteners like maple syrup.

"If you record the sound of bacon in a frying pan and play it back, it sounds like the pops and cracks on an old 33 1/3 recording. You could substitute it for that sound."

➡ Tom Waits, musician

Lettuce

Vegetarian burgers typically have a fat, juicy Portobello mushroom drenched in tangy, stringy cheese, or perhaps a slab of feta, grilled with fresh herbs. But a great burger often has both lettuce and tomato.

The crisp crunch of lettuce, usually iceberg or peppery arugula (rocket) in a more upscale burger, does add flavor, but it's more about a change in texture. Beef, cheese, and the bun are each quite soft and chewy, yet it's a good handful of lettuce that offers the mouth a different component to enjoy.

Eating the Burger

Tomato

Tomatoes have had a place in burgers for even longer than lettuce, due in part to the similarity in flavor with the ketchup garnish. They also offer a different texture and, if juicy and ripe, a slight tang that can beautifully offset beef's savory taste.

Some people might argue that neither lettuce nor tomato are necessary, but they certainly have a place in the burger affections of many.

onion

Onions form both an element of some patties and a topping of many burgers as well. Before the development of cheeseburgers, a slop of onions, often pulled from the same hot plate as the meat was cooked on, would be the only ingredient many of the original diners and burger restaurants added to a burger. Especially when slightly caramelized, best done by slowly frying in butter, the softened, sugary onion can add a different level of texture and flavor. Its sweetness offsets the umami quality of beef and the yeasty quality of the bun, but it is also common to find onions cooked into patties for a different flavor effect. Rather than creating the soft, almost gooey texture of a caramelized onion topping, this alternative gives the burgers crunch and a slight acidity. Onions cooked into patties are more often found in homemade recipes than in restaurant burgers, but provide a satisfying crunch wherever they are.

Pickle

Pickles (gherkins), or pickled cucumbers, are what you get when you put a West Indian or burr cucumber—like a garden cucumber but smaller—into a brine or vinegar solution and leave it to get really tasty. As with onions, the purpose is to add a shard of different flavor to the largely savory, umami burger, in this instance a sour, vinegary one. Traditionally a German or Eastern European delicacy, pickles are also very popular in Japanese and Middle Eastern cuisine, and are often made at home. They hark back to a time when people stocked up on food that could be preserved for the winter, but the flavors, while never subtle, can also be used to wonderful effect in an age when anything we might want is now available year-round at the local supermarket or delicatessen. A vital addition to most people's burgers, onions and pickles show that the balance of tastes in a burger is as important as good beef and a good bun.

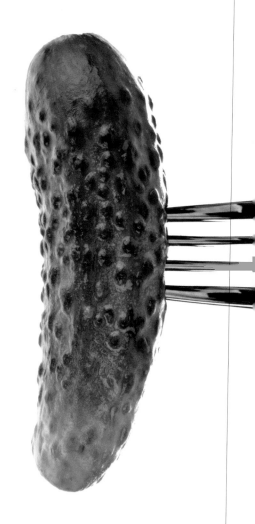

Heinz Ketchup

There may be fifty-seven Heinz varieties, but only one is synonymous with the hamburger, the Tomato Ketchup. The tomato was discovered in Mexico by Spanish conquistadors in the sixteenth century and initially thought by many in the Old World to be a poisonous plant. This delusion persisted until the late nineteenth century, when it was discovered that not only did tomatoes not kill you, they also made an excellent, sweet base for an array of spiced sauces that were popular among Americans and Northern Europeans.

The word "ketchup" comes from the Indonesian *kicap* or *kecap*, a thick soy sauce often used to flavor meat and fish. This gave its name to an array of different sauces produced to spice up the flavor of preserved, and often salted meat, adding both moisture and gustatory interest. The sweet and sour flavor of tomato ketchup developed and became immensely popular. Heinz introduced its first Tomato Ketchup in 1876 and brought out a variant without preservatives in 1906. It is the company's most popular product, with well over 650 million bottles sold each year in more than 140 countries.

French's Mustard

The launch of French's mustard, known then as French's "Cream Salad Brand" mustard, was auspicious given its long associations with hamburgers and fries (chips). George French, the condiment's inventor, revealed it to the public at the St. Louis World's Fair in 1904, a location and date well known to hamburger fans for the claims of Fletcher Davis (see page 25), who asserted that he brought the meal to world prominence there. In 1926, French's was sold to the English firm Colman's, already well-known mustard makers.

With its distinctive bright yellow bottle and tangy, acidic taste, the mustard is well suited to the fatty and savory flavors of a hamburger, and not too sharp or spicy to dominate in the taste buds to the detriment of the rest of the meal. The mustard was initially served with hot dogs, but quickly made the obvious leap to hamburgers.

In 2015, Heinz developed a sweet mustard at the same time that French's brought out a tomato ketchup.

Fries

Fries (chips) are known throughout North America as French fries. Indeed, though fries are intrinsically associated with North America's most popular food, potatoes are originally from South America and were only popularized in Europe after they were discovered by the Spanish in Peru in the early sixteenth century. In the early nineteenth century, the French, ever the gastronomic pioneers, found that tossing potatoes in oil made them fluffy and light, rather than stolid and starchy. The process was refined and the potato strips got thinner until, by the end of that century, they came to resemble what we now know as French fries. Potatoes were certainly eaten in this form in the United States at this time, but it was the return of soldiers from the battlefields of Europe after World War I that really saw the popularity of the French fry soar.

This coincided with the development of safer, cleaner deep fryers, which allowed the potato, with its perfect marriage of water and starch content, to blossom into the vastly popular, omnipresent side we know today. Fries—which, like the burger, you can eat with your fingers—are the perfect accompaniment—a combination of sweet fattiness and salty flavors that both enhance and complement the fatty but more savory flavors of the burger. Waxy potatoes, like the Idaho baking potato most often used to make French fries, have a higher sugar content than many other varieties, which adds a pleasingly caramelized tang. Fries also provide the hamburger meal with its most realized form of vegetable, salad greens (leaves) aside (and the tomato, which is a fruit anyway), adding balance and satisfying our desire to consume all the major food groups in the tastiest way possible.

Coke

There are many soft drinks associated with burgers, but one stands head and shoulders above the rest and that is Coke, the most democratic of soft drinks. Immensely popular across the globe, there is only one country in the world where Coke or a Coca-Cola Company-owned soft drink is not the number-one seller: in Scotland, the orange-colored Irn Bru, manufactured by A. G. Barr, outsells everything and also goes very well with hamburgers. Coca-Cola products are available in almost every country in the world.

Coke was created in 1886 as a medicinal drink containing kola nuts and coca leaves, and was carbonated to make it more refreshing. It is now sold by the central company as a concentrate to licensed bottlers around the world. The bottlers then add water and sweeteners and distribute the drink in cans or bottles or sell it through taps in restaurants or licensed premises. Earl R. Dean created the brand's famous bottle in 1915, basing it on a cocoa pod, having been unable to find a picture of either a kola nut or a coca leaf.

As with other large brands like McDonald's, Coke is associated throughout the world with the United States, and its branding and bottle have become synonymous with the country and, by extension, with globalization and capitalism. Indeed, there are many similarities between Coca-Cola and the large burger brands: they are all heavily involved in sports sponsorship, celebrity endorsement, and cross-promotional activity with films and television programs. There are even a number of recipes for burgers that require the patty mix to be flavored with Coke; there is, it seems, no end to the links between the hamburger and the soft drink. Sweet, refreshingly carbonated, and enervating, Coke is the perfect drink with which to wash down the pleasantly heavy and fatty mix of a hamburger meal.

Nick Solares

Food writer and photographer

Nick Solares is a photographer and food writer with a particular interest in the burger. He is also restaurant editor of Eater, New York and host of *The Meat Show*. Solares has been documenting great burgers across the United States, with a specific focus on New York, since the mid-1980s, despite hailing originally from the United Kingdom.

For Solares, perhaps especially because he comes from elsewhere, there's something indisputably American about the burger: "It's a delicious object ... the closest thing America has to a national dish. It's ground [minced] beef and a hamburger bun. You can do anything you want to a hamburger and it's still a hamburger if those two components are fulfilled."

Solares feels that local, cultural cuisine has been important in developing the burger's flavor profile and interest. He says, "You can fulfill the architectural obligations of the hamburger but add a local resonance, like steamed-cheese burgers in Connecticut or chilies in Arizona. That's the symbiotic power of the burger."

Interestingly, for Solares, what he wants to eat and what he wants to write about are not always the same thing: "What I want in a hamburger is the simplest, most elemental version of the burger. But it would be very boring to only write about that.... If I'm looking at the hamburger intellectually, then it's about the regional expressions. But if I'm looking at it as a comfortable object in my life, then it's the one around the corner from my house." And he does look at burgers intellectually. It's hard to disagree with Solares when he says that when "people write about food in a sociological way, it's implicitly an intellectual exercise.... I'm talking about the history of a restaurant or the theory of sustainability, not just whether something tastes nice."

It's not only the history of restaurants that is sublimated into the history of the burger. Solares says, "The burger's story is the story of America. Unlike any comfort food I can think of, it's postindustrial. White Castle invented the hamburger in that respect—everyone can recognize it. And then it became the national dish. It also became a common thread that ran through American culture." He continues, "It's a triumph of capitalism and industry as well. The slider was born of austerity. By the postwar era, you start to see burgers becoming bigger. Now the average burger in a restaurant is 8 ounces [225 grams], 2 ounces [50 grams] too big as far as I'm concerned. I'm not sure it could have happened anywhere outside the U.S., the beef, a transient society, the invention of lunch (which is very American)—it's the mobile society."

The resurgence of the burger came, in part, against the backdrop of a new austerity, as Solares explains: "The crash of 2008 coincided with the Minetta Tavern opening and April Bloomfield making the burger the centerpiece of that menu. Everyone was eating steaks and suddenly everyone's expense accounts dried up.... And the burger is cheaper, but people also needed comforting, almost a reversion to childhood. It's implicitly nostalgic. The first hamburgers you eat resonate in your memory. There's something about when times get tough, people want nostalgia, and they don't have a lot of money, so the burger is ideal."

Whatever it says, there's no doubt that Solares' intelligent take on the hamburger will continue to be relevant to our appreciation of this most American of food items. As he says, "Food tells a much greater story than just keeping us alive."

Josh Ozersky

Food writer and burger connoisseur

Josh Ozersky was an American food writer, and he was considered a preeminent hamburger expert until his death in 2015. He was the author of *The Hamburger: A History* and was the founding editor of *New York* magazine's Grub Street blog and a columnist for *Time* and *Esquire*.

Ozersky was an academic by inclination, a carnophile by proclivity, and one of the funniest, most gifted food writers of his generation. He bestrode serious commentary on the hamburger like a beefy colossus.

His slim but packed 2009 volume *The Hamburger* stands out among its small peer group for its range of references and the sheer pizzazz of his writing. Ozersky was clearly infatuated with all kinds of meat, but his great ability was to extrapolate from food wider cultural and historical importance. *The Hamburger* did just that, situating its subject in a wider commentary with an array of sources and allusions that were testament to the author's lifelong passion for food and to his learning. As he said in an article for *Vanity Fair* in 2009, "If you really get the hamburger, if you acknowledge its godlike semiotic power, its ubiquity, its iconic combination of a matchless pillowy white bun and a craggy, sizzling pan of brown and unctuous meat … I mean, that's America."

Born in Miami, Ozersky chose not to pursue a career in academia, drawn by the bright neon and even brighter food scene of New York in the early '90s. Ozersky's advocacy of cooking and eating meat led to his founding Meatopia, a festival of carnivorous culinary confections that bills itself as the "Woodstock of Edible Animals." He also worked as a consultant on the South Beach and New York Wine & Food Festivals.

Despite his many commitments, Ozersky always stayed true to the basic premise that a food critic should get out there and eat the stuff he or she enjoys and then write lovingly about it. A piece on Shake Shack from *Esquire* in February 2015 shows the evocative quality of his prose, so descriptive you can almost taste the food:

A HAMBURGER IS SUPPOSED TO BE BROWN, NOT GRAY; BROWN CRUST TASTES GOOD, AND PROVIDES A CRAGGY, TACTILE UNDERCRUNCH BELOW A VISCOUSLY SMOOTH LAYER OF MELTED AMERICAN CHEESE. (AND IT GOES WITHOUT SAYING THAT IT IS MEANT TO BE COVERED BY AMERICAN CHEESE, WHOSE MELTING PROPERTIES ARE, LITERALLY, DESIGNED FOR THE BLANKETING OF BURGERS.)

Ozersky passed away shortly before he was to attend the James Beard Awards, one of America's foremost celebrations of culinary achievement. He was also a former winner, this accolade testament to his standing in the industry. The reaction to his death was still greater testament to his enormous popularity. He is sadly missed by hamburger lovers everywhere.

5

The Idea of the Burger

There is something about a hamburger that stirs echoes in all of us. While not wholly atavistic, there is a basic pleasure to be derived from eating with our hands, a sense, particularly for children, of barriers broken down. There are good sensory reasons why eating with our hands is more pleasing: the food stays near our olfactory glands longer and produces a longer lasting, more intense flavor. But, to put it simply, we are all at one level when we are eating a hamburger.

There is social equality to the hamburger because of this lack of formality, of rules; the exclusivity of "fine dining" is tossed away and replaced with a *joie de vivre* of succulent meat, dripping sauce, and sticky fingers. Because of its portability, the burger is also often associated with trips to fairs or the beach, or with a meal snuck in before or after going to the movie theater. The burger suggests shared experiences beyond just the eating of it. This is why it is so strongly associated with childhood, fun and adventure, and family.

The television presenter Rylan Clark-Neal, on the 2015 series of *Celebrity MasterChef* in the United Kingdom, was asked to prepare a meal that evoked someone or something he loved. He made what, for copyright reasons, he termed a "Cheerful Meal," which reminded him of childhood birthday parties with his family. He tasted the fast food that he was basing his meal on, then sought to replicate it using advanced cooking techniques, including his own take on fast-food fries (chips). This involved blanching the peeled and sliced potatoes in boiling water, draining them, and soaking them in a mixture of sugar and corn (golden) syrup before freezing. He then cooked them from frozen to mimic the flavor of a burger restaurant's fries. He also replicated burger sauce and made his own ketchup. Not many cooks go to such lengths to evoke a happy childhood, but Rylan's efforts, and the positive reception of the judges, show that the hamburger's power to conjure up happy memories is unquestioned.

On a less cozy note, near the beginning of *Rabbit, Run* (1960), Harry Angstrom, the neurotic antihero of John Updike's novel, flees home. He feels hemmed in, by memories of an athletic college time he can't recover, by his alcoholic wife Janice, by an ailing career demonstrating culinary equipment in cheap stores, and by a pressing sense of his own unimportance. He drives away from his outwardly satisfying but claustrophobic family life. And then:

He stops at a diner whose clock says 8:04. He hadn't intended to eat until he got out of the state. He takes a map from the rack by the door and while eating two hamburgers at the counter studies his position.... The hamburgers had been fatter and warmer than the ones you get in Brewer, and the buns had seemed steamed. Things are better already.

Here the burger is both relative and absolute, a symbol for Angstrom of the potentially better life that he could have were he to move away, but also of something that exists everywhere in America, a comforting, reliable product of the suburban culture in which Angstrom resides.

Angstrom longs to forge his own life and identity in much the same way as the pioneers did heading west—the direction that he initially tries to drive in but ends up failing to because of having to follow roads. The West, the frontier, as the British-born observer of American life Alistair Cooke put it, is "a state of mind: the idea still of El Dorado, of getting away from it all, of leading a new and luckier life under that 'big sky,'" and this is what Angstrom craves. This was the great wrench of the 1950s and '60s, the postwar boom era whose neuroses and ructions Updike explores in his novel. As a symbol of both material gain and cultural homogeneity, the hamburger appears often throughout the art of this period.

But as culture changed and people began to question the ideas and myths with which the burger had always been so closely intertwined, so too the burger's place in that culture changed and it became a focal point for more critical questions.

Above: Creative
director Olle
Hemmendorff's
interpretation of
the Air Max 90,
commissioned by Nike
Sportswear, 2008.

Above: Fashion
designer Jeremy
Scott's Moschino
bags inspired
by McDonald's.

June 1-7, 2015 / **The Third Bush** Jeb is not the George. By Jennifer Senior

See No One, Go Out Never, Do Nothing: A Guide p.xx / Ultimate Dance-Music Playlist p.xx / New Books by Dead Authors p.xx

Saving Gordie Howe p.xx / **U.S.A., Sports Cop** p.xx / **The Margaret Mead of Park Ave.** p.xx

NEW YORK

The Amazing Journey of the Lowly Burger
Once a slab of garbage-meat, now a prized plaything of fancy chefs, Wall Street investors, and Silicon Valley engineers.
By Benjamin Wallace

THE 11 TYPES OF NEW YORK BURGERS

This town is now flooded with high-ambition ground-beef sandwiches. Here, a taxonomy of the new world.

By **ROBIN RAISFELD** *and* **ROB PATRONITE**

1. RATIONED
Intentionally scarce burgers that have developed cult followings.

American Cut's In-House Burger, $14
A daily tweet reveals each night's number of burgers available at the bar—a figure that hovers between 11 and 15. There's dry-aged rib eye in the blend, onions caramelized in bourbon, and beer cheese made from Fontina, Cheddar, and Brooklyn Lager.

Maialino's Late-Night Burger, $15
Nick Anderer's Italian take (Gorgonzola, house-cured pancetta, escarole, on rosemary brioche) is available only between 10:30 p.m. and midnight and only in the front barroom. Have a bowl of pasta for dessert.

Raoul's Burger au Poivre, $19
Competition is fierce for the dozen daily orders (and the nine bar stools where they're consumed). The patty's pepper-crusted, the cheese is triple-crème Saint-Andre, and the sidecar of au poivre sauce puts it deliciously over the top.

2. CLASSIC
New York's burger tradition traces back to bars and coffee shops like these.

Joe Jr.'s Cheeseburger, $5.50
The big, floppy burgers are perfect—loose and crumbly and smashed with gusto on the griddle by a guy who's juggling a western omelette and an order of flapjacks in between smooshes. And the hustle-bustle old-school coffee-shop atmosphere is unsurpassed.

P.J. Clarke's Cadillac Burger, $14.85
This bacon cheeseburger with decades of history has a coarse grind and a crusty sear. It also has the illusion of height, thanks to its jaunty perch atop a thick slice of raw onion on the plate—a trick, it's said, to keep the bottom bun high, dry, and unsoggy.

J.G. Melon's Cheeseburger, $11
No ballyhooed "blend," no fancy-pants bun, no name chef—just a couple of nimble grill cooks working a flattop with a grimy, weathered patina that must impart more than a little magic. The grind is loose, the shape lumpen, the surface nicely charred.

3. GOURMET PUB
Updates on the plainspoken, rib-sticking, hefty Irish pub burger of yore.

Two8Two Pub Burger, $13.50
The signature five-ounce burger with roasted poblanos is terrific, but for sheer beefy excess, the half-pound pub—an ecstasy of grease and fat just barely contained by its standard-issue squishy bun—can't be beat.

The Spotted Pig's Char-Grilled Burger, $21
Some say this dish earned the Pig its Michelin star, and on most nights there's at least one on every table. The short-rib-heavy half-pound patty stands up to its mantle of salty-creamy Roquefort, and don't bother asking—the chef won't hold the cheese.

The Breslin Bar & Dining Room's Char-Grilled Lamb Burger, $22
April Bloomfield's Spotted Pig sequel wears a veil of feta and rings of red onion, and aficionados who claim a burger is not a burger unless it's beef allow it as the exception to the rule.

ILLUSTRATION BY JASON POLAN

4. *GRASS-FED*
The p.c. burger for ecominded eaters.

Grazin's Uncle Dude, $21
Like the owner's Hudson Valley farm, whence comes the meat, this restaurant is Animal Welfare Approved and might possibly serve the most guilt-free burgers on the planet—even when adorned with Cheddar, bacon, jalapeño relish, and chipotle mayo.

Reynard's Gruyère Burger, $19
Whole animals from upstate farms like Kinderhook and Slope are broken down by an in-house butcher every week, which means chef Sean Rembold always knows exactly where his grind comes from.

El Colmado Butchery's Hamburguesa With Bacon and Cheese, $16
Seamus Mullen's "butcher's burger" hits all the obligatory locavore notes (New York State meat, house-cured bacon, house-pickled vegetables) and all the hoped-for organoleptic ones, thanks in part to some extra beef fat in the blend and on the bun.

Telepan's Bacon Cheeseburger, PRIX-FIXE ONLY
The Cheddar is Cabot, the bacon is Nueske's, the brioche bun is housemade, and the beef comes from a family-run Missouri farm. If you want a slice of tomato, come back when they're in season. Served as part of a $28 prix-fixe lunch or $32 prix-fixe brunch.

5. *OUT-OF-TOWNERS*
National chains that have improved the local landscape.

BurgerFi's Cheeseburger, $6.94
Concretes? Check. Chicago dogs? Check. This Florida import has taken many pages out of the Shake Shake playbook, but its cheese-burger holds its own: a double by default, with good beefy flavor and a proficient melt.

Steak 'n Shake's Single Burger With Cheese, $7.49
At this venerable midwestern chain and Shake Shack inspiration, the patties are pressed so flat they're almost 2-D, yet somehow still juicy—unless you're talking about the Signature Steakburger, a fancier blend permitted to retain its unsmashed plumpness.

Smashburger's Classic Smashburger, $5.39
Named for the classic fry-cook technique whereby a ball of fresh ground beef is, literally, smashed on a butter-slicked griddle for ten seconds. The resulting texture—crisp, lacy outer sear; loose, crumbly grind—is a marvel.

Umami Burger's Umami Burger, $11.50
The food-lab focus on the fifth taste can seem shticky, but the proof is in the juicy, loosely packed patty, bedecked with propri-etary powders, dusts, and sprays, not to mention shiitake mush-rooms, roasted tomatoes, and a Parmesan crisp.

6. *DRY-AGED*
The biggest trend today: burgers that taste like full-flavored beefsteaks.

Emily's Emmy Burger, $19
One approach to funky dry-aged beef: Juxtapose it with equally bold, bordering-on-baroque accoutrements like Grafton Ched-dar, cornichons, charred onions, and the Korean-inspired "Emmy" sauce. (Not to mention the pretzel bun.)

Church Street Tavern's Tavern Burger, $19
The wild-card addition of beef heart makes this house-ground dry-aged blend as rich and funky as any out there, Minetta in-cluded. Plus good Cheddar, bacon-onion relish, and a brioche bun with enough squish to satisfy the Martin's crowd.

The Gander's Cheeseburger, $16
Jesse Schenker's lunchtime burger is a beautiful thing: a thick puck of dry-aged beef, loosely packed to allow all those succulent fat molecules enough space to do their job. It's one of the best dry-aged-burger bargains in town.

Minetta Tavern's Black Label Burger, $28
Before Minetta, New York burgers weren't listed on menus as "dry-aged." Now it's commonplace. The Black Label is still remarkably rich and costs only two bucks more than the day it debuted in 2009, which is not nothing considering beef prices.

7. *HIGH-LOW*

Unassuming and familiar, like the burger-joint burgers of your youth, but tricked out.

The Brindle Room's Sebastian's Steakhouse Burger, $15

The key is not the upmarket dry-aged beef nor the super-crunchy pan-seared crust. It's the incongruence of processed American cheese, caramelized onions, and the squishy commercial bun.

Bowery Meat Company's Cheeseburger, $22

On paper, it sounds fancy: tomato aïoli; brioche bun; raclette cheese. But this might be the only 30-day dry-aged seven-ounce LaFrieda patty that gets swiped with mustard, In-N-Out style, before it's seared on the plancha.

Alder's Cheeseburger, $13

It may look ordinary, but, as often happens with a Wylie Dufresne production, looks are deceiving. The man grinds his own beef, mixes it with salted kelp to boost the umami factor, brushes his buns with beef fat, and makes his own American-style cheese.

Parm's Patty Melt, $25

The beef they use for this Tuesday-night-special patty melt goes where no patty-melt beef has gone before: into a LaFrieda meat locker, where it's aged for 60 days. Plus great smashed potatoes on the side.

8. *NEW-WAVE BAR*

As bar food has gotten better, so has the bar burger.

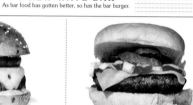

The NoMad Bar's NoMad Burger, $18

An elegant bar burger for an elegant bar: tall and imposing, but with the acquiescent bite of a fast-food burger and extra fat in the stealthy form of bone marrow and beef suet ground into the dry-aged blend.

Pork Slope's Cheeseburger, $11

Proust had his madeleines; Dale Talde has McDonald's cheeseburgers. This is his homage, down to the eerie precision with which he's replicated the familiar tang of the signature condiment mix of ketchup, mustard, and chopped onion.

Bar Sardine's Fedora Burger, $13

The smoked Cheddar and barbecue mayo are key and give this mouth-waterer its distinct flavor profile. In a nod, perhaps, to the Cuban-style burger variant called the frita, a cache of extra-crispy potato sticks adds textural complexity and audible crunch.

The Commodore's Cheeseburger, $7

The sort of saucy, fully dressed two-hander that expresses a commitment to condiments and a reliance on napkins. Chef Stephen Tanner has many deeply held burger beliefs; minimalism doesn't appear to be one of them.

9. *STACKED*

The double, a West Coast fast-food style, is challenging the single-patty hegemony.

El Quinto Pino's El Doble, $12

If gussied-up, ethnicized burgers are rarely good, this is the Basque-inspired exception. It comes with Idiazábal cheese, pickled onions, cornichons, and "salsa especial." (You can get it on Monday nights at sister restaurant Txikito, too.)

The Dutch's Double Cheddar Burger, $21

The special sauce is rich and tangy. The two slices of cheese are well melted. The sesame-seed bun from Orwasher's bakery is spot-on. What's most exciting about this burger, though, is that it's a dry-aged double—a unicorn of the stacked-burger world.

Hard Times Sundaes' Triple Burger With Cheese, $9.50

Three smashed patties, a molten seal of American cheese, a butter-basted Martin's potato roll. The secret ingredient? The cumulative flavor of a well-seasoned (i.e., never cleaned) flattop griddle.

Wilma Jean's Double Bacon Burger With Pimento Cheese, $15

The boutique bacon adds oomph without stealing the show. The Mississippi comeback sauce makes other special sauces seem less so. The tangy housemade pimento cheese holds it all together.

338   Cultural Impact

10. ODDBALL GENIUS
Not every burger conforms to convention.

Le Rivage's
French Onion Soup Burger, PRIX-FIXE ONLY
A canny impersonation of the bistro warhorse in hamburger form, with béchamel, stock-braised onions, and Emmenthaler, on a Thomas's English muffin. It's available only as part of a prix-fixe menu; $25 lunch, $29 dinner, and $39 pretheater.

DB Bistro Moderne's
the Original DB Burger, $35
When Daniel Boulud stuffed braised short ribs, foie gras, and preserved black truffles into a ground-sirloin shell, he forever changed the face of upscale burgerdom. It might not be a weekly habit, but it's definitely a bucket-list burger.

Ramen.Co's Original Ramen Burger, $8.04
American beef burger meets crisp-chewy grilled-ramen "bun." Worldwide hysteria ensues. The most perplexing thing about this mash-up of two of the most fetishized foods of recent history: What took so long?

Korzo's Original Korzo Burger, $16
Once you wrap a grilled burger in flaky dough as if it were an overgrown empanada and toss it in the deep fryer, does it really matter if the beef is grass-fed? Also sealed within: bacon and Emmenthaler cheese.

11. SHAKE SHACK STYLE
Danny Meyer sparked a small-pattied, squishy-bunned,
American-cheesed, special-sauced movement.

Shake Shack's Shackburger, $5.19
What began as a pop-up hot-dog cart has evolved into a fast-casual juggernaut. You already know its proportions are perfect, its construction solid. What's remarkable is how consistent it is no matter where you find it—from Citi Field to the MGM hotel in Vegas.

Schnipper's' the Schnipp, $7
From the brothers who brought you Hale & Hearty soups comes this convincingly greasy contender, unabashedly Shackian in construction and proportion. The patty might be a little too densely packed, but otherwise, it hits the spot.

Blue Collar's Cheeseburger, $5.45
It might seem a little smaller than Shake Shack's, but what this unassuming burger lacks in size it makes up for in good, fresh, beefy flavor. Plus no lines and no greasy vibrating patron pagers.

Genuine Roadside's the Classic Burger, $8
As evocative of California as Meyer lemons and fish tacos, this Gotham West beaut is loose and juicy and well seasoned, not to mention properly dressed (that means lettuce, tomato, pickles, and sauce).

And Yet.
Which One Is Best?
A heated argument among our experts.

ADAM PLATT: My desert-island burger is the one at **Little Owl**. It's got that LaFrieda stamp of excellence. Old-fashioned Vermont Cheddar, little bit of bacon. I think the key is the bun, which they bake on the premises. **ROB PATRONITE:** I like it, too, Platty, but I'd say it's a neighborhood-restaurant burger, not a destination burger. That's partly why it's not in our taxonomy. I'm surprised you singled out the bun, because I've found it to be a little stiff and unyielding—maybe that's why the burger isn't as cohesive as I'd like it to be. **AP:** *Not cohesive.* You're a Goddamn burger snob. **ROBIN RAISFELD:** Context is important for me. It's got to be casual. So I'm going with the burger at **Hard Times Sundaes**, a truck in Mill Basin. It's just a simple four-ounce smash burger cooked on the griddle. It's all about the grease—it's like a condiment. They use a Martin's bun. The cheese isn't so much melted as absorbed. It holds it all together like glue. **AP:** It's in a truck. It will be gone in six months, unlike Little Owl. **RP:** If I had to pick one burger style, I'd go with the high-low. And the epitome of this style is the burger at **Bowery Meat Company.** It sounds fancy-pants, but it's not. It's Josh Capon's first dry-aged burger, and he gets an amazing crust on it. It's tender, juicy, and super-crumbly. **ALAN SYTSMA:** What do you think of the raclette cheese? To me, that's what undoes the BMC burger. **RP:** I love it. It's the ultimate melter, the Kraft Singles of fancy burger cheeses. I'm surprised more chefs don't put raclette on burgers. **AS:** My pick, **NoMad Bar**, is a bunch of very haute chefs doing a very refined version of a burger. But I think they've made an effort to maintain the Americana appeal of it. It's a cheffed-up patty, but it has the sensibility of a fast-food burger. The cheese is clothbound Cheddar. The onion is marinated in white balsamic and— **AP:** White balsamic, oh, for God's sake, it's totally haute. **RP:** It's true. They serve it with a pickled carrot. No one wants to eat a pickled carrot with a burger. Do you think it has enough of a sear on it? **AS:** People complain that it's mushy and that there isn't a lot of sear. I'm more interested in that pink medium-rare center. **RP:** But that's the point. You can have it all. The crusty sear and the juicy interior. That's the ideal. **AS:** I'm not missing the sear. There aren't many places that do a deep sear, and you get a nice medium-rare. **RP:** Well, BMC does!

"Once a slab of garbage-meat, now a prized plaything of fancy chefs, Wall Street investors, and Silicon Valley engineers."

→ **Benjamin Wallace, New York magazine**

339

wimpy the character

In 1934, Edward Vale Gold founded Wimpy Grills in Bloomington, Indiana (see page 42). The chain was named after J. Wellington Wimpy, a cartoon character from the *Popeye* series and created by Elzie Crisler Segar in 1931. Eating burgers was Wimpy's all-consuming obsession; his sole motivation for doing anything was to grub together enough money to satisfy this longing. This usually involved some form of convoluted and unsuccessful long-con fraud, with the hungry antihero pleading, "I'll gladly pay you Tuesday for a hamburger today."

Life imitated art by spinning it on its head and Wimpy the chain became a provider of burgers rather than a petitioner for them. The comic-strip character is believed to be based on someone Segar had encountered in real life, either H. Hillard Wimpee, a journalist colleague at the *Chicago Herald-Examiner* in 1917 who, while fond of a hamburger lunch, was rather less enamored of paying for it; or William Schuchert, manager of an opera house in Chicago where Segar also worked, who loved burgers and the sound of his own voice.

Wimpy was a popular character, his gluttonous pursuit of burgers allied to a warmth and intelligence that saw him play the "straight man" friend to the wild, spinach-fueled Popeye. But his catchphrase has become an epigram to invoke a lack of financial prudence, the desire to acquire at any cost in order to satisfy materialistic and consumer-driven needs.

This, of course, is the dark side of the American Dream, embedded in recent memory at the time of Wimpy's creation due to the Wall Street crash of 1929. That crash had been caused by relentless speculation, and Wimpy's speculation—a burger today for payment tomorrow—sums up in a very basic way the deep fears Americans had at the time, that borrowing led to an illusion of safety and that, worse still, there were those out there who sought to exploit the ingenuous and generous in order to profit from them. Ironically, the upsurge in popular entertainments like cartoons was a direct result of the need for whimsy and cheap, readily available entertainment to forestall the ill effects on a national conscience caused by the evisceration of the American financial system. But hidden in such whimsy was this sort of carefully phrased moralizing that warned Americans against giving too freely of their burgers in case tomorrow's payment never came. By 1935, the burger was such a potent and widely recognized symbol of basic consumer gratification that it would have made little sense for the object of Wimpy's desires to be anything else.

Wimpy reappears in an episode of *Family Guy*, called "McStroke" (2008), in which well-meaning but bumbling Peter Griffin saves the owner of hamburger restaurant McBurgerTown and is gifted a lifetime's supply of free burgers. He eats too much, has a stroke, and tries to sue the restaurant for causing it. His attempted litigation fails miserably because the restaurant has an army of lawyers and Griffin has no evidence; indeed, Brian, the anthropomorphic family dog, points out that Griffin was hoist on his own guzzling petard. At one point in the episode, as Griffin stands outside a typically suburban McBurgerTown, shaking his fist and railing against the restaurant for causing his condition, Wimpy sidles up to him and utters his famous catchphrase, delivering it in a tremulous voice because he too has suffered a stroke.

Family Guy is famous for its cultural references and Wimpy's appearance signifies just how closely associated he still is with the hamburger; his greed for them also reflects Griffin's, as does his inability to see that his problems are of his own making. In this, the burger is again the symbolic symptom of American greed, not its cause.

In another, equally satirical, cartoon we find the same duality of greed and concern forestalled. Robert Crumb's *Zap Comix #2*, published in 1968 in San Francisco, depicts a slavering, trenchcoat-wearing man waiting desperately for a hamburger from an overweight diner chef, echoing Wimpy's compulsion. The chef serves the customer his burger and the two gaze lovingly at it, the customer saying, "Ho ho! Now woudja take a look at that hamburger" and the chef replying, "Wot a beauty! Wot a winner!" The burger and attendant sauces then develop faces and warn the customer of his impending disaster: "Listen pal, I'll fill you in! That burger knows the score!" The customer wolfs it down anyway, munching and gulping with masticatory abandon, before being told by the sauces and the chef that

it is his turn to die. On leaving the restaurant he is run over by a truck, another symbol of consumerism, and sits on the curb in rags, weeping and bemoaning his fate and the "lousy no good dirty lowdown hamburger." However, on seeing another couple of customers striding into the same restaurant, he is restored to his former state, declaiming in words framed by musical notes that all he needs is "another hamburger!"

There was a growing sense in the 1950s and '60s, articulated here by Crumb, that the boom of suburban America and the explosion of individual wealth and capitalism (in part encouraged as being antithetical to Communist Russia) were sowing the seeds of future problems, just as the boom of the 1920s had led to the Great Depression.

Art

The appropriation of classic American icons like the burger for the purposes of satirical humor in art was part of a general movement that paved the way for Pop Art, another style in which the burger would find itself the subject of exploration. The 1960s and its preoccupations gave birth to postmodernism and forms of art comprising, to quote fine-arts scholar Anne D'Alleva, a "recycling of old images and commodities," a world of "imitations with no originals;" this is the world of hyper-reality. Most famously, Andy Warhol produced screen prints of mass-produced items from initial hand-painted works and, in doing so, according to *The 20th Century Art Book* from Phaidon, "questioned both authorship and the validity of uniqueness" by repeating motifs and subjects again and again.

In 1985–6, Warhol painted *Hamburger*, an acrylic-on-linen image of a small, squashed burger, with the patty poking out from the bun but little else discernible in the way of garnish or filling, and the word "Hamburger" in uppercase lettering underneath. The image is also used in a double version with different coloring. The compact, unadorned burger looks unappealing, mass-produced. The image, of course, like every Warhol, was subject to its own mass production. Cynical humor suffuses the piece, an American cultural icon transformed into something that looks barely appetizing but is so immediately recognizable that the caption underneath is, in absolute terms, an unnecessary addition. Warhol is commenting on popularity, advertising, and the unquenchable nature of modern consumerism, and the burger is a perfect site for that comment. It is a classic recycling of an old image and places the iconic burger firmly within its social context as an object of advertising and consumption.

The burger's availability to all appealed greatly to Warhol. As he says in his book *The Philosophy of Andy Warhol*, "What's great about this country is that America started the tradition where the richest consumers buy essentially the same things as the poorest. You can be watching TV and see Coca-Cola, and you know the President drinks Coke, Liz Taylor drinks Coke, and just think, you can drink Coke, too.... All the Cokes are the same and all the Cokes are good." The same could be and indeed has been said of the hamburger.

"My name is Andy Warhol and I just finished eating a hamburger."

➡

Andy Warhol, 66 Scenes from America

Perhaps Warhol's most famous interaction with the burger was, however, not his own artistic creation. In 1981, Danish filmmaker Jørgen Leth directed and edited *66 Scenes from America*, a series of short vignettes exploring American cultural history and the iconic in the everyday. He persuaded Warhol to be filmed eating a Whopper from Burger King, a segment of the film that lasts about four and a half minutes as the artist unwraps the burger, tips out some Heinz ketchup (from a glass bottle, not Burger King's own), eats the burger, and then crumples up the waste and puts it back into the bag. He then seems to pause and think, before saying to the camera, "My name is Andy Warhol and I just finished eating a hamburger." In the opening moments of the scene, which is shot statically from a camera directly opposite where he is sitting, the logos of the Burger King bag and the ketchup bottle are clearly visible.

The most famous artist in the world has the camera turned on him to record him participating in the most commonplace of American pastimes, eating a burger. We are left to guess whether his apparent discomfort is a result of becoming the subject of someone else's work or because he actually didn't enjoy the burger that much, but the piece is a fascinating example of how an icon like the burger can unite the everyday and celebrity, mass consumption and art.

Warhol may be the most famous artist to use the burger in this way, but by no means the only one. Wayne Thiebaud, a contemporary in New York in the 1960s, who worked in advertising before becoming a full-time painter, is also known for nostalgic, warm work recalling or invoking classic features of American life. His pastel *Three Burgers* (2000) is almost juvenile in its composition and exaggerated color scheme, and is part of his general fascination with the output of production lines, like cakes or pies or, indeed, burgers.

Warhol and Thiebaud both had works in the exhibition "New Painting of Common Objects" in Pasadena, California, in 1962, which is regarded as the first museum survey of Pop Art. Also on show was Ed Ruscha, who would go on to work with painting phrases or words onto photos, sometimes using his own typeface, Boy Scout

Previous spread: Artist Andy Warhol eating a Burger King Cheeseburger with Heinz Tomato Ketchup in the film *66 Scenes from America*, 1981.

Left: Photographer David LaChapelle's *Death by Hamburger*, 2001.

Next spread (left): Artist Andy Warhol's *Hamburger*, synthetic polymer and silkscreen inks on canvas, 1986.

Next spread (right): *White Tower Hamburger*, Reginald Marsh, 1945.

Cultural Impact

Cultural Impact

"You know the President drinks Coke, Liz Taylor drinks Coke, and just think, you can drink Coke, too."

➡

Andy Warhol, ***The Philosophy of Andy Warhol***

Utility Modern. One such phrase, painted in capitals over a black-and-white photo of the word "Now" is Wimpy's very own "I would gladly pay you Tuesday for a hamburger today." While there is no visual reference to burgers in the piece other than the word, it is worth quoting what curator Margit Rowell, says of his work: "Through his interpretation of cultural icons and vernacular subjects ... as well as his renderings of words and phrases in countless stylistic variations, Ruscha proposes a modern landscape based on keen observation and wry humor." Another artist from that show, Roy Lichtenstein, did for hot dogs in 1964 what Warhol would do for burgers twenty years later.

Claes Oldenburg's sculpture *Two Cheeseburgers, with Everything* (1962) seems to drip with goodness, stuffed full of salad and cheese and sauce and dark patties of meat. The objects are, however, made from thick burlap cloth that was soaked in plaster and then painted over with enamel. The two burgers are squeezed side by side to make a sculpture not dissimilar in size to what the real object would be, conveying life-likeness in color and dimension, but being utterly inedible. In the same year Oldenburg also created a massive hamburger sculpture in canvas, entitled *Floor Burger*, which looks a lot less appetizing than *Two Cheeseburgers, with Everything*.

The acquisition of *Floor Burger* by the Art Gallery of Ontario in 1967 was so controversial that art students in the city made a 9-foot (almost 3-meter) high Heinz ketchup bottle and demonstrated outside the gallery with it held aloft, before trying to get the gallery to accept it as an equally valid work of art; they also bore a placard sporting the memorable phrase "Don't Burger Up Our Art Gallery." The protest was unsuccessful and the work is still in Ontario, though it is periodically loaned out.

While Oldenburg's work is firmly in the same field as Thiebaud's and Warhol's—an examination of materialism and consumerism—inventive use of materials in sculpture added a texture to the art burger, bringing it even closer to the object we find in everyday life that it intended to be consumed. Of the three, Thiebaud is perhaps the least critical of such cultural shifts and the most nostalgic.

Oldenburg's influential production of exaggerated sculptures of burgers found perhaps its apogee in David LaChapelle's *Death by Hamburger* (2001), a hyper-real photograph in which a model is crushed by an enormous inflatable burger, only her legs visible from underneath the massive object. The burger is made of vinyl and the photograph is beautifully glossy, the colors enhanced; the danger inherent in the lure of consumer objects like burgers is all too obvious as LaChapelle—a protégé of Warhol, who saw his work in New York in the 1980s and gave him a job photographing celebrities at *Interview* magazine—nods to Pop Art but stages his own critique of contemporary society.

All of these artists sought to explore ideas of mass production and commoditization: as the old, grand narratives of pre-postmodernism fell down in the rush of images and socially produced culture that defined the postmodern age, the burger was an ideal focus for the hyper-real. An immediately recognizable object, one familiar in a variety of forms to almost anyone in the world, easily identifiable with advertising and consumer culture: the hamburger was truly a gift to Pop Art.

Cultural Impact

Burger Ninja

Martin Swift's highly rendered pen and ink illustrations investigate ideas of gender, sexuality, childhood uncertainty, and science fiction. His introduction to food art came from commissioned illustration and collaborations, and when PornBurger's Mathew Ramsey proposed that they work together, Swift jumped at the chance: "I couldn't say no. I suggested doing an abbreviated graphic novel combining tropes from classic Japanese Chanbara cinema and American burger culture. I wanted to juxtapose a culture that has grown from ashes to fetishize certain aspects of American culture with an iconic American cultural fetish."

Swift says, "I think decades of cultural nostalgia have elevated the burger to a cult status." Its use in his work made artistic sense, therefore, but he is quick to point out that "I don't think I admire any hamburger art more than the original thing. It is a work of art unto itself."

Swift's favorite burger is "just a medium-rare classic cheeseburger with a little ketchup and mustard. I think I like them because they are simple and difficult to screw up."

Above: Artist Martin Swift's *Burger Jin*.

Fat & Furious

Cultural Impact

Studio Furious are Thomas and Quentin, the iconoclast French designers. They started out on their own burger odyssey when a playful project to cook, photograph, and then eat a range of bespoke, studio-made burgers spawned *Fat & Furious*, which became a burger design maelstrom of creativity and went viral.

According to Thomas and Quentin, though, "We didn't set out to make a project. We took the burger spontaneously and transformed it." That transformation was possible because the basic shape and concept of the burger are so easy to identify, which allowed the playfulness of *Fat & Furious*: "What we like about the burger is that it's so iconic and so it's fun to play with layers, to play with how it's supposed to be cooked and made."

That architectural solidity of the burger's construction is part of what sent the pair in the imaginative directions they have taken: "Everything looks good between two buns. If you keep that bun you can do anything you want, it will always be a burger…. Even though we know it's originally from the U.S., the French love the burger. It's a real craze here. I don't think we look at the burger as a U.S. iconic meal—it's global now." The universality of the burger is beautifully and simply summed up by the worldwide inspiration and appeal of the Fat & Furious project: "There are some food types that start somewhere and then become everyone's."

Fat & Furious's reconstruction of the burger has taken many amazing forms, and Thomas and Quentin are probably most proud of the work they did for Le Calamar, a restaurant in Geneva, for which they created the wonderfully titled *Dr. Jekyll and Mr. Burger*. They also played with a food crossover to create a sushi burger for a collaborative project between Tumblr and *MasterChef* USA, which is their most shared creation online.

Studio Furious has since left the Fat & Furious project behind. Nonetheless, its success has encouraged Thomas and Quentin to take that same spirit of invention and fun into other areas: "Generally we like to play with images; it all started with the burger, but now we are doing Asian food, high-fashion clothing, all sorts of things." That does not mean that they have forsaken the burger altogether, of course: "We used to cook the burgers for the project, but now we much prefer to go and eat a really great burger in a restaurant. Our favorite place in Paris is PNY." The gravitational pull of the burger is, seemingly, inescapable, but Studio Furious wouldn't have it any other way.

Opposite: Fat & Furious's *Burger Blanc sur Fond Blanc*.

Sleazy McCheesy

Sleazy McCheesy describes his artwork as "a combination of humor and the things that inspire me, mostly my friends and my favorite films." His first burger-related piece was a painting of the Hamburglar beating up Ronald McDonald, which he found so much fun to do that from then on he only wanted to make paintings that made him laugh. Indeed, humor and burgers go together for Sleazy. His favorite comedians, Bill Murray, Dan Aykroyd, and John Belushi, all appeared in a *Saturday Night Live* skit called "The Olympia Restaurant," which depicted a fictional café where only three items on the long menu—the cheeseburger (pronounced "cheeburger" by Belushi), chips (not fries), and Pepsi (not Coke)—could be successfully ordered.

Sleazy reckons the hamburger is "the sexiest food group" and inspires an exciting combination of cultural ephemera: "All the original McDonald's characters are amazing. I really like all types of vintage drive-in burger-stand artwork and logos, too. But mostly, it's about the fun of making great art."

Opposite (left):
Artist Sleazy
McCheesy's
*The Good, the Bad
and the Cheesy*.

Left: Artist Sleazy
McCheesy's *Frank*.

Next spread (left):
Artist Sleazy
McCheesy's *Went to
the Bar*.

Next spread (right):
Artist Sleazy
McCheesy's *Double
Fisting*.

If there is an art form to which the hamburger truly belongs it is cinema and television. Burgers often appear in TV series, especially animated ones, as props, for example in *The Jetsons* (1962–87), or as parts of the plot, such as the barbecue scene in the *American Dad* episode "Homeland Insecurity" (2005), in which Stan hosts a block party.

In 2011, Fox launched an animated sitcom, *Bob's Burgers*, featuring the Belcher family, who run and live above a small, diner-style hamburger restaurant called Bob's Burgers. The show is apparently set in New Jersey, though this is never officially stated, and the restaurant is forever on the verge of collapse and subject to a series of disasters, such as fire or vermin infestation, alluded to in the opening titles. Just as *The Simpsons* (first aired in 1989) has a changing episode-based joke in the lines that Bart writes on the blackboard at the beginning of each program, so does *Bob's Burgers* have a changing daily specials board, featuring a new burger each time, usually with a punning title. These include the "Kales from the Crypt Burger," the "Beet-er Late Than Never Burger," and the "We're Here, We're Gruyere, Get Used To It Burger."

The show has had some crossover success as well, most noticeably when Fatburger rebranded some of its restaurants as Bob's Burgers as a promotion. Characters from the show have featured in *The Simpsons*, *Family Guy* (1999–), and *Archer* (2009–), and it has garnered critical acclaim, including an Emmy in 2014. *Family Guy*'s McBurgerTown, mentioned earlier (see page 340), also features an episode ("Baby Not On Board," 2008) in which Stewie gets a job at Fatburger and is sacked for eating fish-stick (fish-finger) sandwiches and then vomiting profusely.

Fictional burger joints feature in other animations, too. In *Beavis and Butt-head* (1993–2011), the duo work at Burger World, replacing the menu items with things like Butt Nuggets, frying dead mice and insects to serve to customers, and generally being disgusting. In *The Simpsons*, Krusty the Clown owns Krusty Burger, a global behemoth that, among other things, serves the "delicious crime against nature" that is Burger 2, made from cows that are fed other cows.

THE LONGEST
CHARD BURGER

Left: The family
helps film the
restaurant's Super
Bowl commercial in
the "Easy Commercial
Easy Gommercial"
episode of *Bob's
Burgers*, 2014.

Next spread: Eddie
Murphy and Louie
Anderson in the John
Landis film *Coming to
America*, 1988.

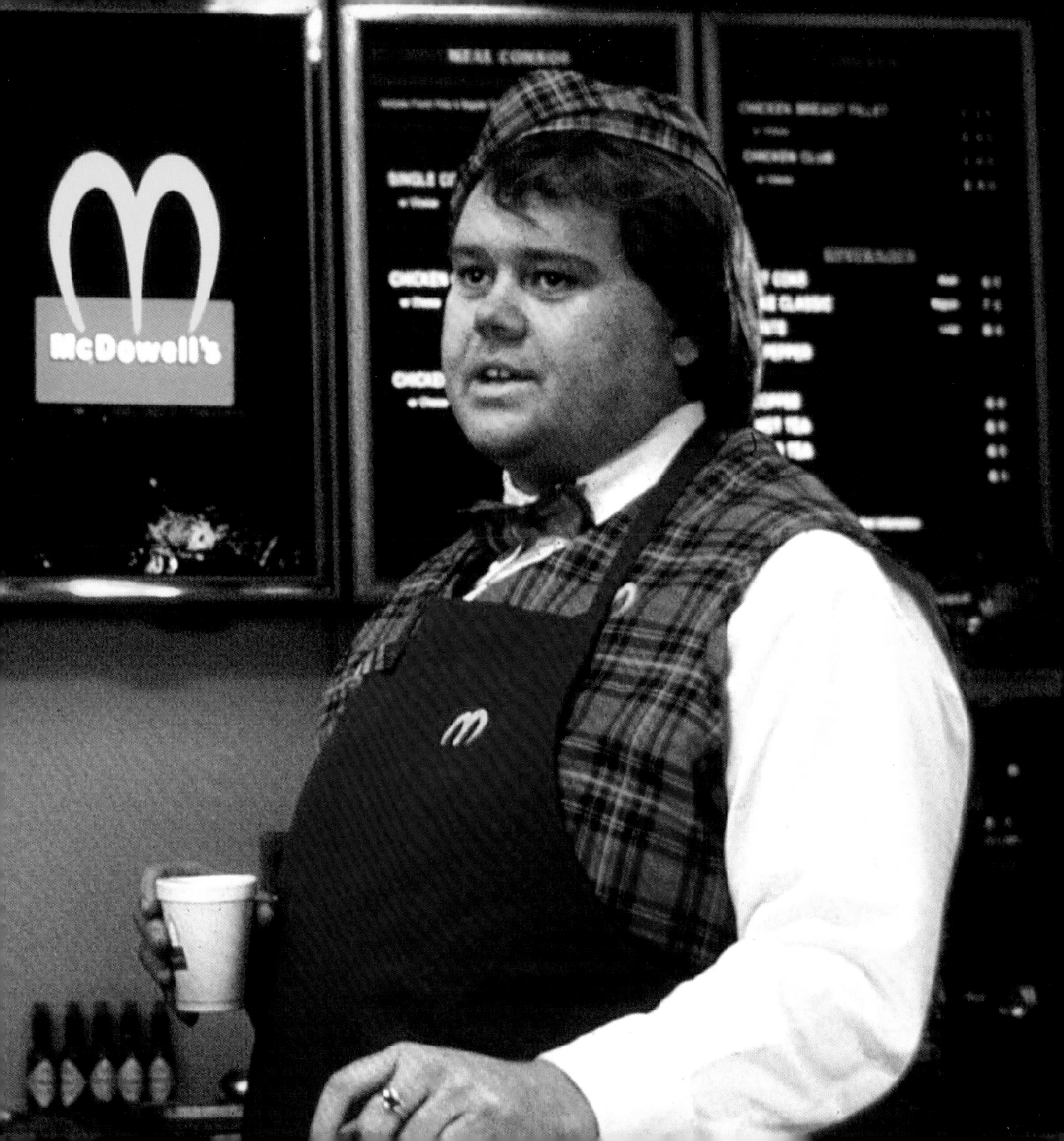
McDowell's

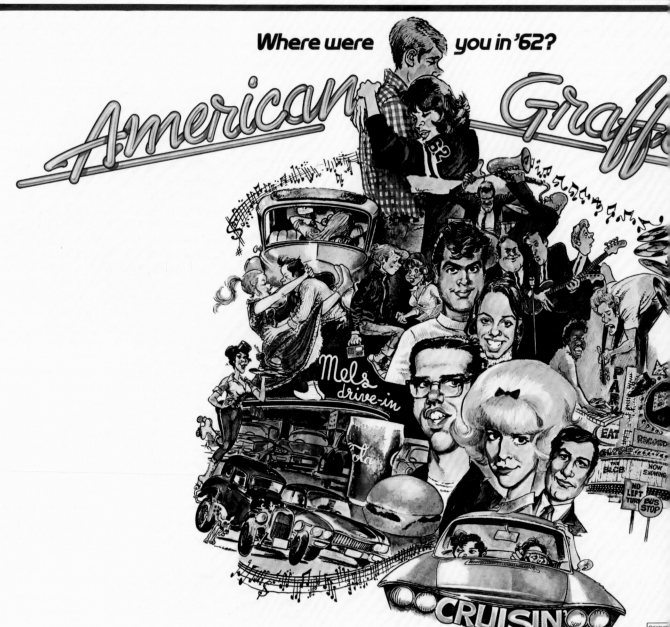

Where were you in '62?

American Graffi

Mel's drive-in

CRUISIN

"AMERICAN GRAFFITI" • A LUCASFILM LTD./COPPOLA CO. Production • Starring RICHARD DREYFUSS • RONNY HOWARD • PAUL LE MAT • CHARLIE MARTIN SMITH • CANDY CLARK • MACKENZIE PHILLIPS
Written by GEORGE LUCAS and GLORIA KATZ & WILLARD HUYCK • Directed by GEORGE LUCAS • Co-Produced by GARY KURTZ • Produced by FRANCIS FORD COPPOLA • A UNIVERSAL PICTURE • TEC

Of course, films feature hamburgers and hamburger restaurants, in ways that overlap with the more adult cartoons and develop the themes seen in Pop Art uses of the food. *Moscow on the Hudson* (1984) is a romantic comedy set in the late Cold War era. Robin Williams plays Vladimir, a Russian musician who defects to the United States while visiting New York to play with the Moscow State Circus. He defects with dreams of freedom and love and, of course, a better economic situation, this being a slightly propagandist number. Indeed, as a New York cop says when Vladimir defects, "This is New York City; a man can do what he wants." However, Vladimir quickly encounters the harsh realities of immigrant life and learns that what he wants and what he can actually do might not be exactly the same thing. He has to take a series of low-paid jobs, including one in a McDonald's restaurant, where he famously takes an order and then, having stuttered his way through the various food items requested, tells the customer to "Come back McSoon."

Along with the idea that America is the land of opportunity, the film is also a hymn to the immigrant origins of the United States; as Vladimir says in his still halting English, "Everybody I meet from somewhere else." In McDonald's we see an obvious symbol of American capitalism and equality, but also, in the prominence of the hamburger in the film, a conscious echo of the food's immigrant origins.

There are further echoes of this in the Eddie Murphy comedy *Coming to America* (1988), where Murphy and his co-star Arsenio Hall, playing an African prince and his advisor, flee their homeland to assert their independence and find true love in the United States. They work at McDowell's, a clear rip-off of McDonald's, and the owner Cleo McDowell is being investigated by McDonald's for untold copyright infringements. McDowell lists the various overlaps and similarities between his small, family-run restaurant and the massive chain, before proudly announcing, "But they use a sesame seed bun. My buns have no seeds." The film even shows McDowell stealing ideas from a McDonald's operations manual. Once again the hamburger restaurant, and specifically McDonald's, is a symbol of the American dream for an immigrant.

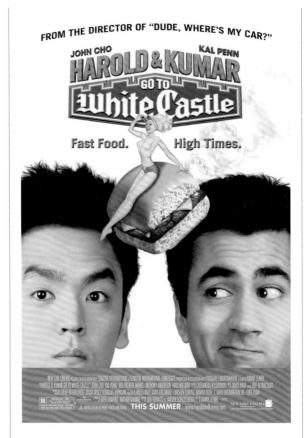

Left: Poster for the George Lucas film *American Graffiti*, 1973.

Above: Poster for the Danny Leiner film *Harold & Kumar go to White Castle*, 2004.

367

A number of films written and directed by Kevin Smith feature a fast-food restaurant called Mooby's. The Mooby character, a golden calf, first occurs in *Dogma* (1999), where fallen angels Bartleby and Loki enter the boardroom of the company that owns the rights to the Mooby doll and its various franchised products. In an earlier scene some of the characters have eaten in a Mooby restaurant.

Mooby recurs in *Jay and Silent Bob Strike Back* (2001) as the Ronald McDonald figure of the Mooby's chain; one of its restaurants then becomes the setting for much of *Clerks II* (2006). The restaurant in which the film was shot was a shutdown Burger King in Buena Park, California, though the Mooby slogan "I'm eatin' it" is a play on McDonalds' "i'm lovin' it." The films show the proliferation of such restaurants and their associated merchandise across America, as well as demonstrating how they provide work and social hubs for working-class American kids. A very similar use, discussed more fully in Josh Ozersky's *The Hamburger*, had appeared several decades earlier in George Lucas's *American Graffiti* (1973).

Perhaps the film auteur most closely associated with the hamburger is Quentin Tarantino. In much the same way as Kevin Smith creates a universe where themes and features run across the films, so Tarantino crams his films with interior references and inside jokes. One is the Hawaiian-themed Big Kahuna Burger chain, which appears in *Reservoir Dogs* (1992), *Pulp Fiction* (1994), and *Death Proof* (2007), as well as in Tarantino's collaborator Robert Rodriguez's films *From Dusk Till Dawn* (1996) and *The Adventures of Sharkboy and Lavagirl in 3-D* (2005). The blurring of reality and fiction continued when, working with his El Rey Network, Rodriguez developed a spin-off TV series of *From Dusk Till Dawn* and, in March 2015, fitted out a restaurant in Austin, Texas, to look like a Big Kahuna franchise to film an ad for the series.

In *Pulp Fiction*, Samuel L. Jackson's hitman Jules Winnfield describes the Big Kahuna hamburger as "the cornerstone of any nutritious breakfast," before asking where the burgers come from. On learning that they are from Big Kahuna, he says he has heard their burgers are tasty, but has never had one; he then eats one and famously exclaims, "Mmm, mmm, this *is* a tasty burger …

"Big Mac's a Big Mac, but they call it *Le Big Mac*."

↓

John Travolta's character, Vincent Vega, *Pulp Fiction*

Left: Actor Samuel L. Jackson, eating a Big Kahuna burger, in the Quentin Tarantino film *Pulp Fiction*, 1994.

I do love the taste of a good burger." The two hitmen (the other Vincent Vega, played by John Travolta) then recap an earlier conversation in which the differences between America and Europe are explored, such as the Quarter Pounder being called a Royale with Cheese due to the metric system and the Big Mac being called *Le* Big Mac.

Tarantino's references to pop culture permeate his films. The burger chain responsible for Mr. Blonde's meal and soft drink in *Reservoir Dogs* feeds poor victims and his sidekick in *Pulp Fiction*, and so on. Tarantino clearly has a special affection for burgers and their purveyors, the iconic American diner and the sleazy, tacky fast-food joint.

And this, ultimately, is the fate of the hamburger in popular culture, to be ever-present and evocative. There is no doubt that as a symbol, the hamburger has served an extraordinary purpose in art of various types. But as we have seen in the burger's origins, its very cultural malleability meant that it was destined to become a metaphor for America or for consumerism gone wild. Though, of course, we should never forget the burger's ability to be, as the Samuel L. Jackson *Pulp Fiction* character Jules Winnfield says, just tasty.

Opposite: Krusty Burger's Krusty the Clown, a character from *The Simpsons*, attends the "Taste of Springfield" press event at Universal Studios Hollywood, 2015.

Left: Kevin Spacey and Marissa Jaret Winokur at Mr. Smiley's drive-thru in the Sam Mendes film *American Beauty*, 1999.

Next spread: Flint Lockwood, the protagonist of the animated film *Cloudy with a Chance of Meatballs*, 2009.

Left: Actor Humphrey
Bogart, at the
racetrack in Santa
Anita, California,
c. 1945.

Cultural Impact

Left: Actress Marilyn
Monroe, 1952.

Left: Boxer Muhammad
Ali appearing in
a UK television
advertisement for
Birds Eye's Quarter
Pounder, 1981.

Cultural Impact

Left: Singer Gene Simmons, on the TV show *Extra* at The Grove, Los Angeles, California, 2012.

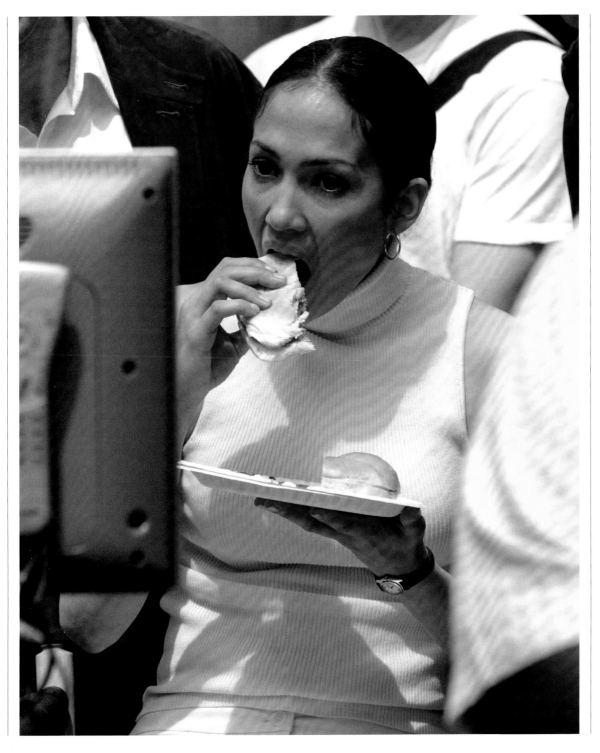

Left: Singer and
actress Jennifer
Lopez, on the New York
film set of Wayne
Wang's *Maid in
Manhattan*, 2002.

Next spread: Paul
and Linda McCartney
launching her
vegetarian burger
line, The Savoy Hotel,
London, 1991.

Cultural Impact

Left: Actress Candice Bergen, c. 1951.

383

Cultural Impact

Left: Actor Neil
Patrick Harris, in
the episode "The Best
Burger In New York"
on the television show
How I Met your Mother.

Left: Actress Farrah
Fawcett, c. 1973.

Cultural Impact

Left: Actress Angela Lansbury, in costume for the film *The Court Jester*, with actor Basil Rathbone, at lunch in the Paramount Studios commissary, c. 1955.

Cultural Impact

Left: The film
character Borat,
played by Sacha
Baron Cohen.

(U.S.) Burger Bash

The Blue Moon Burger Bash of the New York City Wine & Food Festival, hosted by longtime television celebrity Rachael Ray every October, is perhaps the most prestigious Best Burger competition around, along with the Burger Bash at the South Beach Wine & Food Festival in Miami in February. These events are headlining culinary showcases in the United States and feature blind tastings of the burgers by chefs and celebrities to determine who gets the crown. The recent king is American restaurant chef Josh Capon (of the famed Lure burger at Lure Fishbar in New York City), who in 2015 won his fifth "people's choice" award in six years for a cheeseburger with onion and bacon jam and a secret sauce.

Above: Bachi burger at the Amstel Light Burger Bash hosted by Rachael Ray, South Beach Wine & Food Festival, in Miami, Florida, 2016.

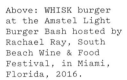

Above: WHISK burger
at the Amstel Light
Burger Bash hosted by
Rachael Ray, South
Beach Wine & Food
Festival, in Miami,
Florida, 2016.

Above: Red Robin
gourmet burger at the
Amstel Light Burger
Bash hosted by Rachael
Ray, South Beach Wine
& Food Festival, in
Miami, Florida, 2016.

Above: Toro burger
at the Amstel Light
Burger Bash hosted by
Rachael Ray, South
Beach Wine & Food
Festival, in Miami,
Florida, 2016.

Above: Eden Eats
burger from Eden
Grinshpan at the
Amstel Light Burger
Bash hosted by Rachael
Ray, South Beach Wine
& Food Festival, in
Miami, Florida, 2016.

Above: Met Back Bay burger at the Amstel Light Burger Bash hosted by Rachael Ray, South Beach Wine & Food Festival, in Miami, Florida, 2016.

Above: ROK:BRGR burger at the Amstel Light Burger Bash hosted by Rachael Ray, South Beach Wine & Food Festival, in Miami, Florida, 2016.

(UK) National Burger Day

Cultural Impact

National Burger Day is a celebration of all things burger in London, centering on a series of open-air parties that host a staggering array of street food burger vendors. Run since 2013 by online men's magazine *Mr. Hyde*, National Burger Day was held near the iconic Battersea Power Station in 2014, at Street Feast in Dalston Yard in 2015, and at Canada Water in 2016. The event also encourages hundreds of restaurants across the UK to discount their foods on the big day to introduce more customers to the sheer joy of the burger.

Left: Bangkok Burger, Slider Bar, 2015.

Above: The Candy Bacon Special, Mother Flipper, 2015.

Above: Pickleback
Slider, PYT Burger,
2015.

Above: US v. UK
burger, Smokestak,
2015.

Above: Fried Calamari
Butter Burger,
B.O.B.'s Lobster,
2016.

Above: Le Royale with
Cheese Slider, Le Bun,
2014.

Bite Me Burger Co.

Making the world a burger place
Eat & Get Out!

BurgerFuel

Fuel For The Human Engine

Burger King

Have it your way
Burger King, where you're the boss!
The Fire's Ready
Your Way, Right Away
The Best Food for Fast Times
Sometimes, you gotta break the rules
America Loves Burgers and We're America's Burger King!
Burger King, Home of the Whopper
Wake up with the King
It takes two hands to handle a Whopper

Byron

Proper Hamburgers

Carl's Jr.

Some guys don't do 49 cent Tuesdays.
At Carl's Jr. you're into something good!
Don't bother me, I'm eating.
Making people happy through food.

Carney's

Probably the best hamburgers and hot dogs ... in the world!
Long live the burger!

Checkers Drive-In Burgers

High Performance Human Fuel
little place. BIG TASTE
Devour the night!
Feast On

Cheeburger Cheeburger

Big Is Better

Ed's Easy Diner
The name says it all!

Fatburger
The Last Great Hamburger Stand

Fergburger
Ferg Loves You.

Fuddruckers
World's Greatest Hamburgers

Grill'd
Burgers done good

Hardee's

Where the food's the star
Hardee's. Come on Home
Delicious Food. To fit your lifestyle

Hard Rock Cafe

Love All—Serve All.

Hungry Jack's

The burgers are better at Hungry Jack's

Jack in the Box

We don't make it until you order it
Love Bacon? Marry It.

Johnny Rockets

American Original
The Original Hamburger

McDonald's

i'm lovin' it
There's a difference at McDonald's you'll enjoy
What you want is what you get
It's a good time for the great taste of McDonald's
Nobody can do it like McDonald's can
You deserve a break today ... at McDonald's
We love to see you smile
What we're made of
Did somebody say McDonald's?

No Name Saloon

Helping People Forget Their Names Since 1903

Red Robin Gourmet Burgers

Red Robin *Yummm*

Smashburger

Smash, Sizzle. Savor.

Burger Slogans

Sonic Drive-In

Sonic's Got It ... Others Don't
It's not just good ... it's Sonic good

Wahlburgers

Our Family, Our Story, Our Burgers

Wendy's

Do what tastes right
Wendy's. Quality is our recipe
It's better here
Where's the beef?
It's waaay better than fast food ... It's Wendy's.

White Castle

White Castle. What You Crave.

Trivia

In the U.S. people eat about **thirteen billion burgers** annually.

McDonald's sells **seventy-five burgers** every single second.

If all the hamburgers eaten in America in a year were laid in a straight line, they would circle the Earth **thirty-two** times.

The average American eats **three burgers** a week.

One in **eight** American adults has been employed by McDonald's.

It takes walking **9 miles** (14.5 kilometers) to burn off a Burger King's Double Whopper.

Burgers account for **40 percent** of all sandwiches sold.

According to the producers of *Guinness World Records*, the largest commercially available hamburger to date was recorded in the United States in 2012. It weighs **777 pounds** (352.44 kilograms) and is prepared by Juicy's Foods and Ovations Foodservices for Juicy's Outlaw Grill, Corvallis, Oregon, USA. The cost: **five thousand dollars**!

Black Bear Casino Resort near Carlton, Minnesota, unveiled a burger weighing an unbelievable **2,014 pounds** (914 kilograms), and it measured **10 feet** (3 meters) in diameter. This colossal burger had the usual trimmings such as onions, pickles (gherkins), lettuce, and cheese.

The Heart Attack Grill in Las Vegas produces the world's most calorific burger. The Quadruple Bypass consists of four half-pound (225-gram) patties, three tablespoons of lard, twenty slices of bacon, eight slices of American cheese, twenty slices of caramelized onion, eight tomato slices, one tablespoon of mayo, three tablespoons of ketchup, one tablespoon of mustard, and a bun. That adds up to **9,982 calories**.

White Castle is the United States's oldest hamburger fast-food chain, established in 1921. At that time their famous "sliders" were sold for **five cents** each.

The New York City food truck 666 Burger offers a **$666** burger coined the "Douche Burger." It's made with a patty of Kobe beef wrapped in gold leaf, foie gras, caviar, lobster, truffles, imported aged Gruyère cheese (melted in Champagne steam), kopi-luwak-infused barbecue sauce, and Himalayan rock salt.

The most expensive burger (**$5,000!**) can be found at a Las Vegas restaurant called Fleur (formerly Fleur de Lys), at the Mandalay Bay hotel. The patty is made of Kobe beef and topped with foie gras and truffles, then served with a drizzle of special sauce, French fries (chips), and more truffles on the side. The meal includes 1990 Chateau Pétrus wine.

During World War I, American soldiers called hamburgers "**liberty sausage**," and during World War II, the hamburger was often known as the **Liberty Sandwich**.

McDonald's Big Mac was previously named the "**Aristocrat**" and "**Blue Ribbon Burger**," both of which failed in the marketplace.

Mexican fast-food chain Taco Bell started out as **Bells Burgers** in 1950, serving fifteen-cent hamburgers.

The Hamburger Hall of Fame is located in **Seymour, Wisconsin**.

In 1990, **30,000 people** lined up to eat at the first McDonald's in Moscow.

In 2012 as part of a marketing campaign, Wimpy in South Africa had burgers with sesame seeds spelling out various messages in **braille**. These were presented to blind consumers and their reactions were filmed.

In 2000, **Kim Jong-Il**, then leader of North Korea, said that he created the hamburger.

In the Middle East, Pizza Hut sells a **cheeseburger pizza**.

In Australia, Burger King is called **Hungry Jack's**.

In the U.S., there are **1,700 people** listed in whitepages.com with the last name "Hamburger" and **26,000 people** with the last name "Burger."

McDonald's mogul **Ray Kroc** didn't get into the burger business until he was in his **fifties**.

Elvis Presley allegedly liked to top all his burgers with bananas, peanut butter, syrup, and egg.

Glossary

50/50 BURGER
A burger containing a patty made using half ground (minced) bacon, half ground beef. Another variety contains half kangaroo meat and half bacon.

AIOLI
A mayonnaise seasoned with garlic.

ALABAMA SAUCE
A mayo-based barbecue sauce.

AMERICAN CHEESE
A processed cheese made from a blend of milk, milk fats and solids, other fats, and whey protein.

AMERICAN MUSTARD OR YELLOW MUSTARD
A very mild mustard colored with turmeric.

ANGUS BURGER
A burger patty made with beef from Angus cattle. Several fast-food chains market an "Angus burger."

AUSTRALIAN HAMBURGER
Also known as "The Lot," this consists of a beef patty topped with tomato, lettuce, grilled onion, cheese, bacon, beet (beetroot), pineapple, and a fried egg, all served in a split bun.

BANQUET BURGER
A name sometimes given to a hamburger topped with bacon and cheese.

BARBECUE BURGER

A burger containing a patty made using a mix of ground (minced) beef, onions, and barbecue sauce. It is then grilled, and often more barbecue sauce is added and that caramelizes during cooking. The bun is also spread with barbecue sauce.

BARBECUE SAUCE

A dark brown sauce with vinegar and tomato paste (purée) as a base and various spices and sugars added.

BLUE CHEESE

A cheese containing veins of blue mold, resulting in a distinctive flavor. The many varieties include Stilton and Danish blue.

BØFSANDWICH

The Bøfsandwich or Danish Gravy Burger from Jutland, Denmark, consists of a ground (minced) beef patty topped with sliced pickled beets (beetroot), served in a split bun, covered in beef gravy, and topped with crispy roasted onions.

BRIE

A soft, mild, and creamy cheese with a firm white outer skin.

BRIOCHE BUN

An originally French sweet bread made from enriched dough.

BUFFALO BURGER

Containing a patty made of meat from the American bison, this has less cholesterol, less fat, and fewer calories than beef hamburgers.

BURGER BUN

A soft white bread roll in which a hamburger is typically served (see page 316).

BURGER RELISH

A thick, sweet, and slightly spicy relish with bell peppers and tomatoes as the main ingredients.

BUTTER BURGER

Originating in Wisconsin, this consists of a beef patty topped with American cheese and grilled onions, then covered with a large scoop of butter and served in a split bun.

CALIFORNIA BURGER

In the Midwest and East Coast of the United States, this refers to a hamburger served with lettuce, tomato, and onion. In the Western states, however, it means a cheeseburger with added guacamole or avocado, plus bacon.

CARAMELIZED ONIONS

Finely sliced onions, cooked down to form a sweet and sticky condiment.

CAROLINA BURGER

Originating in North Carolina, this is served with "everything"—cheese, chili con carne, onions, mustard, and coleslaw.

CHEDDAR CHEESE

A firm smooth cheese originally made in the village of Cheddar in Somerset, UK.

CHEESEBURGER

A grilled patty topped with melted cheese and served in a split bun. While American cheese is typically used, cheese of any type may be added.

CHILI BURGER

A burger in which the patty is topped with chili con carne.

CHILI OR CHILI CON CARNE

A spicy stew with chili peppers, ground (minced) beef, and tomatoes as the main ingredients.

CHIMICHURRI BURGER

A popular burger in Buenos Aires, consisting of a beef patty topped with onion, cheese, and chimichurri (Argentinian parsley sauce) and served in a split bun.

CHUCK

Beef from the shoulder muscles, which makes the meat tougher; it is considered one of the more flavorful cuts.

CURRY BURGER

A patty of beef, chicken, or lamb, seasoned with curry powder and often yogurt, onions, and bell peppers, then served in a traditional bun.

DEEP-FRIED BURGER

A patty deep-fried in oil, then served in the traditional way.

DIJON MUSTARD

A medium-hot mustard originating in Dijon, France.

EMMENTAL CHEESE

A yellow, medium-hard cheese that originated in the area around Emmental in Switzerland. It is riddled with holes, giving it a distinctive appearance.

ENGLISH MUSTARD

One of the hottest varieties, and bright yellow in color. The most famous brand of English mustard is Colman's, which was first produced in 1814.

EXTRA LEAN AND LEAN MINCE

Extra lean beef contains no more than 10 percent fat; lean beef 17 percent fat.

EXTRA-RARE OR BLUE

Of a steak or burger, cooked very lightly, so that the center is very red and cold.

FLAT TOP

A flat cooking top, which creates an extremely hot and even surface.

FRENCH MUSTARD

A dark brown mustard with a mild and sweet flavor, created by the English company Colman's in 1936.

FRESH-GROUND (MINCED) BEEF

Fresh patties as opposed to frozen.

GOAT CHEESE

A soft cheese made from goat milk, and with a distinctive flavor.

GOOBER/GUBER BURGER

A beef patty topped with lettuce, tomato, and a large scoop of peanut butter, served in a split bun. The goober originated in Missouri in the United States.

GOUDA

A yellow Dutch cheese made from cow's milk that originated from Gouda in The Netherlands.

GRASS-FED VERSUS GRAIN-FED

The majority of cattle in the United States is raised on pasture and finished in feed lots where the animals are fed barley or maize (corn). This creates more marbling in the meat. Grass-fed beef is not "finished" in this way, has less fat, and is considered to have a distinctive taste.

HAMBURGER PRESS

A metal device that shapes ground (minced) beef into a patty.

HAMDOG

An American hybrid dish that consists of a hot dog wrapped in a beef patty that is deep-fried, covered with chili, a handful of French fries (chips), and a fried egg.

HAWAII BURGER

A beef patty topped with teriyaki sauce and pineapple.

JUICY LUCY

A cheeseburger with cheese cooked inside the patty, creating a molten center.

KETCHUP

A slightly spicy sauce made primarily from tomatoes and vinegar and used as a relish.

KOBE BEEF

Strictly (although the term is sometimes used more loosely), a Japanese beef from Wagyu cattle, renowned for its flavor and tenderness.

LUTHER BURGER

Also called the donut burger and originating in the southern U.S., in Georgia, this consists of a beef patty topped with bacon and cheese and served in a split and toasted glazed donut.

MAYONNAISE

A thick, creamy condiment made of egg yolks beaten with oil and vinegar.

MEDIUM

Cooked until firm but still pink in the center.

MEDIUM-RARE

Cooked until warm but still reddish in the center.

MEDIUM-WELL
Cooked until still slightly pink in the center.

MEDIUM MINCE
Medium-ground (minced) beef with a maximum of 23 percent fat.

MINCE
Ground (minced) meat, typically beef.

MONTEREY JACK CHEESE
Sometimes shortened to Jack cheese, an American semi-hard cheese originally from Monterey, California.

NAAN BURGER
A burger that uses naan bread instead of the traditional yeasted bun.

PASTRAMI BURGER
A patty topped with cheese and thin-sliced pastrami and served in a split bun.

PATTY
A small rounded cake of ground (minced) meat, the basis of the traditional burger.

PEPPER JACK CHEESE
An American semi-hard cheese spiced with jalapeño peppers.

PORTUGUESE BUN
A sweet bun made with milk.

PRETZEL BUN
A bun with a salty dark brown crust, a close texture, and a slightly sweet taste.

PRIME RIB
Beef taken from the sixth to twelfth ribs of the cow and that is tender and heavily marbled.

RARE
Of beef or a burger, cooked only briefly so the outsides are charred but the center remains cold and red.

REGULAR BEEF
Beef containing a maximum of 30 percent fat.

RICE BURGER
A popular style of burger in East Asia where the bun is made of compressed cakes of rice. It was created by the MOS Burger fast-food restaurant chain in the late 1980s.

ROLL-STAMPED BEEF
The United States Department of Agriculture's (USDA) grading system of quality of meat.

SALMON BURGER
A burger containing a patty made from salmon. Salmon burgers are especially common in Alaska, where they are routinely offered as an alternative to beef hamburgers.

SHAMI BURGER
A popular street food in Pakistan, this consists of a lamb mince and lentil patty topped with scrambled eggs, onions, and ketchup, served in a split bun.

SIRLOIN
Tender and lean beef from the hindquarter of the animal.

SLIDER
A small hamburger, but the term may also refer to any small sandwich served on a slider roll.

SLOPPER
A cheeseburger or hamburger served open-faced on a grilled bun, and covered in red or green chilis and fresh onions.

SLUGBURGER

Served in northeastern Mississippi, this consists of a patty made from a mixture of beef or pork and soybeans, then deep-fried in oil. It is typically served on a bun with mustard, pickles (gherkins), and onion.

STEAK BURGER

A burger containing a patty made with ground (minced) or sliced beefsteak meat.

STEAMED BURGER

A burger patty steamed under a metal dome on a hot plate.

SWISS CHEESE

As used in the U.S., this means a hard cheese with an elastic texture, slightly nutty flavor, and the characteristic holes of genuine Swiss cheese.

TERIYAKI BURGER

A burger that has teriyaki sauce on top or worked into the patty.

TRENCHER

A thick piece of stale bread that substituted for a plate in medieval food service.

VADA PAV

A spiced potato patty deep-fried in a batter made from gram flour (an Asian flour made from pulses), served with chutney and between a split bun or the Indian Ladi Pav bread.

VEGGIE BURGER

Also known as a garden burger, this contains a patty made of tofu, Quorn (the meat substitute product), beans, grains, or an assortment of vegetables, which are ground (minced) and formed into patties.

WELL DONE
Cooked until gray-brown throughout.

WHOLE-GRAIN MUSTARD
A mustard containing whole mustard seeds, creating a rich and thick texture.

Bibliography

CHAPTER 1: ORIGINS

Brogan, Hugh. *The Penguin History of the USA*. London: Penguin, 2001.

Dee, Tim. *Four Fields*. London: Vintage, 2014.

Friedman, Thomas L., *The Lexus and the Olive Tree: Understanding Globalization*. New York: Farrar, Straus & Giroux, 1999.

Jenkins, Keith. *Re-thinking History*. London: Routledge, 1991.

McLamore, James W. *The Burger King: Jim McLamore and the Building of an Empire*. New York: McGraw-Hill, 1997.

Ozersky, Josh. *The Hamburger*. Yale University Press: New Haven, 2008.

Perman, Stacy. *In-N-Out Burger: An Unauthorized Behind-The-Counter Look at the Fast-Food Chain That Breaks All the Rules*. New York: HarperBusiness, 2009.

Rozin, Elisabeth. *The Primal Cheeseburger: A Generous Helping of Food History Served Up on a Bun*. London: Penguin, 1994.

Smith, Andrew F. *Hamburger: A Global History*. London: Reaktion Books, 2008.

Tolbert, Frank X. *Tolbert's Texas*. New York: Doubleday, 1983.

More information about Isicia Omentata can be found at http://www.culture24.org.uk/history-and-heritage/archaeology/art527224-the-1500-year-old-recipe-that-shows-how-romans-invented-the-beef-burger.

CHAPTER 2: THE MODERN BURGER

More information about In-N-Out's secret menu can be found at http://www.in-n-out.com/menu/not-so-secret-menu.aspx.

CHAPTER 3: RECIPES

Motz, George. *Hamburger America: One Man's Cross-Country Odyssey to Find the Best Burgers in the Nation*. Philadelphia: Running Press, 2008.

— *The Great American Burger Book: How to Make Authentic Regional Hamburgers at Home*. New York: Stewart, Tabori & Chang, 2016.

CHAPTER 4: EATING THE BURGER

Pollan, Michael. *Cooked: A Natural History of Transformation*. London: Penguin, 2013.

Segnit, Niki. *The Flavour Thesaurus: Pairings, Recipes and Ideas for the Creative Cook*. London: Bloomsbury, 2010.

CHAPTER 5: CULTURAL IMPACT

Cooke, Alistair. *Alistair Cooke's America*. London: BBC Books, 1973.

D'Alleva, Anne. *Methods and Theories of Art History*. London: Laurence King, 2012.

Grandinetti, Fred. *Popeye: An Illustrated Cultural History*. Jefferson, North Carolina, and London: McFarland & Company Inc., 2004.

Hirsch, Foster. "Afterword" in ed. Carlos Clarens, *Crime Movies: An Illustrated History of the Gangster Genre From D.W. Griffith to Pulp Fiction*. Cambridge: Da Capo, 1997.

Phaidon Editors. *The 20th Century Art Book*. London: Phaidon, 1996.

Updike, John. *Rabbit, Run*. New York: Alfred A. Knopf, 1960.

Warhol, Andy. T*he Philosophy of Andy Warhol: From A to B and Back Again*. New York: Harvest, 1977.

For more about the controversy surrounding Claes Oldenburg's burger sculpture, see http://artmatters.ca/wp/2012/10/ago-history-the-controversial-arrival-of-claes-oldenburgs-floor-burger/.

Index

Credits

Image courtesy of the Advertising Archives: 341; /© Birds Eye: 377.

Alamy Stock Photo/A.F. Archive: 364–65, 372–73; /Bon Appetit: 308; /ClassicStock: 74–75; /Sean Pavone: 162–63; /Stock Connection Blue: 120–21; /Finnbarr Webster: 324.

© 2016 The Andy Warhol Foundation for the Visual Arts, Inc. /Artists Rights Society (ARS), New York and DACS, London 2016: 343, 346, 350, 352.

© ARS, NY and DACS, London 2016: 347.

Death by Hamburger, 2001 © David LaChapelle. Used by permission of Art + Commerce: 344–45.

Art Burger Sushi Bar: 250–51.

Art Gallery of Ontario, Toronto, Purchase 1967. Copyright 1962 Claes Oldenburg: 349.

Balans Soho Society: 278–79.

Barracuda Diner: 166.

Bauer-Griffin: 385.

Big Fernand: 205 t, 205 b.

Bite Me Burger Co.: 285.

Bleecker Burger: 288–89.

J. Bull: 40.

Burger & Lobster: 207, 208–9.

Burger Burger: 238, 239.

Burger Joint, Le Parker Meridian: 159.

Burger King Corporation: 90, 91.

Burger Liquor: 240–41, 241 b.

Burger Ninja: 354 t, 355 t, 354–55.

Burger Table: 254–55, 256, 257, 291.

Burger Theory: 202, 203 l, 203 r.

Burgerim: 185.

The Butchers Club Burger: 232, 233, 234, 235.

Byron: 174–75, 176–77, 178–79, 180 tl, 180 bl, 180–81.

Josh Capon: 287. Recipe on pages 286–87 copyright © Josh Capon.

Carl's Jr.: 44–45, 46–47, 47 l, 48, 49.

Cha Chaan Teng: 297.

Chur Burger: 229, 230–31.

Corbis/Creativ Studio Heinemann/Westend61: 323; /Neil Wilder: 389.

Chris Coulson: 394–95, 395 r, 396 l, 396 r, 397 l, 397 r.

Anselmo Ramos, Chief Creative Officer, DAVID The Agency: 88–89; 92.

Jerry Dean: 130.

Dickie Fitz: 295.

Dirty Bones: 242, 243, 244–45.

Dirty Burger: 218–19, 219 r.

Ed's Easy Diner: 146–47, 148–49.

Elevation Burger: 168.

The Ellaphant In The Room for *New York* magazine: 273.

Fat & Furious: 356.

Fat Hippo: 196, 197, 198–99, 199 r.

Fatburger: 50 t, 50 b, 51.

Fergburger: 154, 155.

Five Guys: 138–39, 139 r, 140 l.

5 Napkin Burger: 183.

Foundry 39: 298–99.

Fuddruckers: 134, 135.

Guillaume Gaudet: 281.

Getty Images/Archive Photos: 382; /H. Armstrong Roberts/ClassicStock: 76–77; /Bettmann Collection: 4, 22–23, 24 b, 82, 83; /Tim Boyle: 60–61; /Monty Brinton/CBS: 384; /Car Culture: 80–81; /Eric Charbonneau/WireImage for Vanity Fair Magazine: 69 r; /Chicago History Museum: 42; /Richard Corkery/NY Daily News Archive: 59 bl; /Alfred Eisenstaedt/The LIFE Picture Collection: 386–87; /J. R. Eyerman/The LIFE Picture Collection: 383; /Tiziana Fabi/AFP: 335; /FOX: 362–63; /Robbin Goddard/Los Angeles Times: 64–65; /Godong: 118–19; /Hulton Archive: 29, 52–53; /Jim Heimann Collection: 43, 72, 78, 79 l, 79 r; /Bill Johnson/The Denver Post: 54; /Wolfgang Kaehler/LightRocket: 56–57; /Joseph Klipple: 375; /Gene Lester: 374; /David McNew: 59 tl; /Movie Poster Image Art: 366–67; /MPI: 21; /National Motor Museum/Heritage Images: 24 t; /Neilson: Barnard 390, 391 l, 391 r, 392 l, 392 r, 393 l, 393 r; /Pool Photographer/WireImage: 66; /Alberto E. Rodriguez: 370; /Art Shay/The LIFE Images Collection: 53; /Brendan Smialowski/Stringer: 140–41; /SSPL: 26, 27; /Stock Montage: 28; /Noel Vasquez: 378.

Gordon Ramsay BurGR: 224–25.

Gourmet Burger Kitchen (GBK): 156–57, 157 r; 282–83.

Haché Burger Connoisseurs: 161 tl, 161 tr, 161 bl, 161 br.

Hard Times Sundaes: 200.

Olle Hemmendorff: 334.

Acknowledgments

I dedicate this book to my wonderful "Mommie Dearest," Shirley.

To: Todd Dalton, Debbie Dove, Bryan Cohen, Lisa Balcombe, Jonathan Beck, Marc Schneiderman, Andy Lowe, Roz Lowe, Richard Atlas, Jayne Bateson, Tim Bulmer, Dustin Miller, Suzanne (Pookey) Costello, and Sarah Martin for your support and encouragement throughout this project.

To my amazing team: Alex Stewart, Ella Edigy, Caroline Hamilton, and Heather Welsh.

To Jeff Vespa for your incredible photography and passion for this project. You are a true burgerista!

To Michael Bierut and Jesse Reed at Pentagram for their fantastic design.

To Emily Takoudes, Clare Churly, Elizabeth Clinton, and the Phaidon team for making this book possible.

Special thanks to all contributors, photographers, and chefs and to: Andrés Anhalt, Sat Bains, Katherine Balmer, Tom Barton, Anton Belmonte, Elliott Bergman, Becky Billingsley, April Bloomfield, Daniel Boulud, Edwin Bragg, David Bressler, Matt Bullington, Jon Burgerman, Tom Byng, Josh Capon, Graydon Carter, Berry Casey, Adrian Chilton, Roy Choi, Citizen Relations, CM Communications, Manuel Coelho, Chris Coulson, Phyllis Cudworth, DAVID, the agency, Justus de Nijs, Rob Dean, Ben Denner, Connie Dickson, Anita Duquette, Mathieu Durand, Robert Earl, Phil Eeles, Fat & Furious, Cristina Fedi, Adam Fleischman, Randy Garutti, Kara Giglio, Rachel Gillman Rischall, Mimi Gilmour, Joe Grossman, Andre Guerrero, Beth Hadrill, Jenny Harris, Gideon Hart, Dan Haydock, K. Heller, Paul Hemus, April Hess, Hans Hess, Christopher Hodgson, Robert C. Jackson, Ole John, Nick Jones, Zan Kaufman, KBPR Group, Jamie Klingler, Anthony Knight, the estate of Ray Kroc, Pat LaFrieda, Jørgen Leth, Lauren Lewis, Eric Lupfer, Kevin McAulay, Fernando Machado, Tom Maher, Angie Mar, Ana Claudia Mascitto, Dan Mendelson, Tom Monaghan, George Motz, Janie Murrell, Jerry Murrell, Devonie Nicholas, Sean Norvett, Scott O'Byrne, Liam O'Keefe, the estate of Josh Ozersky, Tom Paine, Dipak Panchal, Jeremy Park, Daniel Patterson, Mark Peacock, Aarik Persaud, Mike Phillips, Wolfgang Puck, Gordon Ramsay, Mathew Ramsey, Adam Rawson, Roche Communications, Amy Sadowsky, Sauce Communications, John Schauerman, Anthony Sheridan, Amy Sherman, Sleazy McCheesy, Nick Solares, Tjalf Spanaay, Brian Stein, Cokey Sulkin, Martin Swift, Quentin Tarantino, Tomas "Tommi" Tómasson, C. J. Tropp, Warren Turnbull, Mindy Valone, Paul Wahlberg, the estate of Andy Warhol, James Warrillow, Whitney Museum of American Art, Andy Wiederhorn, Christina Wilson, Cathy Winn, Jay Wisse, Bill Wolfe, John Wolfe, Marisa Zafran, and Andrew Zurica.

Phaidon would like to thank Michael Bierut, Vanessa Bird, Clare Churly, Adela Cory, Geraldine Hendler, Mandy Mackie, João Mota, Jo Murray, Jesse Reed, and Caroline Taggart.

NOTES

> All herbs are fresh, unless otherwise specified.
> Eggs and individual vegetables and fruits, such as onions and apples, are assumed to be large (medium), unless otherwise specified.
> All sugar is superfine (white caster) sugar and all brown sugar is cane or demerara unless otherwise specified.
> All milk is whole (full-fat) at 3 percent fat, homogenized and lightly pasteurized, unless otherwise specified.
> All salt is fine sea salt, unless otherwise specified.
> Cooking times are for guidance only, as individual ovens vary. If using a convection (fan) oven, follow the manufacturer's directions concerning oven temperatures.
> Exercise a high level of caution when following recipes involving any potentially hazardous activity, including the use of high temperatures, open flames, slaked lime, and when deep-frying. In particular, when deep-frying, add food carefully to avoid splashing, wear long sleeves, and never leave the pan unattended.
> Some recipes include raw or very lightly cooked eggs, meat, or fish, and fermented products. These should be avoided by the elderly, infants, pregnant women, convalescents, and anyone with an impaired immune system.
> Exercise caution when making fermented products, ensuring all equipment is spotlessly clean, and seek expert advice if in any doubt.
> When no quantity is specified, for example of oils, salts, and herbs used for finishing dishes or for deep-frying, quantities are discretionary and flexible.
> Both imperial and metric measures are used in this book. Follow one set of measurements throughout, not a mixture, as they are not interchangeable.
> All spoon and cup measurements are level, unless otherwise stated.
> 1 teaspoon = 5 ml;
> 1 tablespoon = 15 ml.
> Australian standard tablespoons are 20 ml, so Australian readers are advised to use 3 teaspoons in place of 1 tablespoon when measuring small quantities.

Phaidon Press Limited
Regent's Wharf
All Saints Street
London N1 9PA

Phaidon Press Inc.
65 Bleecker Street
New York, NY 10012

phaidon.com

First published 2017
© 2017 Phaidon Press Limited

ISBN 978 0714 87398 5

A CIP catalog record for this book is available
from the British Library and the Library of Congress.

Commissioning Editor: Emily Takoudes
Project Editor: Clare Churly
Production Controllers: Mandy Mackie, Adela Cory
Design: Jesse Reed and Michael Bierut, Pentagram

Printed in China

David Michaels has worked in conceptual design and branding for many retail and hospitality projects including Walt Disney, LVMH, Pepsi, MGM Resorts, W Hotels and MTV. His passion for hamburgers began at a young age and he has been obsessed ever since. In 2007, he opened Bite Me Burger in Sydney. David lives in London.